What Others Are Saying About This Book . . .

"Grace Robbins has written an explosive tell-all about one of my favorite authors—the wild and wonderful Harold Robbins. He did it . . . She did it . . . And then he wrote about it . . . Sexy fun."

—Jackie Collins, *New York Times* best-selling author

"The book is a fascinating and racy frothy read—magnificently written, and built with plenty of scandalous and salacious detail."

—Barry Krost, award-winning producer

"If you want the hot skinny on one of the world's most interesting authors, Harold Robbins, look no further than one of the world's most interesting women, his wife. Grace was always as much a part of the royal Hollywood social scene as Harold. They enlivened every major event I ever attended, and when they went home, they left everyone with something to talk about. Now Grace gets it all down on paper, remembering everything, and leaving out nothing. Every anecdote in *Cinderella and the Carpetbagger* is worth repeating. Every chapter is worth reading twice. Misunderstood as often as he was toasted, Harold was one in a million. He gave as good as he got, and thank god Grace was in the background, taking notes for posterity. I laughed, I wallowed in nostalgia for a time that will never come again, when people were originals and fame was something you could take to the bank. I gulped down every juicy minute of this funny, outrageous memoir. Do not take a pill before you go to bed with this book, because you will not be able to put it down until the sun comes up."

—Rex Reed

"This sweet little memoir will not grab the Vatican's blessing."

—*New York Post*

"50 Shades of Grace! I couldn't put *Cinderella and the Carpetbagger* down, I couldn't eat, I couldn't sleep. The pages turned themselves. You will enjoy this!"

—**Monique Van Vooren, Actress/Author**

"This racy romp through a life and style nobody could dare dream of is so sizzling and hot you'd better wear gloves to turn the pages! It's the fastest high-speed roller coaster through the valley of the rich to the mountain of the famous so buckle up for a ride unlike any other. Even more incredible is that its fact: it's not fiction—although it's about a man who wrote and sold more graphic stories of 'sex drugs and rock 'n' roll' than any other author in history. Grace Robbins pulls back Hollywood's bedroom drapes to reveal tales to tantalize and torment. She not only hands you the VIP invitation to party with the jet-set privileged around the world, she escorts you through their platinum playgrounds in an easy and warm read you won't put down. A jet to go for lunch. A yacht to go for dinner. A mega-mansion for breakfast champagne. $50-million here for baubles and beads—a mere bagatelle! I tried on my television show to bring a hint of it, but Grace does much better with the first ever real look at what went on when the cameras were shut off. You'd expect it in a fantasy work of fiction but this is ten times more dynamite and dramatic because it was real life and more electrifying than anything that could be on reality television. You have been warned. It's HOT! Very hot! Dangerously hot! Sexually hot! It couldn't get any hotter—and that's just one page of the orgy party in the hills of Hollywood. Little wonder then when Harold Robbins was alive and the center of every party he was hailed as the man whose life was even bigger, better, bolder than the tall tales he created for his books!"

—**Robin Leach,** *Lifestyles of the Rich & Famous*

Cinderella
and the
Carpetbagger

My Life as the Wife of the
"World's Best-Selling Author,"
HAROLD ROBBINS

GRACE ROBBINS

BETTIE YOUNGS BOOKS

Disclaimer: This is a true story, and the characters and events are real. However, in some cases, the names, descriptions, and locations have been changed, and some events have been altered, combined, or condensed for storytelling purposes, but the overall chronology is an accurate depiction of the author's experience.

Cover Design by Tatomir Pitariu
Text Design by Jane Hagaman
Senior Editor: Elisabeth Rinaldi
Author photo of Grace Robbins by Timothy Fielding, Timothy Fielding Studios

Burres Books and Bettie Youngs Books are distributed worldwide. If you are unable to order this book from your local bookseller or online or from Espresso, you may order directly from the publisher.

BETTIE YOUNGS BOOK PUBLISHERS
www.BettieYoungsBooks.com
info@BettieYoungsBooks.com

ISBN: 978-0-9882848-2-1
ePub: 978-0-9882848-4-5

Library of Congress Control Number: 2012952599

1. Robbins, Grace. 2. Robbins, Harold. 3. Marriage. 4. Authors' Spouses—United States. 5. Authors, American—20th Century—Biography. 6. Relationships. 7. Famous Authors. 8. Beverly Hills Housewives. 9. Lifestyles of the Rich and Famous.

Printed in the United States of America.

To Harold—
who gave me the greatest gift of all,
my daughter, Adréana

"All good stories have a beginning, middle, and an end, although not necessarily in that order."

—Harold Robbins

Contents

Part 1—The Beginning

Part 2—The Middle

Part 3—The End

Acknowledgements

This work has been a life in progress. So many years to cover, so many experiences, so many memories, and thus so many people to thank. I'd like to thank my publisher, Bettie Youngs of Bettie Youngs Book Publishers, who believed in me and this work and has helped mobilize me into sharing it. Thank you as well to her excellent staff, especially Adrian Pitariu for the sexy and snazzy cover; Jane Hagaman for the beautiful interior text and design; and, Elisabeth Rinaldi for her sensitivity in editing. A big thank you to my masterful PR agent, Arlene Howard of Arlene Howard and Associates, and to my agent and best go-to guy any gal could ever hope to have in a dear friend, Gilbert Holmes, who took my book "out of the closet" and made sure it got published.

For all of those experiences, one thing is for sure, our lives are never lived in a vacuum, and I'd like to thank so many who have shared the journey with me, especially those who over the years have held my heart and hands in so many ways. To my friends Monique Van Vooren, Geoffrey Bradfield, Anita Jaffe and Joseph Sirolla who were there for me in New York. Larry Flynt, Beverly Cohen, and Marci Weiner who were there for me in Los Angeles—and my many other wonderful friends. I must not forget my brother Gary, his wife Libby and the Palermo clan. And lastly, to the loves of my life, my daughter Adréana; her husband Jeff; and, Luke my sweet dog.

Sharing one's memoir is quite an experience, exhilarating while also being one that creates vulnerability, because it does invade one's privacy. But, my life—lived for some thirty years with the gregarious and very visible "world's bestselling author," Harold Robbins—has been in the public eye, so I do hope this book allows a glimpse into the times of the sixties, seventies, and eighties to be seen for what they were, irreplaceable.

PROLOGUE

The Beginning of the End

The sixties! Ah, those psychedelic sixties. The era of JFK, the Vietnam War, free love, the Beatles, Marilyn Monroe, Elvis, and more free love. It was the beginning of "Sex, Drugs and Rock 'n' Roll." And Harold Robbins's books were flying off bookstore shelves. The public just couldn't get enough of Harold's steamy sex scenes, filled with his bigger than life characters each more interesting than the next. Harold put being high and living high on the front lines of the sexual revolution, and suddenly I found myself smack dab in his pages.

It has been said "with wealth comes great responsibility." With Harold came (more) of everything. The homes got bigger, the cars more exotic and expensive, the drugs turned from bags to bowls, and the sex was filled with an endless pool of partners.

Our parties evolved into two polarized types. The first were laden with celebrities and covered by the press, with invitations sought after and accepted by the crème de la crème. They were parties in the old Hollywood tradition—black ties and gowns. Glamorous, grandiose functions attended by hundreds of people, either held in a grand hotel or at one of our sumptuous homes, where tents were set up with delectable goodies for the indulgence of anyone who wished to partake. One tent, in particular was for foot massages with expert "massage therapists."

On this summer, moonlit night our party was of the second type—a very secret affair and one definitely not meant for the scrutiny of the press. Aside from specialty cocktails served up by legendary bartender Scotty Bowers and catered appetizers, a large crystal bowl was placed on a cocktail table filled with high-grade cocaine. Anyone desirous of a snort could dip into it as though scooping sugar for a cup of coffee. Most did.

By midnight the collective mood of our guests was charged with electricity. At Harold's direction, we had "elevated." I looked around. Our guests were decidedly anticipatory, looking forward to the delights of the "next," which were about two minutes away. An equal mix of men and women was present. Most of the men were handsome and all of the women were undoubtedly beautiful, a group Harold called "the hip of the hippest." Before I knew it, all were naked, although a few of us had bath towels draped discreetly over parts of our bodies. I had long overcome my nervousness at such affairs, but a recurrent question was foremost in my thoughts: "Grazia, what's a nice Sicilian girl like you doing here?"

"Here" was the master bedroom of our ten thousand square-foot mansion in the famous hills overlooking Beverly Hills—a bedroom so enormous that most apartments would fit easily within its space. It was decorated in various shades of champagne with silk upholstered walls, satin covered chaises, a mirrored ceiling, and a down comforter massive enough to encompass the entirety of our custom-made, emperor-sized bed. I had designed the room for romance, its sensuous decor meant particularly for Harold and me alone, but now there were all these people.

I had never met any of them before, nor would I again after tonight. Where they had come from I had no idea; Harold did not go out and find liberated people as much as they found him, such was his reputation. I was certain most of the people felt as if they had walked into the pages of one of Harold's novels, and in a way they had, for nothing we did was immune to Harold's pen.

My eyes scanned, avoiding bedroom eyes and swaying bodies, seeking Harold. I did not see him; for a moment I panicked. Was he already with one of those beauties? That was against the rules—*his* rules, although at times he had come to break them with abandon. Then I saw the door to the bedroom open, very slowly, then wider, the gesture of a Robbins's entrance. Suddenly he was there, framed in the doorway, a small man, towel tied around his waist, a naughty smile on his face—a smile I had adored through the years, one of a guilty little boy caught with his hand in the cookie jar. Unfortunately the innocence of his smile had become more and more difficult to appreciate: Harold was now almost sixty years old.

He stepped forward, tugging gently into the room a curvaceously nude young woman who carried a chalkboard and pointer. We were now at the beginning of another orgy, a one-ring circus with Harold as ringmaster, orchestrating with what he thought was masterly flair. I looked at the woman beside him and wondered what nuance he was adding tonight. What new fun did he have in store for us now?

The truth is Harold *was* fun. He was creative, and his schemes were usually unique, regardless of the circumstances. From my first encounter with him, he had always been full of life, energy, and mischief, with a touch of mania and a great deal of imagination. He made no qualms about it—he liked "the good life," and the good life to Harold meant "pushing the envelope."

Tonight the girl with the chalkboard was an extension of that continual effort; she was a Linda Lovelace look-alike—the real Lovelace being the star of the immensely popular X-rated film *Deep Throat*, which had turned the act of fellatio into a phenomenal, silver-screen success. Oh, she was right up Harold's alley!

I looked around. Everyone was enraptured. It was another memorable event in the "World of Harold Robbins," a world that had come to dominate every moment of my life. I couldn't believe this actually was happening in my bedroom, but it was, and somehow I was taking it in stride. In fact, I'd had a great deal of training and guidance from my husband, and no matter my reservations, I admit to this day it was exciting.

"Leave it to Grace and Harold to invite a sex therapist to lecture at an orgy," someone whispered with a giggle.

"Linda" continued tapping the blackboard, "Ladies, I want you to imagine the most beautiful, the biggest, the largest, the grandest, the looooongest cock in the world—just like those I see rising before me," she said, flattering the men immensely, even though some of them didn't deserve the compliment. "Now, girls, choose the one you want—oh, you lucky fellows!—and follow my instructions."

Rapid scampering and nervous giggling ensued as men and women paired off. I had never seen such enthusiasm at one of our orgies, but then we'd never had a chalkboard lecture by a naked teacher. A young woman scurried by me, saying in a flash, "Hi, Grace! How unique! This is wonderful!" It was confirmation again that I was living up to my reputation as one of Beverly Hills' premier hostesses, although the ritual unfolding before my eyes was truly Harold's doing. Everyone quickly found a partner—everyone, that is, except Harold, "Linda," and me.

"Miss Lovelace" became clinical. She drew a large circle on the board. "All right ladies. I want you to put your fingers gently around his cock and slowly insert it into your mouth, at all times never forgetting the big 'O' represented on the chalkboard. Remember, the real 'O' is at the very bottom of your throat, and it's becoming larger and larger and larger . . ."

"What good students!" I said aloud and rushed to Harold. The only person I wanted to try out the instructions on was my husband.

Eventually the class came to its climactic end. There was unanimous agreement the party had been one of "the most far-out orgies ever." It was written plainly on the faces of the guests, whoever they were; each immensely content. It took what seemed an endless amount of time for them to sort out their clothes and shoes, but eventually the last happy guest left.

"That was a great party!" cried Harold enthusiastically. "That 'Linda' was dynamic. Don't you think so, darling?"

I nodded agreement. We were in our bedroom, and we collapsed on the huge bed, alone at last. Harold took me in his arms. "I love you, Tiger," he whispered.

"I love you, too, Harold."

My words were sincere, even though I had begun to feel that certain scenes from our life were like outtakes from Fellini's *La Dolce Vita*. But instead of the hero being a Roman gossip columnist, he was the world's best-selling novelist who happened to be my husband.

"We live one good, sweet life, Tiger!" He drifted off to sleep.

Later, while he snored softly, I stared at the mirrored ceiling in the dark of night, wondering how all of this had come about. How had I ended up at an orgy in an opulent mansion in Beverly Hills, California? What attracted me to a man who felt compelled to invite strangers into our lives and into our bedroom? To be sure it had not always been that way. No, my life with Harold Robbins had started very differently, very innocently, and very sweetly, a long time before . . .

Part One

The Beginning

"Birds do it, bees do it,
Even educated fleas do it.
Let's do it, let's fall
In love!

—"Let's Do It," Cole Porter

1

Serendipity

*I*t was September, 1962. I lived in Manhattan, the hub of the nation, where life swirled about with great vigor. I was twenty-eight years old, a casting director at Grey Advertising, and married to a handsome artist who resembled Steve McQueen. As for me, I'd been told that I looked a lot like Elizabeth Taylor. Most people thought I was radiantly happy, but I wasn't—or even close to it.

I held a secret. Tom was an incurable alcoholic (I hadn't a clue at first, cognac and more cognac even in his corn flakes). I was living in a state of chronic, growing depression. I managed to mask my feelings at the office. When others laughed, I laughed with them. When their spirits were low, I tried to lift them.

Casting days were the best. Days of casting babies who talked "baby talk" for Ivory Snow. Dozens of giants and dwarfs for Jif peanut butter, and skating monkeys too. The driver for Greyhound bus ("and leave the driving to us"). Not excluding the Revlon beauties and the mighty P&G housewives.

My four-year marriage to Tom Horky was not just falling apart, it had hit rock bottom and shattered: no love left between us. Tom had stopped working. "I will not prostitute my talent for commercials." I was paying our bills; our sex life had receded to memories. I was having sporadic but meaningless affairs, while Tom was becoming a full-blown alcoholic. The sum total of it was a weight I couldn't lift from my heart no matter what I did. I was lonely, caught up in the debilitating secret of continual marital strife. My friends knew nothing about it, and my parents were aware only that Tom and I were having financial problems. To survive with my mental health intact, I needed a miracle.

One Friday I felt so knotted up I thought I would explode. I wanted to unwind, but I didn't know how. Often after work, some of us would meet at the Monkey Bar or at Cheerios—two nearby cocktail lounges—to initiate the weekend, but I wasn't in a mood to socialize. In passing I mentioned my uneasiness to Peggy Ann Ellis, a hands and feet model whom I had cast often in commercials. I ran into her late in the afternoon at one of the contract studios where we filmed commercials.

"Hi, Grace," said Peggy. "How are you?"

"Not so well," I moaned.

"What's the problem?"

"Work . . . life . . . things—all of the above," I said.

"Wanna go have a cocktail and talk it over?" she asked.

"I don't think that would solve my problem, Peggy," I told her. "What I need is a long, long weekend away from work, away from home, away from everything."

She laughed knowingly. After a moment of reflection, she said, "Hey, why don't you and Tom go stay on my yacht for the weekend?"

Don't ever think the only moneymakers in the modeling business are women and men with beautiful faces. Peggy made gobs of money just showing her hands and feet, and she had a yacht to prove it. Loving boats and water, I did not have to think twice about her offer. I accepted without hesitation. I wanted to unwind and relax, all by my lonesome, and this was my chance because I knew that Tom, who had become sulky and reclusive, would not want to transport his bottle from one place to another.

When I got to our apartment that evening, Tom was already drinking. His commercial art career, which had been promising when we married, had slowly gone down the drain where the contents of his bottle should have gone. I told him about Peggy's offer. He shook his head no. Alcohol already had set firmly in his system. He wasn't going anywhere, except to the refrigerator for ice, and then back to the couch.

"No, I don't want to blow the weekend on a damned boat," he said, and then added, "but you go." I threw some things in a bag and caught a taxi to the Seventy-Ninth Street boat basis, inhaling the momentary elixir of cool autumn air through an open taxi window. I just wanted to loosen up and forget my problems, if only for a couple of days.

Night had fallen by the time I found Peggy's boat moored in its slip. It was beautiful, not large but well-kept with all the luxuries a small yacht could afford. I hung up my clothes and settled in for the weekend. I mixed a drink in an effort to relax, although I could hardly be called a drinker. No matter what I did, however, I couldn't seem to loosen up. I wandered around, from bow to stern, inside and outside, but the lapping water, the crisp autumn night, even the glistening stars could not dispel my mood. I remembered seeing a library—really just a small collection of books—in one of the rooms in the yacht. I decided reading might help me settle down.

I don't know why I chose the book I did. It was an unusual choice because it was fiction, which I seldom read; since college, my reading had been almost exclusively about business and advertising. The book was a hardback, a really big one, about eight hundred pages: *The Carpetbaggers.* The title rang a slight bell in my head, as if I had heard it before, but I wasn't sure. Whatever. I slipped it off of the shelf—it felt like a brick—and retired to bed, thinking I would read myself to sleep.

From the first page the book did everything except put me in a doze. I had certainly not read anything like it before. I considered myself fairly sexually sophisticated, but I had never, ever, read anything remotely similar to what the characters were doing in the episodes unfolding in the pages before me.

The backdrop of the novel was the motion picture industry, from 1925 to 1945, and I suspect any sophisticated reader in those days would have recognized the real prototypes of the fictional characters, ranging from Howard Hughes to Jean Harlow. I wondered: had the author known the real people? It was the first book I had ever read that moved forward at a continuously mounting pace, building and building, climbing and climbing toward its climax with an ever-increasing energy. I didn't want to put it down; couldn't.

I would read a few pages and then pause, wondering how a person could write such a story. It was wonderful and titillating and sexy and sinful, and far removed from the daily regimen of my life. I thought: Who wrote this? How could he open himself up like this? How could he divulge such things? Had he lived these moments and experiences I'm reading about? Did he make them up? If so, what an imagination! I looked inside the dust jacket, but there was no biography of the writer. He was a man named Harold Robbins, whom I assumed was dead. I began reading again. As I flipped the pages, devouring each one as rapidly as possible, I became more and more amazed.

I breezed through the weekend with *The Carpetbaggers* in my hands, my eyes pinned to every word. I finished reading it Sunday night, just in time to go home. I called a taxi and returned silently through the streets to our apartment on West Seventy-Second Street.

"Why so quiet? What's wrong?" asked Tom a few minutes after I got home. He was already firmly planted on the couch, hardly lifting his head even to speak. "Didn't you enjoy the weekend on the boat?"

"I had a wonderful time," I said vaguely.

"Who was there?"

"No one, just me."

Tom's failure as a commercial artist, along with my success in the advertising business, had given him a massive inferiority complex. He wasn't a jealous person, but he had an innate need to know everything that happened to me out of his presence.

"What did you do?" he asked.

"Oh, I just read."

"Read?" His face screwed up. "You mean like a book?"

"Yes, a book," I said.

"What was it about?"

"I don't know, Tom. About nothing," I lied. "It was just a way to kill time."

We said nothing more. I could smell the heavy odor of brandy on his breath as he dozed off.

The next morning, I rode by taxi through Central Park on my way to the Grey Advertising offices at Park Avenue. As always, I was putting on my makeup in the cab. The ride should have been routine, but it wasn't. I couldn't help but think about *The Carpetbaggers* and its author. Who was Harold Robbins and when did he die? I wished I had met and known him. The story of Jonas Cord and Nevada Smith and Rina Marlowe and Jennie Denton and David Woolf were locked in my mind as if they were real people, although bigger than life. When I tried to let them out of my head, they wouldn't go. They were immured there, vibrant and full of energy. They weren't like the characters in Hemingway and Fitzgerald; they were alive, and I wanted to identify with them.

Once ensconced in my office, Harold Robbins and his book went by the wayside. I had a casting session, and *The Carpetbaggers* was suddenly far from my mind. Little did I realize the needed miracle in my life was on the verge of happening. It started with a telephone call. I had just dismissed several actresses and models who were auditioning for a P&G soap commercial, and I had flopped down at my desk to catch my breath. The call was from talent agent Archer King.

My acquaintance with Archer predated my first job in the advertising business, which had been as a receptionist at Biow, the firm made famous and rich by its television client "I Love Lucy." When I dropped out of college, not knowing exactly what to do, I had flirted with the idea of becoming an actress. I had majored in speech and drama in lieu of education, which was my parents' wish. My only claim to fame as a thespian had been playing Hermia in an amateur collegiate production of Shakespeare's *A Midsummer Night's Dream*.

During an interlude between college and career a new friend had "discovered" me, observing a talent that really didn't exist.

"Have some pictures made and I'll set up an appointment for you with Archer King," he said. "He's one of the best talent agents in Manhattan. Let's see what he can do with you."

I followed my mentor's advice, spending some of my mother's hard-earned money to get a series of photographs shot and made into what agents called a composite. My friend followed through on his promise and a few days later I was sitting in Archer King's office. To say the least, Archer was not very responsive to my momentary career goal. He interviewed me briefly; I told him about my one and only theatrical experience, when I was a junior at Queen's College in Flushing. He shrugged unappreciatively and studied my photographs.

"Why does a nice young Sicilian girl like you want to become an actress?" he said. Before I could respond, however, he continued: "Not that you're so young, Grace but you're so inexperienced."

My god, I thought, I'm only nineteen years old and still a virgin!

Archer knew, of course, that I was out of my element, just a kid with limited experience, and one who still lived at home with her parents. I think he was trying to be gracious, but the words came out the wrong way. He did not sign me up.

A couple of years later, when I became a casting director at Grey, I contacted all the agents to let them know who I was and what I was doing and that I was interested in meeting their clients. I called Archer, but until that Monday morning after my weekend on Peggy's yacht, I don't believe I had ever talked with him about anything other than business, and most certainly he had never invited me to lunch. So if his call wasn't a surprise, his request, or demand, was.

"Hello, Gracie," he said.

"Archer, I hate being called Gracie. How would you like to be called Archie?"

He laughed. "Whatever you say, Grace. Listen: I'm taking you to lunch today, and don't say no."

I was taken aback. "Archer, after all this time, you've never asked me to lunch a single time. You've never even sent me a gift." I was jokingly referring to the common practice of "payola" involved in casting. Agents usually sent a small gift when one of their clients was hired, never money, just a token of appreciation. In those days none of us considered the impropriety of such an act, and the truth is I was slightly miffed that Archer would call me out of the blue, demanding a sudden luncheon engagement.

"Nevertheless, I'm taking you to lunch today," he repeated.

"Why today of all days?"

I think he was afraid I was going to decline because he suddenly said, "It's not really my lunch. It's Harold Robbins' lunch, the writer."

My heart fluttered. I couldn't believe his words. It was as though I were suddenly in a dream, clicking away fantasies like so many frames in a homemade movie. Harold Robbins, the writer? I was stunned. "I thought he was dead," I said.

Archer laughed. "He's alive and well, and he'd like to meet you."

I could not speak or think clearly enough to ask how Harold Robbins knew of me or why he wanted to meet me. I didn't even say, "I just read his book!" Instead, I said coldly, "Okay, what time and where, Archer?"

When I got off the elevator on the ground floor of our office building at noon, Archer was waiting for me in the lobby. Robbins was staying at the old Americana Hotel, a couple of blocks away.

The air was crisp and fresh and cool in the street, a welcome relief from the long hot summer that had just ended. As we walked briskly, I felt tingly. I looked down at my "Tape Measure" dress from the well-known shop of the same name on Madison Avenue. It was apple green, and its color set off nicely my Mediterranean complexion and dark hair; I was satisfied with the way I looked. I think Archer expected me to quiz him about Harold Robbins and his unexpected luncheon invitation, but I remained collected—determined to be cool.

The Americana was an old standard for the rich and famous. It was a nice hotel, but not in the five-star class of the Waldorf-Astoria. When Archer tugged me into an elevator and asked the operator for the penthouse suite, I didn't blink an eye. He looked at me curiously, no doubt expecting a question from me as we ascended, but I remained silent, confidently in control of myself, if only for the moment.

We exited the elevator and walked down the corridor to a suite with double-doors. Archer knocked and the doors opened immediately. Standing at the threshold was a very unimposing middle-aged man, shiny-bald pate, with pure white hair fringing his temples and running along the sides of his head. He was not tall, only five-feet-eight, nor did he seem particularly muscular or athletic, although he had not yet gone to fat. His eyes were almond shaped, and they were riveted to me.

"Harold, meet Grace—Grace, Harold."

"Hello, Grace!" said Harold enthusiastically. His eyes never left me. They were blue-brown with an uncanny ability to change shades as if they belonged to a chameleon. Ignoring Archer, he took my extended hand and swept me into the suite as though he had been awaiting my arrival with bated breath. Archer trailed after us. Whatever my emotions were concerning this man whom I had dwelled upon through the course of the weekend and my morning ride to work, I kept them in check. It wasn't easy, for as we entered the living room I saw two women sitting side-by-side on the couch. Not two anonymous women, but two housewife-type actresses whom I had interviewed that very morning. I had to bite my tongue to keep from asking, "What are you two doing here?" What saved me from losing my poise, I believe, was that Harold's eyes were still locked on me. They just wouldn't let go, not for a moment.

It did not take long for me to surmise the two actresses were somehow my connection to Harold Robbins, but I didn't want to know the true reason was for this serendipity. The women had been in my office only hours before, and Archer knew everyone in the advertising world, but . . . no, I didn't want to know. I wanted this chance meeting to be like the make-believe I had conjured in my mind the night before. After all, on Peggy's yacht, I had wished that I had met the author of *The Carpetbaggers* before his demise; and now, realizing he wasn't dead but very much alive—and that his blue-brown, almond-shaped eyes were pinned on me—my wish had come true. To this day I don't know exactly how my invitation to Harold's suite for lunch came about. I never asked him because I never wanted or needed to know. It just happened. It was a miracle.

I don't think I had developed a mental picture of Harold before we met, even after reading *The Carpetbaggers*. Perhaps after Archer invited me to lunch, I had assembled some vague image in my mind. I expected him to be younger, probably because my experiences up to then had been with men of my own age or even younger. But this man, with his balding head and white hair—he seemed so old! In fact, he was forty-eight and it was because of his dynamism and allure that any negative idea regarding his age soon faded from my mind, although not before I made a few more observations.

His age may have been exaggerated because he looked tired. He had bags under his eyes, which I rationalized away by thinking, *He's a writer, and he probably works deep into the night.* He was dressed casually, and I wondered why his pants were so baggy, especially at the seat. I disposed of that question also. I attributed his baggy pants to the fact he probably sat in front of his typewriter most of the day, including right up to the time we had arrived, or rather when the "housewives" had arrived. At some point I realized I was making excuses for him because I wanted to like him. As it turned out, I would make excuses for him for much of the next twenty-eight years.

One of the models had also noticed his attire. "What kind of shoes are those?" she asked with a laugh.

"Hush Puppies," he replied without taking his eyes away from me for even a glance at the woman.

In the years to come, I was to learn that Harold had a tendency to make a production out of any—and everything. It was one of his greatest gifts and, I'm sorry to say, one of the aspects of his creativity for which he was most ridiculed and criticized. He could turn the simplest social pastime into a wonderful merrymaking activity or into a solemn ceremony of pomp and circumstance, depending upon his momentary whim. One never knew what to expect.

He did not fail that day at lunch. It started with a bottle of Dom Pérignon, then a second bottle, then a third. It was more wine than I had ever had at one sitting! There was much small talk, which I don't remember, but the fact he seldom took his eyes off me was unnerving.

Finally he seated us at a rectangular dining table with the flourish of a movie director preparing to shoot a scene. It was a long table and Harold placed me at one end with Archer seated to my left, the actresses were seated across from each other. Harold took the chair at the other end of the table, facing me, his eyes still glued to me, not even averting when he suddenly tossed a hand in the air and snapped his fingers. Seemingly from out of nowhere a horde of waiters in black tie appeared, and lunch was served. It was more than lunch—it was a sumptuous feast: caviar, pommes soufflés, lobster tails, and more Dom Pérignon. My usual lunches had always been rather light, alone or with friends, if not just a sandwich in the office, but this—why, it was outrageous . . . and wonderful.

Harold avoided talking about his writing, fending off relevant questions. As far as I knew, *The Carpetbaggers* was the only book he had written. In time I realized he was a wonderful listener, a student of human nature who was always learning from others. He usually gave each person equal time, prompting his guests to talk, especially about themselves, and he would listen as though what they were saying was the most important thing in the world—but not this day. I'm sure Archer and the models got their two-cents worth into the dialogue, but seldom did Harold look at the speaker; his eyes continued to hold me in such a steady gaze that I actually became uneasy.

To this day, when I become nervous, I begin to talk. That day I really began to talk. I became loquacious (no doubt with great assistance from the champagne,) and I talked and talked and talked, with Harold's ears taking in my every word, his eyes my every gesture. I talked about the advertising business; I talked about casting; I talked about—I talked until Harold suddenly came into sharp focus at the opposite end of the table, an incredibly sly smile on his face that seemed to indicate he knew some little secret I wasn't privy to. I stopped in midsentence, looked around the table, and realized we were alone. Archer was gone; the actresses were gone; even the waiters had vanished.

"Where did everyone go?" I asked.

Harold continued to smile. "They said to say goodbye," he offered casually. "Don't worry about it. We can stay and continue talking. I'm enjoying it immensely. The others just didn't want to interrupt you. Archer had an appointment and the girls had a casting session."

"A casting session!" I looked at my watch. It was three o'clock. "My god!" I cried. "I have to go! I had my own casting session at two-thirty. With babies, for Proctor and Gamble!" I leaped up and bolted for my purse. "I'm going to have babies crawling all over the place, and a lot of angry mothers!"

"No problem," said Harold with a chuckle. He stood up and took my arm. "Come on, I'll walk you back to your office. It'll be faster than a cab."

Outside on the sidewalk, I tried to walk as briskly as possible, but Harold hung back, purposely slowing the pace. I would stop and wait for him to catch up. "Really, I have to get to my office," I kept telling him, and then I would hasten forward.

As I scurried, then stopped and waited, then scurried again, Harold and I somehow had a broken conversation that I later realized was chock-full of information. No doubt he had seen my wedding ring during my monologue at the hotel; I had certainly seen his.

"How long you been married, Grace?" he asked.

"Four years."

"What's your maiden name?"

"Palermo."

"Italian, huh?"

"Sicilian."

"Born in Brooklyn?"

"Uh-huh."

He smiled to himself. "What's he do—your husband?"

"He's an artist."

He shrugged nonchalantly, and then told me his own marriage was to a woman with whom he lived in Connecticut. "Twenty long years," he said with a sigh.

"Twenty?"

"Yeah. Name's Lillian," he said. "What's your husband's name?"

"Tom."

He dropped back and stared at the display window of a store. I waited, eager with the need to go. He caught up again. "I commute back and forth," he said, and after a pause he asked, "Any children?"

"Only my husband."

He laughed and continued talking. He had a daughter, not with Lillian but with a woman he'd had a brief but tragic relationship with some years before. He had given the daughter, Caryn, his surname, and had even tried to gain custody of her. His voice seemed bitter when he spoke of the girl's mother, Yvonne, and he quickly shifted gears and launched into a new subject as if to escape a bad memory. He had worked many years at Universal Pictures, starting at the bottom and climbing the executive ladder before turning to writing; he pointed out with glee that his office had been in the building directly across from mine. The proximity of our offices gave us some kind of mystical bond, although I had only been at Grey a year and Harold hadn't worked at Universal for half a decade.

At last we were near the corner of the block opposite from Grey Advertising. Harold was trailing again; I hurried to the corner and stopped at a red light. He caught up with me and grasped my arm, not harshly but gently. "Hold up a minute," he said. "I want you to take a look in this window."

"But Harold!" I protested. "Really—"

"Just one second," he said calmly. "That's all we need. Believe me, the advertising world can wait. Products will still sell and capitalism won't come to a halt." He tugged me to the show window of a small but exclusive jewelry store. "Take a look in this window."

I gave the showcase a cursory glance. "Really, Harold, please," I protested. "I'll have bawling babies all over my office. Their mothers are going to be furious with me."

"Do you see something in the window you would like?" he asked, unperturbed by my anxiety.

"I really, really have to go."

"Just point at something," he said.

I fluttered a hand in frustration and pointed, not really at anything specific. A pendant was the only item in the window that remotely caught my attention; it was a gold, heart-shaped frame, with a dangling pearl suspended from the cleft of the heart on a small gold chain—very pretty. Harold shrugged; the light changed; and we crossed the street.

He left me at the elevator in the lobby of the Grey building. It was anything but climactic. He did not even kiss me on the cheek; he just shook my hand as though we'd just had a business meeting.

"Thanks for the wonderful lunch," I told him.

"I'll give you a call," he said, and with that he was gone.

When I got upstairs, I hardly had time to think about Harold Robbins. The babies were indeed waiting for me in a storm of squalls, their mothers uptight and silently peeved at another rude casting director. Somehow I got the job done, although for the first time in months my heart wasn't devoted to the task at hand.

It was five thirty before the session wrapped and my office was empty. I collapsed in my chair. Almost immediately I heard a woman's high-pitched voice echoing in the corridor outside. "Grace Horky? Grace Horky?" I stood up and peeked out the door. A small woman, even tinier than I, stood there with a small package in her hands.

"I'm Grace," I told her.

"This is for you, Mrs. Horky," the woman said. She giggled, almost with embarrassment—she apparently knew who the package was from. It was a beautifully wrapped gift box with a card from the jewelry story across the street. By this time Claudia, Grey's other casting director, had come out of her office, which was adjacent to mine. She saw the box in my hand.

"Oh!" said Claudia. "A little payola from a satisfied client?"

"No," I responded, "but I think I know who sent it."

I went back into my office and opened the box. It was the heart with the dangling pearl I had so hurriedly pointed at in the jewelry store window. I opened the card. It read: "Ah, those Sicilians! —Harold."

2

"Getting to Know You"

The next morning Harold called me at my office. "Did you receive a delivery yesterday?" he asked.

"Yes," I told him, "but I think it's customary to say something like 'I'm sorry, but I can't really accept it. I hardly know you.'"

He laughed. "Don't give me that bullshit," he said. I was glad, because I really did love it. "I want you to have it," he continued, "so you will think of me while I'm in France."

"Oh? You're going to France?"

"Yeah."

"When?"

"Today."

"What are you going to do in France?"

"Brigitte Bardot needs a little help from me," he said. There was a hint in his voice, an effort at a double entendre, that his meeting with Miss Bardot, the world's reigning celluloid "sex kitten," wouldn't be all work. Harold was like that. He loved to tease, to insinuate, to surround his activities with mystery, often of the sexual sort.

"I hope you have a wonderful trip," I said.

"Joe Levine is doing a film there," he continued, "and he wants me to help Brigitte with her English." He offered another subtle laugh as though "helping her with her English" was a euphemism for something else.

"Who's Joe Levine?"

"The movie producer," he said. "He makes movies out of my books. You know, Joseph E. Levine." He laughed again. "Next year he's gonna produce *The Carpetbaggers*."

"Harold, have a wonderful trip," I repeated, knowing he wanted me to explore his relationship with Levine (whom I had never heard of) and Brigitte (whom everyone had heard of) with more interest, wanted me to ask questions like, Why on earth would Joseph E. Levine want you to help Brigitte Bardot? After all, Harold had a pronounced New York accent, with hardly the inflection and diction of a language coach. I was curious though, and dying to quiz him, but I remained mum.

"I'll only be gone for a couple of weeks," he said. "I'll call you when I get back."

"Great," I said.

"Be sure and wear that pendant."

"I will, Harold."

"Promise?"

"I promise."

We hung up. I had no idea if Harold would call me again. During the next two weeks, although I thought about him at random when I wore the heart-shaped pendant, he did not overwhelm my thoughts. I had other, more important things to think about.

Tom didn't even ask me where I got the pendant, although I wore it often. His drinking had reached an all-time high, to the degree that sometimes he seemed hardly to see me.

Our marriage had been a mistake from the outset, born of my desire to escape my sheltering parents. Even in college, where I had been a day student, I was subject to my father's curfew. My parents were of an old-world school, determined I enter marriage as a virgin. I was still living at home when I met Tom with some friends at a baseball game after I had gone to work in the advertising business. Tom was good-looking and fun in those days, and I enjoyed his company. One day when my father caught us in the attic of our home in Queens, I blurted out: "Don't worry, Daddy. We're getting married!"

"You'd better!" cried my father.

We did, even though I was the one who instigated it. We had the ceremony at St. Patrick's Cathedral, primarily because a friend of mine had been married there. Although our relationship had never been founded on love, I thought naively we could make the marriage work. Tom *was* a talented artist and in the beginning he did quite a lot of reasonably profitable freelance work, for the most part illustrations for medical magazines. I was unaware he had a problem with alcohol. Until our marriage, I just assumed his drinking was as normal as that of other young men his age.

By the time I met Harold, Tom slept most of the time and woke only to the rattling sound of the ice-cube trays. He *talked* about painting far more than he painted, and the realization that our relationship was doomed was foremost in my thoughts. I continually thought of reasons not to go home immediately after work, and Tom seemed not to care. Alcohol had become his mistress and his demise. Once, I got home just in time to save him from burning to death. He had passed out on the couch and his cigarette had started a fire; smoke and flames encircled him; had I been a minute later, the fire would have been out of control. As long as I worked, paid the rent, and left him enough money to replenish his inventory of brandy, he was satisfied.

One midmorning the switchboard operator at Grey announced: "A Mr. Robbins is holding on line two." I looked at my calendar. It was fifteen days to the day since Harold had left for France to "tutor" Miss Bardot. My heart leaped, but I composed and readied myself before I took his call.

"Good morning, Harold," I said casually into the telephone.

"I'm back! Got in last night," he said enthusiastically. "Did you wear the pendant while I was gone?"

"Well . . . some," I answered cagily.

"Did you think about me?"

"I thought of you, yes, but you didn't consume my thoughts, if that's what you mean."

If he knew I was teasing him, he did not reveal it. Instead, he laughed confidently and said, "Let's have lunch."

The Four Seasons Restaurant was within walking distance of Grey Advertising. I arrived precisely at noon. Harold was already there, seated at what he called his "regular" table. He was sipping champagne, the bottle of Dom Pérignon stationed in an ice bucket at his side. He wore an elegantly tailored, light-brown, sheepskin sport coat, rather like suede on the outside with very fine, soft sheepskin inside, and a dress shirt opened at the neck. He also wore a big smile and a sparkle in his blue-brown eyes. He stood up and spread his arms like an orchestra conductor. "Grace, it's good to see you again," he said warmly, and hugged me as if we were long lost friends.

We sat down, and I asked, "So, how was your trip to France?"

"Here!" he said with zeal. He raised his arm and pulled back the sleeves of his coat and shirt. On his wrist was a big, round watch bejeweled with several expensive heart-shaped diamonds encircling its face. It was very feminine, and when he took it off and handed it to me, I was momentarily speechless. I thought to myself, *Why, this is a really lovely and beautiful gift, and I hardly know this man*. Before I could think of a response, he said, "Look at the back of it."

I turned the watch over. Inscribed on the sterling silver were the words: "Thank you, Harold! BB." The watch wasn't a present for me after all, but a gift to Harold from Brigitte Bardot, for services rendered, whatever they were. I looked at Harold, holding back my surprise and, yes, my embarrassment. He was grinning like the Cheshire Cat. I handed the watch back and said with false enthusiasm, "It's very nice."

"That's what she gave me in return for my help," he said. Again there was the innuendo.

"I'm sure she speaks English perfectly now," I responded sharply, and lowered my eyes to the menu.

Regardless of what my taste buds found appetizing, I realized soon enough that for Harold, eating—whether breakfast, lunch, or dinner—was a scene he had to direct. It was always a production. He poured me a second glass of champagne, snapped his fingers, and a waiter delivered a finely chopped, leafy green salad for two in a crystal-serving bowl, accompanied by a container of beluga caviar, not the usual teeny-tiny tin but a huge, even giant, one. The largest and the very best—that summed up what Harold Robbins was all about.

He looked at me with his ubiquitous grin and again snapped his fingers. The waiter returned. "Please turn the tin of caviar upside down and pour it on the salad," Harold instructed him.

The waiter did as requested, and left. Harold tossed the salad with glee, talking casually as he did so; then he began dividing it on two salad plates. "Have you ever been to the South of France?"

"No, but I'd like to go someday."

"What other places are on your wish list?"

I thought back to my childhood; we kids played a game called "Time" in which two opponents had a face-off of fantasy. A common material subject was chosen, like a cottage, and the point was to enlarge upon its description. A cottage became a house with all the adjectives one could beckon, then the house became a mansion, the mansion a castle, and so forth. I always conjured up magnificent homes and luxurious yachts and fabulous trips, most of them gleaned from the movies.

"Aside from France," I told him, "there's Italy, particularly Venice. And I would like to go to Sicily sometime to visit my mother's family. I would like to go to London; and then there's Capri and Monaco, and I've been hearing a lot lately about Ibiza, somewhere in the Mediterranean."

"Ibiza?" Harold said offhandedly, but it wasn't really a question. "It's off the east coast of Spain, just below Majorca. A great little island."

He finished dividing the salad.

"Here," he said, placing one of the salad plates before me. "Try that"—he had a devilish grin on his face—"and tell me what you think of it."

I took a bite of the salad; it was delicious. Caviar and leafy greens. I had never had it before, nor had I seen it on a menu.

"Well?" he asked. "How do you like it?"

"It's delicious," I responded honestly.

"I made up the recipe myself," he said proudly. "I invented the damn thing."

"Really? What do you call it?"

"The Money Salad!" he cried with a boisterous laugh, and then attacked his own plate. After a moment he said, "Go on, Grace. Talk to me. Tell me about yourself. How long have you been in the advertising game?"

"I've been at Grey for a year, and before that I was with Biow Advertising, and then . . ."

As I rambled on, Harold listened with rapt attention. His eyes were locked on me just as they had been at the Americana Hotel two weeks before, but this time it was less nerve-racking. He had a wonderful talent for disarming people. His celebrity was evident, for many people came by our table to say hello and to chat briefly; each time he introduced me with such flair that I felt like a celebrity myself. None of the people seemed to be close friends, however, just acquaintances. He had a talent, too, for dismissing interlocutors diplomatically but quickly. Then his eyes and attention would fix again on me as though I were the only person in the world who mattered to him. It was flattering indeed!

We ate his Money Salad, which was delectable, and filets mignon, and we sipped more and more Dom Pérignon, propelling me again into a one-woman talkathon, with Harold taking in my every word. He was a better listener than he was a conversationalist. He had an innate curiosity, a desire to learn all he could about a person as quickly as possible. He was not shy, but he did not enjoy talking about himself. I suspected he was a loner, as many creative people are; when I occasionally paused in my monologue to ask him a question about himself, he adroitly evaded it and turned the question back to me. It made me wonder what skeletons were in his closet that he didn't want drummed up. By the time lunch was over, I didn't care. I did not fall in love with him that day, but I certainly liked him, a lot. Today it sounds cliché, but he was the first person in my life who seemed solely interested in what I was all about as a woman, as a human being, rather than as a sex object. It sounds strange—I know—when one considers all the inglorious rumors the gossip mill produced over the years regarding Harold's obsession with sex (which were mostly true).

But the luncheon that day, at least in reference to his attentions on me, was as innocent as a family picnic. When I returned to my office, I had made a new friend, nothing more.

Over the next year, I saw Harold at least once a week, sometimes twice, and occasionally three times, always for lunch at one of the innumerable local restaurants he liked. Although he was dictatorial and had an unquenchable thirst to dominate, I did not mind; during the previous four years I had fended for myself, making virtually every important decision for both Tom and myself. Harold's seeming mastery of every situation was a welcome breather from my world of constant decision making. I did not consider our lunches as legitimate dates but rather as fun meetings, no different than meeting up with a girlfriend or a colleague. We never had dinner, although I joined him for a cocktail at Grand Central Station a few times before he caught the commuter train to his home in Connecticut. After our drink, I would wait on the platform as he boarded. He would turn back and call out from the train, "Hey, Tiger, I'll call you in a couple of days!"—and with that he'd be off to his other world, which I knew nothing about, nor did I want to.

As time went on, I knew something was happening within me, an internal change. I don't know exactly when I fell in love with him; it was gradual, innocent, and without premeditation; absent of sex. I didn't tell a soul about my feelings, not even Harold. After all, he was married and so was I. For that matter, I didn't tell anyone I was even seeing him. It was our secret, Harold's and mine, or so I thought. I began to realize what was happening to me though, particularly on days when we did not meet; then I felt empty and lonely, as if something were missing in my life.

One day when I joined him for lunch, I did a double take. What little hair he had was no longer white: it had been dyed something close to natural brown. I didn't say anything about the color change, nor did he, but he obviously wanted to appear younger than he was. I thought his gesture was cute, particularly since he did it without encouragement from me. For the rest of his life, his hair was always colored.

He was fun, an escape from what was happening at home. I knew little about him, except that he was a successful writer—very successful I began to learn. I made no attempt to pry into his private life, but any astute observer could ascertain that he was not satisfied. I suspected he had been a lonely child, independent of parental guidance, for he never called upon anyone when a problem needed to be solved. He was a decision maker, forceful and persuasive. He could be charming and suave on the one hand, but blunt and caustic on the other if he thought the situation required toughness. Above all, he was generous, the most generous person I had ever met. Nothing fazed him, and he seemed to find humor in every experience. We laughed constantly, which was something I never did at home.

I told him small details about my private life and marriage, even though he often quizzed me more than I felt he should. I told him about my sheltered life while growing up in Brooklyn, about the mask I had learned to use to cover my anxieties and fears, about my mother's hard work as a seamstress, and my father's failures as a businessman, about the dysfunction between them caused by near poverty, about the abuse my father showered on us—my mother, my younger brother, Gary, and me—brought about by random drinking at the racetrack and his loss of self-esteem.

"Did your parents ever consider divorce?"

"Heaven forbid!" I exclaimed. "They're too Catholic for that. Besides, in their strange way, they loved each other. My mother's a saint, a hardworking saint."

Harold sometimes hinted that his own marriage was not made in paradise. He had been married for twenty years; if divorce had ever been in the works, it seemed to me it would have taken place long before. I did not learn until years later that he and Lillian had once divorced and then remarried.

My own life was the same as the day I had met Harold, if not worse. Tom was drinking nonstop and I had come to accept that he was a bona fide alcoholic. Our sex life had diminished to naught, and if Tom ever indicated he was disturbed by it or the lack thereof, it was only in the small inquisitions he held when I came home later than usual, which never had anything to do with Harold. What conversations Tom and I had were banal at best.

"Where have you been?"

"Oh, I had a drink with some of the girls."

"Where?"

"At Cheerios."

"Who was there?"

"No one in particular. Just the regulars."

"What did you talk about?"

"Nothing. Just business."

He would shrug and pour another glass of brandy.

Despite his reticence in speaking about himself, it was impossible not to learn more about Harold Robbins during a year of luncheons and quick cocktails before he caught the evening train. He was well traveled and I had been nowhere. With the exception of having flown to Florida once with Tom to visit some of his relatives and a couple of trips to Fire Island with friends, my sole venture outside New York City had been to Rhode Island when I was two.

Harold would look off into space in disbelief as I unveiled my life, and then he would change the subject, as if to release me from my memories.

"I kidnapped Caryn when she was a baby and took her to Argentina," he said in passing one day.

"You kidnapped your own daughter?"

"Yeah," he answered, "at least that's what they tried to pin on my, after the fact."

I was curious, not only about the child's welfare, but because Harold spoke more frequently, if only in fleeting spurts, about his former lover Yvonne than he did about his wife, Lillian.

"I did it to get Caryn out of her mother's environment," he continued. "Yvonne was ruining the child. She didn't want children; she wanted a career, and Caryn was a handicap to her plans. It's hard to believe, but sometimes Yvonne would actually forget what friend she had left Caryn with when she went to work in the morning. It was a terrible environment for a child to grow up in." He looked off, thinking, and then he muttered, "Fucking terrible!"

"What happened?" I asked hesitantly.

"Well," he began, and then he looked at his watch. "Look, I've gotta catch the train."

The truth is I didn't have to do a lot of research to find out more about Harold Robbins. He was already famous in a small way, or infamous, but he wasn't yet a celebrity. A month after he returned from France, the book, *Where Love Has Gone*, was published with great fanfare. It became an overnight bestseller, although most of the critics derided it as smut.

"I write for my readers," said Harold testily, "not for the reviewers. I don't read my reviews ever."

Where Love Has Gone was Harold's eighth novel. All had been bestsellers, but *The Carpetbaggers*, which had come out the year before I met him, had made his name a household word, although only as the author of the book, not as the man. It was a blockbuster that had gone through innumerable hardback editions and had just come out in its sixth paperback printing when we met that first time at the Americana Hotel.

One night when we were walking to Grand Central Station we passed a bookstore. A huge sign was displayed in the window reading: "Harold Robbins's Latest Smashing Best Seller—*Where Love Has Gone*."

"Look Harold!" I cried excitedly. "They have your novel!"

"Forget it," and he tugged me on down the sidewalk without looking in the window. "Wait till you see what they do with my next book." I thought he was being flip in a conceited fashion, but he wasn't. As far as Harold was concerned, once a book was completed, it was over, finished, done, finito, a part of history. It was the next project he was concentrating on already, tossing ideas about in his mind. "Sometimes they have to ferment for years before I can sit down and write them," he said. He seldom discussed a new project with me, hardly ever in twenty-eight years. He would tell me the basic skeletal idea, but that would be it; he wasn't looking for advice.

"My next book is gonna be about a Latin American peasant," he said without being prompted. "A guy who becomes a revolutionary, and then because of certain circumstances he becomes rich, and when he becomes rich he turns from being a revolutionary into being a playboy diplomat." He did not follow up with the obvious question: "What do you think?" He simply made the statement, almost as though he were talking to himself.

If he was not yet a national figure, he was certainly well known in New York, especially in several restaurants and nightclubs. He always got his table of choice, and he was a favorite of among his peers. He was jaunty and confident, but I began to realize with certainty that he was a loner, even a habitual loner. I later surmised he could count his close friends on the finger of one hand and have uncounted fingers left.

It was during that year, when I was meeting him for weekly luncheons, that he began to become a celebrity. I believe it's also when he began to understand what celebrity status could do for him. I was proud I knew him, although I hadn't revealed to anyone that we often rendezvoused for lunch. It wasn't my style; I liked having my own secrets; besides, it was nobody's business. I just didn't say anything about him.

When you meet someone you've never heard of before and suddenly realize he has a certain claim to fame, the name seems to pop up at every turn. I had never heard his name before reading *The Carpetbaggers* on Peggy Ann's yacht that weekend, but after I met him, the name "Harold Robbins" came to my ears more frequently than I would ever have imagined, and some of the stories attached to it were not exactly Sunday school tales.

There was his apparent liaison with Lena Horne a few years before. The story had managed to land in the gossip columns and scandal sheets, front and center, culminating when Lena's husband vowed to kill Harold. (I suppose adding to the mix was the racial aspect, the affair having occurred in the fifties, some few years before civil rights took over the headlines. But Harold was always ahead of his time, which I believe was one of the secrets of his success.)

And then there was a story about Harold getting into a fight one night at the Latin Quarter, the famous Manhattan nightclub, with Aristotle Onassis over another alleged liaison—with Onassis's then wife, Cristina.

I took the stories with a grain of salt and never asked Harold anything about them. The truth is, I was having too much fun lunching with him. If he as a roué, so what? The people I knew, with discreet reputations, seemed suddenly boring. Harold made me laugh, which was more than the others did.

Although Harold did not tell me about Lena Horne or Christina Onassis, he never pawned himself off as a saint. He enjoyed acting macho and his language was laced with profanities, which in those days seemed strangely quaint rather than crude. He was frank in a low-key way about his past and about sex. He definitely liked women, yet not once did he hit on me. His less headline-laden affairs came out slowly in small dribbles during our conversations. I suppose it was impossible for them not to. It was my father, however, who did the in-depth research after I told my parents one weekend that I had been seeing Harold Robbins, the writer. I had finally confessed to them that my marriage was not doing well.

My mother had never heard of Harold, but my father, who was an avid reader, had. "I've read some of his books," he said. He had also read the tabloids. "Grace, you be careful around that man," he lectured. "He's a lech."

"Why, Daddy," I laughed, "that's exactly what I've always wanted in a man!" My father did not laugh.

Eventually I did learn, if not in sordid detail, more about his liaison with Yvonne Russell-Farrow, the mother of his only child. Unlike the dalliances with Lena Horne and Christina Onassis (if they actually happened), it had a lasting effect on Harold and, although much later, on our own relationship.

Sometime during the mid-fifties Harold had met Yvonne, who was then an actress. She was in the process of changing careers, and soon she became a successful cosmetic executive in New York.

She and Harold had a fleeting but torrid affair. Her newfound career apparently came first; consequently, Harold broke off the relationship. (Contrary to what was written about Harold in later years, he did not divorce Lillian and marry Yvonne.) When he broke off with Yvonne, however, he was unaware she was pregnant. She waited several months before she told him, and by then, it was too late for her to have an abortion.

Harold went back to Yvonne and was with her when Caryn was born. Unfortunately, Yvonne still placed her career above everything else, particularly child rearing. Harold became incensed because he felt she wasn't taking proper care of the baby. His anger culminated when he stole the child away and took her to Argentina.

Yvonne was not to be taken lightly. She pursued Harold to South America, where she filed a civil suit for custody of the child and tried to have him extradited. Harold evaded the summons, returned with Caryn to New York, and was indeed immediately charged with something just short of kidnapping.

"I knew I had lost the battle when Yvonne showed up in court with a Catholic priest on her arm as a witness to her moral righteousness," Harold told me.

Yvonne regained custody after the priest testified that she was a fit mother, and after Yvonne had told the priest that she would raise the child as a Catholic. To Harold's consternation and anguish, she did not comply with her promise. She promptly placed Caryn in a boarding school, which Harold paid for; however, it only served to make Caryn feel rejected by both parents. The legal process cost Harold $500,000.

"I love my daughter," he told me many times. "I love her very much." His words, which I took as being totally sincere, established a growing affinity between us.

While we were having lunch, he said very casually, "I have to go to Hollywood."

I knew *The Carpetbaggers* movie had gone into production, but Harold seldom mentioned it. He had little confidence in moviemakers when it came to translating his books to the screen. "They always fuck them up," he would say, "so if you can't produce it yourself, it's best to just take the money and run." He looked at me.

"Hollywood?" I said.

"Hollywood. I have to go out there on some business."

"Oh? What kind of business?"

"Joe Levine needs to talk to me about something. You know, some crap about *The Carpetbaggers*."

I experienced a twinge of emotion. I had been with Harold two or three times a week since he had returned from "helping" Brigitte Bardot on another Joe Levine movie, and the knowledge that he would be absent from my life for even a week left a hollow feeling in my chest.

"Is Miss Bardot going to be there?" I kidded.

"Brigitte?" he grinned. "Naw, she's in Europe doing another flick." He said it as if he had talked to her every day since his return from France the year before.

"When are you going?"

"Next week," he said. He paused a moment, looking me in the eyes. He seemed to hesitate, and then he said rather forcefully, "Want to come with me, Tiger?"

It was a question, not a demand, but I knew we were suddenly at a midpoint, one of return or of no return. We could go forward or we could turn back. An inner voice immediately told me no, that I shouldn't accept his invitation. We had been having a great deal of fun at our lunches and during our brief meetings at Grand Central Station. But having platonic fun in your own backyard was different than going off with a man on an airplane to a hotel in a far removed location.

It was autumn again and the air was growing crisp—a change of seasons. It had been almost precisely a year to the day that Harold and I had met. From the outset I had gone with the flow, virtuously and platonically. Nothing had happened that would even remotely suggest something illicit. If ever a relationship had developed on innocent grounds, this had been it.

I did not think about the proposition long, even though sex was implicit in his invitation. By this time I was thoroughly hooked, at least in this way: I completely trusted Harold and wanted to be with him. The question for me was quite simple: to do or not to do, to cease and desist or to continue. I tossed it over in my mind, maybe twice, and that was it.

"How long are you going to be gone?" I asked.

"One week." He grinned, waiting for my answer. Then he tossed his hands in the air. "Come on, Tiger. It's Tinsel Town. You've never been there. Hollywood and Vine! The Chinese Theater! The Brown Derby! The Sunset Strip! I'm gonna show you the rounds!"

I thought it over for another fleeting second, and said, "I'd love to go, Harold."

He grinned broadly, snapped his fingers with extraordinary confidence and called to the waiter, "Another bottle of champagne!"

3

California Dreaming

Committing myself to a trip to California with Harold was one thing; implementing the plan was something else.

"I have to go to the West Coast," I told Tom.

"What for?"

"We need some kids for a Proctor and Gamble commercial," I said.

"Why can't you get them here?"

"We need golden kids with beach-blonde hair—preferably some real towheads."

He shrugged. "They're crazy, these advertising people." Then he poured another drink.

The next day at the agency, I confessed to Catherine my plan without revealing whom it was I wanted to escape to California with. Catherine Pitts was a mentor of mine, a sophisticated lady in her mid-thirties who understood my predicament completely.

"Don't worry about it, Grace." She smiled adventurously, perhaps with vicarious pleasure. "You deserve a holiday, and I can easily cover for you."

The second the airplane lifted off from Idlewild Airport (it had not yet been named Kennedy International), I felt a great sense of relief, suddenly lighthearted, totally in the present, oblivious of the past. I looked at Harold. He was grinning mischievously. What was in store for me I did not know, but I was determined to relax and enjoy it.

Harold was in high spirits—not that he usually wasn't, but it was obvious that he, too, felt he was escaping something. Was it Lillian, back home in

Connecticut? Her name hardly ever entered our conversations, and when it did, it was just a passing comment from Harold, never anything revealing. If I knew little about Harold, I knew nothing of Lillian and their life together. I was not a callous person, it simply didn't matter to me. Such was my own misery at the apartment on West Seventy-Second Street.

The flight from New York to Los Angeles seemed to last minutes rather than hours. Everything Harold said was funny, and then too there was the wonderful anticipation I had of California, like a child going to Disneyland for the first time. The hours passed in a burst of energy and champagne; we were in New York, we were airborne, and suddenly we were on the tarmac at Los Angeles International. Harold hailed a taxi.

We drove straight from the airport to the Beverly Hills Hotel. Harold's high spirits continued; he was good-natured, quipping jokes, jotting down risqué limericks. It was September and winter was on the horizon in New York City, but there in Southern California—well, to me it was like the Garden of Eden. Colorful flowers grew everywhere and the streets were lined with an infinite variety of Palm trees. Tall narrow trees with frou-frous on top; short squat trees like giant pineapples. My "Cinderella" adventure had begun; the "Carpetbagger" was eager and confident in new territory.

I had never seen anything like the Beverly Hills Hotel before, at least not in person. We drove up the long driveway flanked by flowers and shrubs and palm trees, and stopped under the wide porte cochére, where uniformed valets greeted us. Harold was in his element; it was impossible not to be transformed along with him into another person, one suddenly carefree and unleashed from all the problems back home. I had forgotten about Tom and New York City and Grey Advertising.

The clerk at the desk knew Harold, or at least acted as though he did, but it was evident Harold was much more of a New Yorker than a Southern Californian. He was blunt, to the point, sometime tactless, but cheerfully funny. Before I knew it, we were outside again. Harold insisted I be given a tour of the grounds. There was an Olympic-sized swimming pool where sun-worshipers were still gathered, even though dusk was falling, and a garden-like atmosphere created by the abundance of brilliant flowers, all read and yellow and white and blue. We followed the bellhop along a lush trail that meandered by the hotel's famous pink cottages and bungalows. It was so very different from the massive high-rise hotels in New York City, and when we were finally in our own bungalow and the bellhop had left with a hefty tip in his pocket, Harold turned to me and said proudly, "This is the number one bungalow, Tiger, *number one*."

"It's lovely," I said, and I meant it.

By the time we were ensconced in the bungalow, it was fully dusk and the evening was unfolding. Harold was on the house telephone, ordering this and that, not once asking me if there was anything in particular I wanted.

"Some caviar and smoked salmon and a couple of bottles of Dom Pérignon," he ordered, "and Chateaubriand with béarnaise sauce for two. This is Harold Robbins," he stated with authority.

So far, he had not made any overt gestures, and I wouldn't let it enter my mind. I asked him if I might take a shower and freshen up.

"By all means, Tiger! This is your home away from home!"

I showered, now wondering when it was going to happen. I didn't care, of course. I was so excited to be away from New York and Tom and the advertising agency, and there was no doubt in my mind that only Harold could have persuaded me to escape.

When I emerged from the bathroom, having primped in front of the mirror for what I perceived as several tantalizing minutes and had changed into what I hoped was sexy California casual attire, a waiter was delivering our order in the living room of the suite on silver trays and in silver bowls with silver lids and with the two bottles of Dom Pérignon stuffed in silver buckets laced with ice. When he left, again after pocketing a hefty tip, Harold sang "Ta-dahhhhh!" without looking at me.

He poured two glasses of champagne, very carefully, and then he turned to hand one to me. "This is the way to live the good"—he stopped in midsentence and midaction, his body frozen, his eyes riveted. He stared at me a moment and then muttered under his breath: "Wow!"

We neither drank nor ate. We made love—passionate, wild, physical, fiery, unmitigated love. It happened with such rapidity—not that it was a quickie; it was indeed a process—that I hardly remember how we began. He simply took me in his arms and we were suddenly kissing and groping and fondling with such rare ecstasy that time was lost. We never even made it to the bed—the couch was closer. What energy, what dexterity. It caused me to sit up and surprisingly ask, "What was that?" "Gotcha," he laughed, with that gleam in his eye.

This first sexual intimacy changed our relationship forever. From that moment forward, and I thought secretly it truly might be forever, I felt unquestionably that I was Harold's girl and I certainly felt that he was my man. New York was a world away, and I didn't care if we never returned again, although I knew we would eventually.

Compared to my few previous sexual experiences, Harold was the epitome of what I thought a lover was supposed to be. Sex was his passion and he reveled in it; it was wonderful, and as far as I knew, it was in *my* sex—that is me, and in me alone—that he reveled. Fortunately, it would remain that way for a long, long time; unfortunately, it would one day change.

In retrospect, I realize the technique of Harold's lovemaking was the culmination of many years of experience. He knew what satisfied a woman and he enjoyed immensely giving that satisfaction. Suffice it to say, he was not a "wham bam, thank you ma'am" type of lover. He was meticulous, slow, and terribly caring.

I don't know how many times we made love during that week, but each time it was marvelous and each time a little different. Harold could have done anything to me that he wanted to do and I would not have complained, for I knew I was truly in love with him. Whatever he wanted to do now—well, I was game, morning, noon, and night.

One of Harold's favorite expressions was, "No day can be a bad day that starts out with a good fuck!" He was serious, and I realized soon enough that his need for sex was rapacious, part and parcel of his nature, and that he was doing his best to make his words come true. I wasn't dissatisfied, nor was he.

It wasn't all lovemaking. We saw the sights. We went to Hollywood and Vine, which was depressing after all I had heard about it—just a seedy intersection in a decaying old Hollywood. We had lunch at the famous Brown Derby (where I saw Bogart sitting alone with his ham and eggs), cocktails in the Polo Lounge at the Beverly Hills Hotel, dinner at Ken Hansen's Scandia on Sunset Boulevard, which was Harold's favorite West Coast restaurant. We took the back lot tour at Universal, where we watched an actual scene from a movie being made, and then we rushed back to bungalow #1 and made love.

One afternoon Harold said, "We're going to Chasen's tonight for dinner."

What he meant was, "Dress up." I believe it was the first time since I had met him that he wore a suit and tie. He looked debonair, very refined, in a tailored Savile Row suit. (Later, he had his clothes made by Doug Hayward in London.) I put on a cocktail dress, jazzed it up with costume jewelry, and high heels.

"Dammit, Tiger, you look absolutely gorgeous!" cried Harold. "You'll put these Beverly Hills ingénues to shame."

On the way to the restaurant in a taxi, Harold explained that Dave Chasen's place was the preeminent eatery and watering hole for celebrities—now that Dave's major competitor, bogus Prince Michael Romanoff, had closed his namesake restaurant in Beverly Hills and retired. Chasen was an ex-New Yorker whom Harold had known since the late thirties. Chasen had been the straight man in a vaudeville comedy team in his early years, but had apparently been better known for his homemade chili than he had been for his comedy; when he decided to open a chili parlor in West Hollywood, several New Yorkers had bankrolled him, including Harold Ross, the owner of the *New Yorker* magazine. I was surprised when we arrived; rather than a chili parlor, I saw a huge rambling white building of distinction; the interior was lush and formal, and I was duly impressed.

The maitre d' (another New Yorker) recognized Harold, and he gave us what was undoubtedly one on the "A" tables, the same service Harold was accustomed to back East. The place was packed, with half of the patrons being Hollywood celebrities, just as Harold had predicted. There was James Stewart with a group of people at one table, Cary Grant and a similar group at another table. George Burns and Jack Benny; Rosalind Russell and Barbara Stanwyck. It became apparent that Harold knew more of the non-celebrities, the writers and producers, than he did the actors themselves. Several people came by our table to greet Harold, including a thin, weathered-looking man in a tweed jacket who turned out to be Dave Chasen. It was as though we were back at one of Harold's haunts in Manhattan.

Finally, we were alone again. We had a booth, and Harold had placed me where I could see out over the main dining room and eye the myriad famous people. His angle was toward the foyer and front door. We were having a good time, an intimate dinner, when Harold's eyes suddenly riveted and his chin fell. He said under his breath, "Oh, fuck! Be prepared for the shit to hit the fan, Tiger."

"What do you mean? What's wrong?"

"Lana's here," he whispered, and he laughed in a special way he had when he was gearing up for confrontation. Confrontation to Harold meant he had to use his considerable wiles to charm someone.

I looked. Lana Turner was standing in the foyer with a tall distinctive man. She was beautiful in a white dress and diamonds that sparkled like stars. It was a well-known fact she had detested *Where Love Has Gone*, which Harold had framed loosely upon her lurid affair with mobster Johnny Stompanato. She had gone on record saying that Harold "had turned the worst tragedy of my life into a cheap, mean, best-selling novel based on cruel fabrications." It didn't help her deflated ego that the novel was still a best seller, piled high in bookstore window. "I hate the man," Lana told people.

"Do you know her?" I now asked Harold, my eyes glued to the foyer.

"No, but I certainly know the man she's with," he said with a grin.

"Who is he?" I asked.

"Ross Hunter, the producer," said Harold.

The Stompanato tragedy had not affected Lana's career negatively, nor had Harold's book, which was so loosely based on the real incident that I wondered what all the fuss was about; furthermore, the book had been published a full six years after the tabloid event. In the episode's aftermath, Turner had made three lavish movies during alternating years, *Imitation of Life*, *Portrait in Black*, and *By Love Possessed*, and all of them had been successful.

"Actually," Harold once analyzed, "my book gave her career another ten years. After all, most actresses of Lana's age are just about over the hill."

She was forty-two years old, and as I watched her, she certainly didn't look over the hill to me. My eyes swept the room; I thought she was the most gorgeous person present.

"She's absolutely beautiful," I said to Harold.

"That she is," he answered. "Second only to you, Tiger."

At that moment the maitre d' led the couple toward a reserved table. En route they passed within a foot of ours. It was true that Lana did not know what Harold looked like, but when Ross Hunter saw him, he stared with a strange combination of friendship and fear. His first inclination seemed to be friendly, and I thought he was going to stop and shake Harold's hand, but he suddenly caught himself, averted his eyes, speeded his pace, and swept Lana by our table without as much as a whisper. Harold grinned and laughed under his breath; he loved it.

The rest of the evening went by without incident, although I was afraid someone would notify Lana that the man sitting at my side was the writer Harold Robbins who had defamed her image in *Where Love Has Gone*. It didn't happen, and when we left for the evening, Harold commented enigmatically, "If I ever get a chance, I'm gonna help Lana."

I had not the foggiest idea what he was talking about. Lana was at the zenith of her career. What help would she need? As usual, however, Harold was thinking ahead of the times.

Whatever business he had in Hollywood was lost in our shuffle of lovemaking. I suspect today there was never a business agenda to begin with, that Harold had used it as a pretext to seduce me on foreign turf. Not once did he mention Joseph E. Levine after we left New York; for all I knew the producer was a fiction of Harold's imagination, used as an excuse whenever he wanted to leave town, a la his visit to Brigitte Bardot in France. It didn't matter to me, then or later. I mean, who on earth would want to break such an idyllic and romantic holiday with business? It simply wasn't in the cards, although there was a brief moment one morning when I thought the fun and games indeed had terminated.

"Listen," said Harold. "Paul Gitlin is coming by our bungalow this morning and when he gets here, I want you to act like you don't speak English."

"What?"

"Just act like you don't speak English," he repeated with a laugh. "You know, like you're a foreigner just arrived from the old country."

His request didn't surprise me at all. Harold's behavior was often antic, but almost always on the humorous side. I shrugged. If that's what he wanted, okay.

"Who's Paul Gitlin?"

Harold explained that Paul was his lawyer, agent, and business manager all rolled into one. He was the executor of the Thomas Wolfe, Sinclair Lewis, and Ayn Rand estates, and he represented, among other best-selling writers, two of Harold's colleagues and acquaintances, novelist Irving Wallace and historian Cornelius Ryan. Paul was on the West Coast for business purposes primarily unrelated to Harold. His office represented several other writers, all of whom had books for Hollywood fodder. Paul was a seasoned negotiator, Harold explained, who thought writers should partake more equitably in the wealth they created for their publishers. "In other words," he said, "Paul Gitlin is a man right up my Hell's Kitchen alley." Then he repeated: "Just act like you don't speak English."

I thought Harold's request was amusing. "Whatever you want," I told him with a laugh.

A short time later there was a rap on the door. Harold looked at me and grinned. "Remember, no English," he whispered.

I nodded, and he opened the door. When Paul Gitlin entered, I saw a person who looked more like a stereotypical writer than Harold ever did. He was Hemingwayesque, with a beard and all the trimmings. He was a couple of years younger than Harold, of medium height, slightly overweight, and dressed as casually as a holiday beachcomber, although he was as much of a native New Yorker as Harold was.

Harold greeted him with great enthusiasm and affection, which Paul reciprocated. I realized immediately that he was more than Harold had confessed: he was Harold's alter ego. After a moment Paul gave me a curious glance and then turned back to Harold.

"Well?" he said with a hand gesture toward me and in a voice that seemed to be a duplicate of Harold's. "You gonna introduce us or what?"

"Hey, don't worry about her," said Harold indifferently. "She's an Italian broad I picked up at one of the studio joints over in Hollywood. She can't speak a fucking word of English. Not a bad looker though, huh?"

Paul observed me, up and down and back again, taking Harold's words in stride as if they were the ultimate truth. I stood there, mutely. It was apparent anything Harold did or anyone Harold was with did not surprise Paul Gitlin in the least.

"Well?" said Harold. "What do you think of her?"

"Not bad," answered Paul as he continued to scrutinize me as though he were checking out a racehorse before the daily double. I felt a little embarrassed.

"What do you mean, 'Not bad?'" cried Harold. "Look at those breasts! Look at that ass! Jesus Christ, man! And the best thing about her, she doesn't understand one goddamned word of English. Not one! She's perfect! She speaks the language of sex!"

Paul stared at me, convinced of Harold's sincerity. I continued to stand there, doing my best to act like a dumb statue.

"You mean, she doesn't even know how to say fucking hello?" asked Paul.

"She doesn't know how to say shit," said Harold. "She's a fucking Sicilian, Paul. What does she need to know how to say anything for? She's got a body and that's what she talks with! Look at her for God's sake!"

Paul looked again. "Wow," he said under his breath. "She has that, Harold. She does indeed."

Harold went to the dresser and splashed on some cologne. "This stuff is lime-flavored, pal. Sicilians, they go nuts for it. They love fruit, you see. Here, try some." He started to spray some of it on Paul, but the latter threw up his arms and backed away.

"I'll pass," said Paul.

"At least you could give her a real inspection," Harold continued. "Touch her up a little. Feel those fucking boobs! Grab one of those buns!"

I don't know if Paul really was going to submit to Harold's request, but that was it for me. I picked up a pillow and threw it at them across the room. "That's enough!" I said.

Harold burst into unrestrained laugher. Paul's face fell; being the goat, he was less amused. His face grew slightly red and he stammered, "Robbins, you . . . you bastard!"

When Paul learned I was not another struggling, out-of-work Hollywood actress seeking an entrée into movies by giving favors, he assumed a different posture.

Harold introduced us, and then he said to Paul, "Grace is the real thing," which seemed an ambiguous comment to me.

"Oh, I'm real all right," I said.

"Hello, Grace," said Paul. He took my hand and kissed me on the cheek. "It's so nice to meet you." He chatted with me a moment, and then turned to Harold. He suddenly had his business hat on.

"When are you gonna get started on the new book?" he asked.

"When I finish my research," Harold answered.

"When are you gonna get started on the research?"

"Soon," said Harold. He grinned. "Goddammit, Paul, don't worry about it. Robbins always comes through."

I knew nothing about the publishing business, and it would be a long time before I understood the importance Paul had played in Harold's career and the importance he would play in the future. Together they had already revolutionized the book business, although I was unaware of it. I was ignorant of the fact, too, that Harold was on the verge of becoming the highest paid writer in the world, if he wasn't already, with of course Paul's help. I was not trying to eavesdrop on Harold and Paul's conversation, but it became clear, whether I wanted the knowledge or not, that Harold's publisher had advanced him $500,000 for his next novel before a single word had been written, which was a considerable amount of money in 1963.

Harold did not have many close friends, but it was apparent to me also, and very quickly, that Paul Gitlin was the preeminent member of his select inner circle. After he left Harold commented succinctly, "Paul and I are a team."

The rest of our week in Hollywood went by in a flash; suddenly it was time to return to New York. I was packing my suitcase to go home, remorseful at the prospect, when Harold said, "Hey, Tiger what's the rush? We're having a great time! Why don't we fly over to Hawaii for a few days?"

"Oh, Harold, I can't !"

"Why not?"

"Because I have a job."

"Call 'em," he said, "call your fucking office. Grey Advertising isn't gonna fall apart in your absence."

He did not have to persuade me further. I made the call, all tied up in knots.

"Don't worry about it," said Catherine. "I'll cover for you. Have a good time."

"Hawaii, here we come!" cried Harold.

4

A Little Bit of Paradise

The flight from Los Angeles to the Hawaiian Islands was vastly longer than I expected and significantly different than the one from New York to Los Angeles. Time could have been at a standstill for all I was concerned, and in a way it was. It was evident to me, although I did not express it, that what had begun as a whimsical relationship had changed dramatically. In retrospect, I perhaps said nothing because I was afraid of misinterpreting the situation. After all, I still knew little about Harold Robbins the man, except that he had written eight books, enjoyed sex immensely, laughed a lot, spent money like it was growing on trees, and strove always to have a good time.

Some things one remembers vividly, and our continuation to Hawaii seems today as though it happened only yesterday. I remember it all, primarily because we had such a fantastic time. Harold stepped up his limerick writing on the plane; his words became more erotic, sometimes crude, but there was such a charm to the way he wrote them that it was impossible for me to be offended. He would suddenly get an idea, quickly jot it down on a piece of paper, and hand it to me. The words were mundane and naughty, but fun:

> *A woman named Grace*
> *Has a beautiful face,*
> *But oh*
> *Her ass is to die for!*

He wrote at least twenty of them, all harmless, and they made the flight to Hawaii pass quickly.

When you're in love and you've never been to a tropical island, then Hawaii is paradise. I had loved Beverly Hills and Hollywood, but this new place was something absolutely ethereal. Our destination was Kauai, the Garden Island that travel books today promote as the island for nature lovers. I had no knowledge of it and didn't know what to expect, although I knew it would be tantalizingly erotic and romantic. Harold was doing the planning and what he had in mind was as close to basic nature as you can get; in fact, it was nature in the raw.

From Honolulu International Airport on Oahu, we took a two-engine puddle-jumper across another ninety miles of ocean to Kauai. It had all the elements romantic dreams are made of, from moody rain forests, sparkling waterfalls, and majestic cliffs, to jagged peaks, emerald valleys, and palm trees swaying in the soft tropical breeze. Even today, two-thirds of the island is impenetrable. Rainbows were commonplace and the beaches were golden, although we weren't going to see much of them.

In those days there was only one hotel on the entire island, the Hanalei Plantation, which consisted of several scattered cottages strung up and down the beach on the edge of the rain forest. It seemed we were at the end of the civilized world, certainly incommunicado because there wasn't a telephone on the island. Each cottage of the hotel complex had its own special name, and after Harold checked us in, he came running back to me with a devilish grin on his face.

"What's the big smile all about?" I asked.

"What do you think the name of our cottage is?"

"What?"

"The Missionary!" he burst out with glee.

His humor was well founded, for during the course of the next few days we were in precisely that position many times over, with certain variations in between. The cottage had a huge king-size bed, square in the middle of the bedroom with a curtain that could be drawn completely around it, giving one the sense of being in a cuddly nest. We seldom left it, not even to eat. The hotel dining room sent our meals over on a tray, the delivery boy rapping on our door—not very lightly, I thought—and then leaving the food on the porch before departing with what sounded like a giggle.

Again, it was not all lovemaking. During interludes we talked, although we seldom left the bed. Actually, Harold talked and I listened—a sudden and welcome reversal of the conversations we'd had during a year of lunches in New York, when I had done most of the talking in response to Harold's questions. By the time he began to reveal himself, he could have been a serial killer for all I cared and it would have made little difference to me. I had no reason to doubt the sincerity of his words, for he wasn't making a confession. Information about him simply seeped out in random pieces. For instance, he inadvertently mentioned his foster parents in a passing comment.

"Foster parents?" I quizzed.

"Right, my real father left me on the steps of the Paulist Catholic Orphanage in Hell's Kitchen when I was a baby. The way it was told to me was that he was at wit's end because he wasn't married to my mother, who died after delivering me. It was all Charles Dickens stuff. It was probably complicated because my father was Jewish and my mother was a gentile."

"What was your father's name?"

"I don't know for certain, but the Paulist Brothers gave me the moniker of Francis Kane."

"Francis Kane? Like in your book?" I was referring to the main character in *Never Love a Stranger*, Harold's first book.

"That's right," he said. "That's me, that character in the book. Francis Kane and his experiences are as close as I've ever come to writing something autobiographical."

The truth is Harold wasn't *anything* like the Francis Kane character. Maybe he wanted to be, but the only similarity he had with his fictional character was that both of them were orphans who became rich. Kane was selfish, ruthless, and cynical; none of those adjectives remotely described Harold when I first met him, not at all. He was generous to a fault, with an extraordinary compassion for those who were less privileged than he was; furthermore, he had tremendous admiration for people such as priests and rabbis who had given up the material things in life in order to pursue a higher, more spiritual goal. No, Harold wasn't in the least like Francis Kane to my way of thinking, but now that he had opened the door to some of the secrets of his life, I was stimulated to learn all I could about him.

"Tell me more," I said. "You grew up in an orphanage?"

He lit a cigarette, inhaled deeply, contemplated a moment, and then exhaled. "That's right. I was an orphan," he continued. "And like every kid, I wanted to be adopted, and every Sunday, potential parents would drop by the orphanage looking for a child to adopt. The Paulist Brothers would line us up and the people would inspect us, as if they were buying cattle at an auction or maybe a slave before the Civil War." He laughed under his breath and took another drag of his cigarette. "When you're rejected Sunday after Sunday— well, it has a lasting effect on your life. You either toughen up and roll with the punches or you develop some kind of inferiority complex."

"You poor baby," I said sympathetically.

"Hey!" he exclaimed. "I didn't think I was second or subordinate to anyone, so I got tough. I don't want anyone feeling sorry for me. I've had a great life, and the best is yet to come, Tiger." He looked at me with a wry smile, and wham!—we were suddenly embraced in mad passion again.

Later, the conversation continued over dinner and champagne in bed. Harold quizzed me continuously, as he had from the very first day we met, but in the course of our marathon conversations in Hawaii, the subject invariably shifted back to him; it could not have been otherwise, for Harold was, after all, very human and in need of a few strokes himself, regardless of the macho persona he displayed in public.

He was born May 21, 1916, which made him over twenty years older than I, but the gap in age seemed to narrow by the day as little secrets were unfolded and revealed. We made love; then we talked and ate and drank; then we made love again. We were rapidly becoming a fused unit, more than a twosome, something of a unique team. We communicated on a whole new level, silently as well as verbally. I began to understand precisely what his silent expressions and gestures meant, and I suppose it was the same for him of me.

Although we were in the Missionary Cottage 90 percent of the time, and shrouded in that draped, four-poster bed almost 100 percent of that time, we did venture out on occasion. The island was rustic at best, but Harold always bought me something—a native princess dress, a piece of costume jewelry, simple things that I adored.

"I was adopted when I was almost twelve years old," he said one day. "That's too late to really bond with your foster parents, although I've always had the suspicion that my foster father was also my real father."

"Really?"

"Yeah, I think he had a guilt complex for having given me over to the orphanage in the first place, and later, when he met another woman and married her, he wanted to make it up to me. But it was too late by then. I never really thought of him as my real father, just my adopted father, like my adopted mother. Their name was Rubin, so I became Harold Rubin."

"Why did they change your first name?" I asked. "From Francis to Harold?"

He shrugged. "Who the hell knows?"

"How did Rubin become Robbins?"

"That was Al Knoph's doing, my first publisher. He thought Robbins was a better name to put on a dust jacket."

It was difficult to absorb everything Harold told me, but I did my best, even when some of it seemed outlandish. I could tell that he enjoyed revealing his inner secrets, which drew me closer to him, and one day he said, "I've never told this stuff to anyone else before, not even to Lillian."

"What were your foster parents like?" I asked.

"They were a nice, old-fashioned Jewish couple, very respectable. My father was a pharmacist and my stepmother, Blanche, well, she was . . . "—his words trailed off.

"Well, she was what?"

He shrugged. "My parents were just too confining—you know?—too much on the straight and narrow. I mean, there's a hell of a difference between Hell's Kitchen and a nice upper-class Jewish neighborhood. I didn't feel as if I belonged in their home, because I didn't. I was a street kid, far more aware of what the world was really all about than they ever were. The situation was a time bomb waiting to explode. And then, or course, it did."

"What happened?"

"First of all I was a little sickly, probably from all the time running around on the streets before I was adopted. In and out of the orphanage, in and out of the weather—you know? I had ear infections, which seemed to bother Blanche more than they did me, although they certainly bothered the hell out of me. And then she thought I ate too much. I was a burden to her, that's all. And then she got pregnant, and with a new baby coming, a baby of her own flesh and blood—well, to make a long story short, the bomb finally exploded—they dumped me back at the orphanage."

"Oh, Harold, no!"

He laughed. "Hey, that was all right by me. I mean, they were still my parents legally, but I was fed up with the regimen they tried to impose. It just didn't fit with my background." He paused, thinking, reliving his past.

"Please tell me more."

"Well," he sighed, "I wasn't exactly a kid anymore. They adopted me when I was pushing twelve years old, and now I was fourteen, and more mature for my age than most teenagers. I'd been around the block a few times—you know? And I didn't want to be confined at the orphanage, so I went out and got a job."

"A job? What about your education?"

"Oh, we had that too. After all, the brothers were of the Paulist order, similar to the Jesuits, so there was heavy-duty education. When I went back the second time, they put me in a public school, George Washington High in Washington Heights, but I was also getting an education in the streets after my classes. You know, smoking marijuana, snorting a little snow when it was available, screwing around with a whore now and then, just exploring."

He grinned, as if he wanted me to pursue the subject of dope and sex further. I didn't, not that it deterred him. He lit another cigarette and went through the usual routine of the chain-smoker that he was, coughing and clearing his throat.

"My first sexual experience was with a street walker. You know, the whore with a heart of gold kind of thing?" He laughed heartily at the memory. "What I mean by that is she didn't charge me any money, at least not the first time."

He looked at me, waiting for my reaction. I wasn't interested in the sordid details of his experience with a hooker, so I took Harold's usual tack and changed the direction of my questions.

"What kind of job did you get?" I asked.

"My first job was stuffing ballot boxes at Tammany Hall for two dollars a vote," he said. "It was my first exposure to politics." He thought a moment, as if he were reaching back in time. "I ran errands for a bookie. One time I was employed as a handyman at the Apollo Theater in Harlem. Now that was something to write home about. I didn't do too much handy work, but it was worth sitting through two lousy movies everyday just to see the burlesque show that followed them. I love strippers!"

I took what Harold told me at face value. I had no cause to doubt him; there seemed to be no reason that he should embellish the facts of his life for my sake, and for the next twenty-eight years he seldom varied the data when he told other people the details of his biography; he had it down perfectly.

He was fifteen when he experienced his first major run-in with what he called "the higher authorities." He was caught "in the act" with a girl at the top of the Washington High School tower. "I was pumping her like crazy when my ass hit the goddamned bell. Ding-dong! And then a couple of burly custodians showed up and beat the shit out of me. After that humiliation was finished, the Brothers expelled me."

"What did you do?"

"I joined the fucking Navy."

"When you were fifteen?"

"Yeah, I forged my father's signature on the papers. It was easy. I always looked a couple of years older than I really was, primarily because I had premature gray hair, even as a teenager."

"And of course you had a girl in every port," I teased.

"Every goddamned one of them. I started in Pensacola with the submarine fleet. We hopscotched all over the Caribbean. I can thank the Navy for my high school diploma and for giving me the time to study Kessler's *Handbook of Accounting*. There's not much to do when you're submerged in a submarine, except read. It was a blessing in disguise. I was good at numbers, which later helped me climb the ladder at Universal."

"How old were you when you were discharged from the Navy?"

"I wasn't discharged. Our sub sank, you see, and I was the only one who survived. I never knew exactly what happened, but suddenly I found myself in the ocean off the coast of Florida. We were all separated quickly in a rough sea. Somehow I latched on to a life vest, so I started swimming hoping like hell I was going toward land." He grinned. "Obviously, I made it to terra firma."

"What did you do then?"

"First, I was given a purple heart. Then there was an inquiry; that's when they discovered I wasn't seventeen yet, so they discharged me. Suddenly I was back where I had started, on the streets in Hell's Kitchen. I went to work for a Jamaican bootlegger who dealt dope on the side. In fact, I once delivered cocaine to Cole Porter." He lit another cigarette.

"My accounting skills helped me move up in the underworld, not that I really felt I was one of them. But it was a way to get a few dollars in my pocket, and I became what they called a 'layoff man.'"

"What's a layoff man?" I asked.

"He's the guy who counsels bookies on how to spread the risk when they have too much riding on one horse."

The days went by, too quickly for me. I was enjoying every minute of my holiday with Harold. He was fascinating and I took in his every word as the end-all of truth. In retrospect, it may sound dull, but it wasn't, making love, then eating and drinking and talking, then making love again, occasionally venturing outdoors, but I was in love and nothing really was ever boring with Harold. My curiosity was constantly stimulated to know more about him.

"How did you escape the mob?" I asked one day. "I mean, once you're with them, aren't you always?"

"Oh, I was still a kid, at least as far as they were concerned, just a kid with an aptitude for mathematics." He lit a cigarette and poured two fresh glasses of Dom Pérignon. "I don't know why, because I hadn't thought about getting a regular job, but one day I passed a grocery store and there was a sign in the window: Wanted, Inventory Clerk, $8 Per Week. I went in, got the job, and became a member of the American work force with the required ethic."

"How long did you work there?"

"Not long, because my day-labor ethic wasn't as strong as I thought it was. I soon developed a get-rich-quick scheme. Know what I mean?"

I knew, because my father had dreamed up plenty of them. There had been a dry-cleaning shop, a TV repair shop, and sundry other failures. "I know all right," I told him.

Harold may have been reading my mind, because he said, "The difference between me and so many others was that my scheme worked to perfection."

"You mean you got rich?"

"I made my first million before I was twenty-one," he said with pride.

"Oh, Harold! Did you really? How?"

"Well, remember this was during the depression. I learned that crops were rotting on the vines in the fields of some of the southern states. They were perishable commodities that could be sold to stores like the one I worked for if they had a distributor. I went back to Hell's Kitchen and begged and borrowed a total of eight hundred dollars from various characters I knew had money in their pockets, whether obtained legally or not. Some of them were even friends!" He laughed. "Then I took flying lessons for a couple of weeks and bought an old single-engine biplane. You know, those with double winds, one on top of the other."

"Like the one Jonas Cord flew in the opening chapter of *The Carpetbaggers*?"

"Exactly. That's why I could write about flying, with accuracy and emotion," he said enthusiastically. "So I flew down to Georgia and circled around for a few days looking for growth fields of vegetables that were going to die on the stem and stalk. I bought whole fields of corn at just fifty dollars down per field. Then I flew back to New York and sold them for cash to stores like the one I had worked for. That gave me enough money to pay off the farmers and ship the product with a hefty return on my investment."

"And you made a million dollars?"

"Actually, I made two million," he said proudly. "I was suddenly in tail cotton, as they say in Georgia. I moved into the penthouse at the Edison Hotel, which was pretty swank in those days. Hell, it cost $625 a month, and that was a lot of money in the midthirties. I was in hog heaven, as they also say in Georgia."

"What did you do then?"

"For one thing I started eating better than I'd ever eaten in my life, until I got trichinosis from eating pork." He laughed again, a new memory coming to the fore.

Although Harold was a nonpracticing Jew who had been brought up in an orphanage by Catholics, he knew a great deal about the Jewish faith. He explained to me the religious taboo against eating pork, and then he continued his story.

"So I was in the hospital recuperating, when suddenly this rabbi shows up. 'What's wrong with you, son?' he asked.

"I didn't want to tell him I had contracted trichinosis from eating pork." He paused and laughed.

"What did you tell him?"

"I looked him straight in the eye and said, 'Sir, please forgive me, but I've caught the clap.'"

I laughed, as I often did at Harold's stories. Some of them seemed so farfetched, yet he related them with such wonderful charm. And why not? He made his living as a master storyteller.

We were walking among the palm trees on the beach one morning when he told me about losing his fortune. It was 1941, and he had invested his two million dollars in another commodities venture. He bought several tons of sugar at $4.85 a pound.

"The price began to skyrocket," he told me, "but I held out on selling what I had. I wanted to make a real killing. Then the war came and Roosevelt froze the price of sugar. Mine was dead on arrival. I was bankrupt. I lost my penthouse suite, everything."

"You gambled and lost," I said.

"Hey, if I weren't a gambling man, I'd still be running errands in Hell's Kitchen," he responded. After a pause he said seriously, "Tiger, you gotta gamble. That's what it's all about. If you're not willing to take a risk, then why in hell keep living? That's why you married Tom. You had to take a gamble. You had to get out from under your parents' umbrella." He paused, and then he continued, "You lost—so what? At least you got out on your own. Sometimes when you gamble and lose, you haven't really lost."

I shrugged my shoulders and nodded, but I remained silent. He looked off into the trees and laughed at a memory. "A few years ago," he continued, "I was fronting for some money men at the gaming tables in Monaco. I lost $180,000 of their money and they weren't very happy with me, to say the least. I was broke and the bastards wouldn't even pay my hotel bill."

"What did you do?"

"I had an Eldorado Caddy convertible and I sold it to a Greek businessman for $10,000 cash," he said. "I paid my hotel bill, bought a plane ticket home, and then I went back to the casino. I put what money I had left, almost $9,000, on one roll of the dice."

"And you won?" I asked excitedly.

"Hell, no! I lost it all." He snapped his fingers. "Just like that, in one fucking fell swoop. I was bankrupt again, but what the hell? I had a ticket home, and I had already learned that no matter how bad things get, they can get worse— but then they can get better also."

"So things got better?"

"Hell, no! They got worse. I sucked in my gut and flew back to New York, trying all the while to figure out how I was gonna start over." He laughed boisterously. "And when I got to my place, there was a fucking IRS agent waiting on my doorstep!"

"What did he want?" I asked naively.

"What did he want?" Shit, he wanted back taxes!"

I laughed, not remotely dreaming that back taxes would be one of Harold's nemeses for the next two decades plus.

In those few moments when we weren't making love or chattering like monkeys, I thought about Harold's life as compared to my own. Mine had been so boring and sheltered that I hardly remembered growing up, only that I was frightened much of the time, of other kids on the street (particularly after we moved to a mixed ethnic neighborhood in Brooklyn), and of my father, who after his many business failures took out his frustrations on my brother and me and my mother, my mother who sustained our family by working as a seamstress in a fur coat sweatshop. Unlike Harold, who had learned to attack and solve his problems, I had developed a crisis mask, always facing my dilemmas with a serene smile on my face, silently and without argument. My past life had been primarily one of dreams, like when we played the "time game" as children; but now Harold, if only for a couple of fleeting weeks, was making a few of my wishes come true.

We were back in the Missionary Cottage when I asked, "What did you do after you lost your two million?"

"I went to work as a shipping clerk in the freight department in the New York warehouse of Universal Pictures for a measly $27.50 a week. I was always watching the books, and one day I discovered an overpayment of thirty thousand dollars. One of the big bosses took note, and after that I began to work my way up the ladder until I was vice president in charge of budgets and statistics. A friend of mine was the head of the story department, Ray Crossett. I had to budget the stories he bought. I was always complaining about the novels Ray kept getting the company to buy. One day Ray got tired of listening to my complaints. He said, 'If you don't like the novels we're buying, why don't you write one yourself?' 'Maybe I will,' I told him, and Ray said, 'Wanna make a hundred dollar bet that you won't?'"

Harold leaned back on the pillows with a broad, triumphant smile on his face. "I took the bet, and over a two-year period I wrote *Never Love a Stranger*. Ray thought the book was terrible, too sexually explicit, but I got an agent and she sold it in ten days for a thousand dollars against 15 percent royalties, to Alfred Knopf, because Alfred's son Pat thought the book was hot shit." He paused. "And you know what, Tiger? It was. Most important though, I won the fucking bet."

"And several hundred thousand copies later the rest is history," I said dreamily.

"Not exactly," said Harold.

He explained that from the outset of publication *Never Love a Stranger* had faced problems with local censors over Harold's descriptions of sex—for example, "I ran my fingers up her thigh and under her dress, the soft warm flesh of a young woman's thigh filled with electricity and fire"—language that seems tame by today's standards, but was virtually taboo in 1948.

"It came to a head in Philadelphia," he continued, "where they banned the book as being licentious, immoral, and antisocial."

"What did you do?" I asked with sincere curiosity.

"I challenged the local obscenity law in Philly," he said proudly, "not in a local court, but in a federal court."

"What happened?"

"I won the damned thing, and after that every major banning organization in the country fell apart because I won the case in the Federal Circuit Court of Appeals. I'll never get credit for it, but I think that suit opened the door for the publication of previously banned books by James Joyce, Henry Miller, D.H. Lawrence, and everybody else. Like Mark Twain, Harold could brag with the best of them, but I think he was always sincerely proud of his efforts against postwar censorship. It was a defining moment for him; certainly he felt it gave him leeway for his later novels.

"*Never Love a Stranger* became a best seller, but I wasn't in the big chips as a writer, not yet," he continued. "I was still working at Universal, trying to write at the same time, which was never easy. In '49, Knopf published *The Dream Merchants*, which did better than *Never*. After that, I wrote *A Stone for Danny Fisher*, which was not only another best seller, but it received some critical acclaim. That's when I got cocky.

"I was sick of Universal," he continued. "I had to fly back and forth from New York to Hollywood so often that I was going nuts. I'd catch the red-eye, sometimes as many as three times a week; I was so damned tired that when the stewardess woke me up upon landing, I'd often have to ask where we were, California or New York?

"I hated being confined in my office, which was a couple of floors below my boss's at the Universal Building. I had to stay three hours later than everybody else because I had to wait for a wire from the West Coast reporting the daily box office tabulations. Since nobody ever checked on me, particularly at night, I decided to have a telephone installed in a booth at my favorite haunt. With the help of a guy I knew at the telephone company, I had the number listed and distributed to the Universal hot shots as my private telephone number at my office. I'd be having a gay old time in the booth at the cocktail lounge, and when someone called me from Universal, they thought I was in my office."

"You got away with that?"

He laughed. "I did for about a year. Then one evening the president called me and told me to report to his office in five minutes. He had stayed late, which for him was unusual as hell.

"'I can't,' I told him.

"'Why not?' he wanted to know.

"'Well,' I said, "'I'm not in my office.'

"There was a long pause, and I knew he was trying to figure out what I meant. He thought he had called my office, of course, which was a two minute walk from his. But my real office, in the joint where I was hanging out across town was, an hour away from Universal. I knew I was in a fix.

"Finally, the boss asked, 'What do you mean you're not in your office?'

"I couldn't think of a good bullshit story, so I told him the truth, without the finer details, that I wasn't exactly in my main office, that in fact I was about an hour away. There was another long pause on the phone, and then the president hung up. The next day I became a full-fledged freelance writer, without ties to Universal." He laughed again and looked at me. "And the rest, Tiger, my dear Grace, is history."

During our last night at the Missionary Cottage, a tropical storm struck Kauai with gale-force winds, crackling lightning, and ear-splitting thunder. To others I'm sure it seemed the island was going to blow away, but not for us. We made love on the big four-poster bed as passionately as the storm raging outdoors. When we were finished, Harold looked me in the eyes and said for the last time on Kauai, "Gotcha again, Tiger!"

5

"My Girl Needs a Fur!"

Neither of us really wanted to go back to New York, but I had my job and I knew Catherine couldn't keep covering for me. Meanwhile, Harold had a new novel to contemplate, research, and discuss with his publisher. All I knew was that it was going to be about a revolutionary figure in Latin America, based on some of the exploits and personality of Porfirio Rubirosa, the rich celebrity playboy from the Dominican Republic.

As the plane lifted above the island, I looked out the window. The cottages gradually diminished until they were just little spots among the trees and on the beach. The spectacular palm forests were gorgeous and the mist-shrouded mountains were the props of a fairyland I would never forget.

This time the flight was long, first to Los Angeles, where we changed planes, and then on to New York. Long, yes, but not long enough for me—I didn't want to go back. I had my memories, my thoughts, but now I wondered: did I have Harold?

He continued nonstop, his lyrics, his jokes, his risqué comments, never once letting up, but also never once giving me even a tiny inkling that our affair was anything but fleeting. I grew nervous. Perhaps I had been mistaken about this man who was old enough to be my father, and as the plane descended toward Idlewild I began having second thoughts. It had been a wonderful, exulting experience, but now I began to surmise the awful truth, that all good things come to an end. There was Tom to think about, although I now knew with certainty that our marriage had to come to an official and legal termination. And I knew, too, that Harold would soon be back with Lillian.

I looked at Harold. He was talking animatedly to the stewardess, laughing. "Buckle up, Mr. Robbins," she said with one of those wide, pearly-white, manufactured smiles. I looked away. God, what misery I suddenly felt! I had enjoyed every moment with Harold. I was in love with him, yet I thought there was nothing I could do about it except keep my thoughts and dreams to myself.

We landed with a hard jolt, and the plane taxied slowly on the tarmac to the ramp. It was dusk and an eerie end-of-journey silence prevailed in the coach from front to back. The plane stopped and we waited for what seemed an interminable length of time as the steps were rolled up to the passenger door. I looked at Harold again; neither of us said anything, such a departure from our marathon talks of the last two weeks. At last we deplaned, retrieved our baggage, and finally stood at a taxi stand in front of the airport. We had hardly spoken since landing, and now we stood waiting at the curb avoiding each other's eyes. I heard Harold sigh, and I followed suit. It was time to part; I would have to go my way and Harold his. A taxi pulled up and the cabby put my luggage, including my cosmetic case, in the trunk. He started to close the trunk, but, no, I wanted my cosmetic case with me. Why, I don't know; I certainly wasn't going to prepare my face for Tom. Then a second taxi pulled up—Harold's. I sighed again and reached for my case. That's when it happened: Harold gently took my hand and pulled it back. I looked at him.

"Tiger, surely you don't think you're going back to your apartment and that I'm going to my house in Connecticut," he said. His words seemed part question and part statement.

My heart leaped. "Well, I—"

"No," said Harold. He shook his head, slowly, then faster. "I don't think so!" This time he was definitely making a statement.

He looked me in the eyes, and it was then I knew with certainty. I was his woman, he was my man, and our life together was only beginning. It was one of the happiest moments I've ever experienced. My fairytale was coming true.

We went to the Plaza Hotel and checked into a suite. By the time we got to the room nightfall had arrived. We were exhausted, and without further ado, without an ounce of champagne, without a morsel of food, without another word, we flopped on the big king-size bed and fell into a deep sleep.

It was Friday night when we arrived. We spent another weekend together without letting anyone of importance know we were back in town. Saturday morning we went to Reuben's Delicatessen, directly across the street from the hotel, where we had what can only be described as an extravagant breakfast.

"I'm starving, Tiger! Let's eat!"

We did, for almost three hours, everything tasted so good, the best blintzes and French toast ever.

"You know what, Tiger? Everything's gonna work out for us because we're gonna make it work out!" exclaimed Harold with confidence. "I'm so fucking happy!"

I don't know if he really knew everyone he called over to our table that morning, but he introduced me to at least twenty people. It was obvious our former New York relationship was a thing of the past. He now wanted us to be an item.

"Hey, Bernie!" he would yell. "Get your ass over here! I want you to meet Grace!"

After we returned to the Plaza, it was much like the time we had spent at the Missionary Cottage in Hawaii. No complaints! We hardly left the suite for the next two days, living on love and room service. I felt totally secure with Harold, happy as a lark, but now that we were back in New York, my thoughts could not help but wander periodically to Tom. "What am I to do?" I finally asked.

"It's simple," said Harold authoritatively. "Call him and tell him you're not coming back."

It was easier for him to say it than it was for me to do, but by Sunday afternoon I had worked up enough nerve to call the apartment. If Tom wasn't sober, he would be by the time my brief statement had sunk in.

"Tom," I said without hesitation, "I'm leaving you."

There was a moment of silence; then he said, "What do you mean?"

"I think you know what I mean," I said. "We both know we haven't had a life together for a long while. It's time to end it, that's all. I'm not coming back."

Another long silence. Finally, he said, "Okay, who's the fucking guy, bitch?"

"Tom—"

"Goddamn it! What's the bastard's name? I'll kill the son of a bitch, you fucking whore!"

I didn't answer; I hung up and turned to Harold. He grinned, rather proudly. I was relieved, but frightened. I felt like crying; tears welled in my eyes. He put his arms around me and pulled me close. "Don't worry, Tiger," he said tenderly. "I'll talk to Tom in a couple of days. He'll get over it; believe me. You're my girl now, and there's nothing he can do to change it." I buried my head in his shoulder.

My concern, however, wasn't solely with Tom. I had to call my parents also. They would not be pleased either, but at least with them I wouldn't have to put up with a barrage of curse words. I had tried to forewarn them, but my leaving Tom would come as a shock nonetheless. While I began to formulate my wording to them, pacing back and forth across the thick carpet, Harold picked up the phone and ordered a bottle of Dom Pérignon from room service.

"We'll get everything programmed this week," he said. "Then I'll spill the beans to Lillian."

What the program would entail, I had no idea, but I felt better. While we were sipping champagne, Tom was apparently fortifying his bruised ego with brandy, because when I finally called my parents, he had already beaten me to it. They were upset.

"Are you okay?" my mother asked.

"I really am," I told her. "I'm with the man I truly love."

They were not easily persuaded. My mother was crying and my father's voice was rising as they passed the telephone back and forth. It was my father's turn. I held the phone away from my ear.

"Where are you?" he demanded. "What are you doing?"

His voice was loud enough that even Harold could hear him. He cupped his hand over the transmitter and whispered to me, "Tell them we'll come out to see them in a few days."

I nodded and raised the phone. "Look, Daddy, we'll come to Queens this weekend. I want you to meet Harold."

"Harold who?" barked my father.

"Harold Robbins."

Another silence fell at the end of the line. After a moment my father said, "You mean, that writer?"

"That's the one, Daddy, the one I told you about a few weeks ago." Before he could respond, I said a quick goodbye and hung up.

The next morning, Monday, Harold and I parted on the sidewalk in front of the Plaza. We had not checked out. Harold was off to Paul Gitlin's office and I was on my way back to my job. Harold flagged a taxi, kissed me passionately on the lips. "Keep your chin up, Tiger. You're gonna be fine. We're gonna be fine. Just fine! It's me and you against the world!" He laughed. "I fuckin' love it!"

Everything at the office was just as I'd left it, except when I arrived the switchboard operator said Tom had called three times. I didn't call him back, but I was concerned he might show up in person. No one said anything unseemly about my extended holiday, but when I thanked Catherine for covering for me she smiled thinly as if she were privy to a deep, dark secret. Before the week was out, a rumor was going around that I was having an affair with playwright Edward Albee, the author of the current Broadway hit *Who's Afraid of Virginia Woolf?*, and whom I had never met in my life.

At noon, Harold called. "Look," he said, "I've been thinking it over. I've decided to go home to Connecticut."

My heart sank. "Oh?"

"Yeah, I guess I'd better," he said mysteriously, letting my imagination run on empty for a moment. Then he laughed. "But I'll be back on the six-twenty. Wanna meet me at Grand Central?"

"You bet!"

"That's my girl!"

I had a couple of casting sessions, and then took an unwanted call from my father. "I hope you know what you're doing," he said.

"I do, Daddy."

"Whatever, you're going to have to talk to Tom," he advised.

"I've already talked with him."

"Well, about this Robbins guy. Like I told you, I've read some of his books, you know, and, Gracie, like I told you, he's a lecher, a woman chaser of the first order. Now, you better watch out."

"Daddy, I've been seeing him for a year."

"And Tom didn't know?"

"Tom's seldom sober enough to know anything."

"Well," he said, "I want to meet this guy. Come on Sunday. Your mother's doing dinner."

"I know, Daddy. It was Harold's idea. Thanks," I said, and felt a new sense of relief.

At 6:20, I was waiting at Grand Central Station in the throes of the commuting crowd, most of them returning to their homes for the evening. It had not occurred to me that Harold would not show up, but when I didn't see him immediately, I began to worry. A second became a minute, a minute an hour. My imagination ran rampant. A thousand questions fluttered in my mind: what if Lillian this and what if Lillian that? I knew that, independent of Harold, I would not have left Tom. I began to feel queasy, and then I saw him. He did not throw his arms around me. He couldn't. He was lugging a suitcase in one hand and an old beat-up manual typewriter in the other. The first thing he said was, "I'm pissed off!"

My heart leaped for the umpteenth time. "Why?"

"Because in my haste I forgot my goddamned Chateau Rothschild! I had three bottles of it!"

"Oh no!" I said, biting my tongue to keep from laughing.

"It's just as well, though," he continued. "My gout has started up." (Gout? Didn't know about that).

We hopped in a taxi. "Park Avenue, near Fifty-Fourth Street," Harold told the driver with enthusiasm.

I looked at him with surprise. The Plaza Hotel was on Fifth Avenue. "Where are we going?" I asked.

"To our new place, darling!" he cried.

I was learning quickly that when Harold Robbins made decisions, he made them promptly and backed them up with action, just like the heroes in his novels. Somehow, he had found time during the day to rent an apartment on a side street off Park Avenue that was within walking distance of Grey Advertising. It was small but comfy, fully decorated, and well-supplied with Dom Pérignon. Our belongings had already been moved from the Plaza Hotel into our new abode. I was thoroughly happy in New York for the first time in years.

We made love and then went out to dinner at a nearby restaurant. I assumed Harold would tell me about his conversation with Lillian, but he didn't and I certainly didn't ask him any questions. He asked me though if Tom had called.

"Yes," I said, "several times, but I didn't talk with him."

"Don't," he said.

"I'm sure he doesn't have enough money to pay the rent," I commented.

"Don't give him a dime," said Harold. "I'll take care of it. Tomorrow morning at eleven o'clock I want you to go to your old apartment and get out of there what you need."

"But what about Tom?"

"He won't be there."

"How do you know?" I asked. "He seldom leaves."

"I know, that's all, so don't worry about it. Just do what I say, Tiger. Everything will be fuckin' fine."

The next morning I did as Harold requested. I left for lunch early and went to the apartment. I had misgivings as I entered, but as Harold had assured me, Tom wasn't there. His brandy bottle sat half-empty on the coffee table; his ashtray was full of butts. My heart was racing; my blood was rushing; the silence scared me. I quickly gathered a few things, started to leave, and then on impulse I went back and took a single painting off the wall. It was a portrait Tom had painted of me when we first married. I was nude, from the waist up. I was holding an enticing apple in my hands, like Eve tempting Adam in the Garden of Eden.

When Harold saw the painting in our new apartment that night, he went nuts with enthusiasm, even praise. "I love it!" he cried. "I just fuckin' love it!"

"Thank you," I said, "but of course Tom painted it."

"I'll tell you one thing. The man has talent, and it's a damned shame he's letting it go to pot! But he's no longer any of our business. We're not gonna worry about him. He's out of your life now."

Harold had "taken care" of Tom, and Lillian too, although I was unaware of what occurred with her. During a whirlwind week, he and Paul put together a plan for both Harold's divorce from Lillian and mine from Tom. I found out later—many years later—that he settled with Lillian for a lifetime alimony payment of five thousand dollars per month. The settlement with Tom he revealed more quickly.

Unbeknownst to me, he had invited Tom to meet him at Paul's office that morning at precisely the time he told me to go to the apartment and get my things.

"And he showed up?" I asked.

"Of course," said Harold.

Using Paul as a forceful legal shield, he had offered Tom a sum total of ten thousand dollars to accept a divorce and cease and desist from any other machinations he may cook up.

"Did he settle?" I asked.

"Of course, darling," said Harold.

For the first time since we had been together, I looked angry. Harold looked surprised. He stared at me curiously. "What's wrong?" he asked.

"What's wrong?" I repeated with more emphasis. "You want to know what's wrong? I'll tell you what's wrong. I thought Tom would think I'm worth more than that! Ten thousand dollars? How insulting!"

Harold doubled up with laughter.

I steamed on the surface for a few minutes, but I was so happy inside I could hardly see straight. Within a few weeks, Tom signed the separation papers and received the payment in a lump sum from Harold. I never saw Tom again in my life, although the divorce was not finalized for another year.

The first week Harold and I were together in our own apartment flew by so quickly. I would go to the office, then meet Harold for lunch, then go back to the office, and then meet Harold for dinner before we retreated to our new home.

As I was putting on my makeup before going to work Friday morning, Harold, who was still lolling about in bed, said casually, "Instead of going to lunch today, I want you to meet me at Di Rizio's."

I didn't have to ask him what Di Rizio's was. Every girl in town knew it was a top-of-the-line New York furrier. Butterflies began to flutter round and round in my stomach. "At Di Rizio's?" I asked cautiously.

"Di Rizio's," he laughed. "My girl needs a fur."

The furrier knew Harold, and perhaps his taste also, for he realized exactly what to bring into the showroom for us to see. Ultimately, there were three beautiful coats to choose from, or at least that's what I thought: a beautiful lynx, a white mink, and a luxurious sable. I was beside myself with excitement. A fur coat! It would be the first one in my life.

I had modeled them all for Harold, but now I didn't know which one I wanted. It was such a difficult choice; they were all so beautiful. "I don't know which one to choose," I said at last.

"What do you mean choose?" said Harold. He turned to the furrier. "She wants all of them!"

I was speechless, but he wasn't kidding. Harold was as "crazy nice" as the Jonas Cord character he had created in *The Carpetbaggers*, and rather than having my first fur, I got my first three furs, all with a snap of Harold's fingers. I had already recognized his generosity, but this was beyond words. It was incredible.

Out on the street Harold said, "In the morning we're gonna have breakfast at Tiffany's."

"They don't serve breakfast at Tiffany's," I said with a laugh.

"Oh, yes, they do," said Harold confidently.

The next morning, surrounded by a sparkling array of jewelry and other extravagant items, Harold showed me what breakfast at Tiffany's was all about, and believe me, it was better than ham and eggs. He chose a magnificent diamond engagement ring that seemed to me as big as a baseball. When he slipped it on my finger, my knees buckled. In all my fantasies never once had I thought such material dreams would ever come true. Yet they were, and what was more fabulous, they were just beginning.

On Sunday, we prepared to go to my parents' house in Queens Village. Harold had ordered a limousine. By now, I had a whole new wardrobe, and I made sure I looked as elegant and radiant as possible. When I was ready to go, I slipped on the sable coat.

"Don't forget to wear your ring," said Harold.

"Are you kidding?" I said. "How could I possible forget it?" I realized Harold wanted very badly to impress my folks and wanted to use every tool at our disposal, but I did also.

Traditionally my family had always eaten our Italian Sunday dinner at 4:00 p.m., but when I mentioned the time to Harold, he said, "Let's surprise them and get there early!"

The limousine pulled up at two o'clock. As I got out, I saw my mother in the garden gathering fresh basil and picking out the choice tomatoes she used in her meat sauce. She had made a bowl out of her apron that was still tied at her waist. When she saw me climbing out of the limousine in my fur coat, she dropped her cupped apron and the herbs and tomatoes fell to the ground. She was in a state of temporary shock.

"Is that your mother?" Harold asked.

"Yes."

"Then go to her posthaste, Tiger," he said softly. "I'll wait here in the limo for a minute."

I went to my mother in the garden. She was silent, speechless, just staring at me.

"Are you okay, Mamma?' I asked.

She inspected me very slowly, and then she whispered like a soft breeze, "Dove vai, mia figlia?" (Where are you going, my daughter?)

I understood my mother's old-world thinking well; what she was really asking was, "Where are you going with your life?" Neither of us knew, but it was apparent that wherever it might be, already I was en route. We embraced and kissed; then I said, "I want you to meet Harold, Mamma."

He joined us then, a little sheepishly I thought, again like a boy who has just been caught stealing from the cookie jar. Of course, I was the cookie he had stolen; at least, that's what my parents thought.

My father was waiting for us in the house. After I introduced him to Harold, he took his good time, carefully scrutinizing him without comment. The ice wasn't really broken until we sat down for dinner. Harold ate and ate, raving between bites about how marvelous the food was. I thought it was all for show, but Harold later said it wasn't, that he really enjoyed the meal that much. My mother was pleased; when Harold asked if we could take some of her sauce home with us, her eyes sparkled.

"He likes my cooking," she said proudly when we were alone in the kitchen.

Harold won my father over more slowly, but it certainly didn't hurt that I looked like a million dollars. The truth is, having been unsuccessful in so many business deals in his life my father appreciated those who were successful, and through his reading and even more his research about Harold since Tom had called, he knew indeed that Harold was one of the best-selling authors in the world. Not once did he mention Harold's past.

There was no question Harold had a good time that day. His writing reflected his own past in reference to troubled families and he enjoyed being with a unit that had not fallen apart, regardless of the circumstances. By the time we left, long after dinner was over, I was certain both of my parents approved of him— but it wouldn't have changed the new course of my life even if they hadn't.

The next morning, when I was putting on my makeup before going to work, Harold remained in bed. He was awake, however, and watching me. I didn't say anything. I was in my usual rush not to be late. Harold folded his arms under his head and grinned at me.

"What's so funny?" I asked.

"Nothing, darling," he said. "I just want you to have a nice day at the office. I know you love your work."

"Aren't you going to your office?"

"Me? I don't have an office."

"I thought you used Paul's office?"

"Sometimes," he said, "but I don't need to go to the office anymore, do I? I've got you now, a working girl, a career girl dedicated to her profession. So today, I'm just going to lie here and think about my next book, while you work to bring home the bacon."

As I left, he called after me with extra but affected vigor, "Have a nice day at the office, darling!"

I returned to the apartment as soon as my workday was finished. Harold was still sprawled cozily on the bed, although I was reasonably certain he really hadn't been there all day.

"Hey, Tiger!" he said as I entered. "How'd your day at the office go?"

This antic continued for several days, with me leaving in the morning— "Well, I'm off to work, darling!"—and with Harold responding from the bed, "Great! Have a nice day, Tiger. I'll certainly be here when you get back."

It was a charade I finally grew tired of. Before leaving the apartment a few mornings later, I said, "Seriously, Harold. You don't really stay in bed all day long, do you?"

"Why not? I don't have anything else to do."

"Don't you have a book to write?"

"Yes, and I'm glad you brought that up," he said. He folded his arms under his head and watched as I applied makeup in front of the dresser mirror. "I'll be leaving soon. I gotta go dig up some facts."

Although Harold didn't talk much about his projects, I knew he did a great deal of research, although I didn't know precisely how. I assumed he would go to the local library.

"Where are you going?" I asked.

"Colombia," he said without emphasis, "down in South America.

"Oh?" I said, trying to maintain my composure. I glanced at him. He still lay casually on the bed, his arms folded under his head. He was watching me with a silly grin on his face. "When are you leaving?" I asked.

"Soon," he said. "I know you're too busy with your work to go with me. And I understand your position, Tiger—believe me. I know you can't leave, wouldn't dream of it."

"What do you mean, I can't leave?" I asked.

"Well, I know you can't go with me, because, after all, you're a career girl, and I wouldn't dare ask you to leave your job. I'm not that kind of man. I wouldn't want to shoulder that overwhelming responsibility. I know how much your job means to you."

I was listening intently, thinking hard, trying to put on my eyeliner, a bit in shock.

He continued: "So, I suppose I'll just have to go by lonesome myself. But I'll think of you all the time I'm away, Tiger. I really will. I promise you I will."

He was angering me, but I didn't want to lose my composure just before leaving for work. "When are you leaving?" I asked without looking at him, still busy in the mirror.

"As soon as I get my bags packed, I guess. Bur really, I don't want you to worry. I'll be thinking of you."

I'd had enough. I threw down my liner pencil and muttered under my breath, "Damn!" Then I grabbed my handbag and left, without saying goodbye. Over my shoulder as I was going out the door I heard Harold say, "Have a great day at the office, darling!"

I walked to the Grey building at double-time. *That bastard!* I thought angrily as I was going up in the elevator. He really is going to go without me. Well, over my dead body! I debarked from the elevator, marched down the corridor, passed my office without as much as a glimpse, and went directly to the personnel office.

"I'm submitting my resignation," I said.

"Effective when, Grace?"

"Today!"

Without another word, I hurried back to clean out my desk. I knew Harold couldn't pack and leave that quickly, and I was determined to head him off. When I turned into my office, I stopped dead in my tracks at the threshold. My desk was covered with flowers, all kinds of flowers—reds, blues, pinks, yellows, pastels galore. They were breathtaking and gorgeous. I rummaged through the stems and petals until I found a card. I held it up; there was no inscription on the envelope. I ripped it open. The note inside read: "Avanti, Tiger!" I knew then why he called me Tiger.

6

The Land of Los Bandoleros

For some time, the seeds of Harold's next novel had been germinating in his head, a sprawling adventure whose main protagonist was a man named Dax, a Latin American revolutionary in the fictional Republic of Corteguay. The idea was larger in scope and characters than *The Carpetbaggers*, and Harold chose Colombia as a location in which to do his research. His choice entailed a twofold reason: one, Colombia had been besieged by revolutionary activity for more decades than anyone cared to remember, and two, his New York doctor and close personal friend, William Hitzig, had a brother who was a medical practitioner in Bogotá, Colombia's capital city, which was in the heart of rebel country. The minute we climbed on the plane in New York, Harold was excited about the prospect of actually meeting some of the revolutionaries.

"I want to go up into the mountains and live with the rebels for a few days," he said. "I need to find out what they're all about, why they're rebelling."

"Why don't you just ask some of the government officials who have to deal with them?" I asked.

"Because it doesn't work like that," he answered. "I need firsthand information, straight from the horse's mouth."

I did not relish the idea of his leaving me alone in a hotel while he lived with what he had begun calling *los bandoleros*, but I honestly did not think it would come to that. Harold liked the comforts of life as much as I did and I could not visualize him in the midst of a rebel camp, living like a peasant bandolero. As it turned out, I didn't know him as well as I thought I did. Luxuries were one think, but when it came to research, Harold avoided few opportunities.

We checked into the splendidly appointed Tequendama Hotel, a new luxury high-rise with gorgeous suites, from where we could see the beauty of the surrounding mountainous countryside. The hotel was centrally located in the surprisingly modern city of two million people. Harold ordered food and drinks from room service, and then he got on the telephone to the South American branch of the Hitzig family.

By nightfall we were sharing dinner with them, a charming couple with three wonderful children, at an exclusive country club on the outskirts of Bogotá, a peaceful setting that seemed as far removed from revolutionary activity as a place could get. The polite, civil atmosphere, however, did not deter Harold from pursuing the object of his visit, los bandoleros. I began to see another side of Harold—the professional writer. He had come to Colombia with a goal in mind; unlike during our trip to Hollywood and Hawaii, I was no longer, at least for the time being, the main focus of his attention. Not that he ignored me; in those days Harold was always considerate and loving, but business was business, and he jumped into the conversation of his expectations with a barrage of unceasing questions for the debonair doctor and his wife. Harold listened with growing impatience to the detailed tediousness of the answers Dr. Hitzig gave him.

"How far away is the *violencia*?" he asked.

"Why just up there," the doctor said, pointing abstractedly, "up there in the mountains. We are not far removed from it at all. In fact, we are but a few miles away."

"What I want to do," said Harold, "is go up there and meet with some of the guerrillas."

Dr. Hitzig was clearly astonished by Harold's statement of intention.

"My dear Harold," he began, "I'm afraid that would be quite impossible. This country is in the midst of a bloody civil war and neither side takes many prisoners. Such a move by you would be extraordinarily dangerous."

"But that's the purpose of my visit," said Harold forcefully and unabashedly. "If I can't find some way of meeting with the guerrillas, then my trip here is for nothing." He looked off abstractedly. "Maybe I should take off into the mountains alone and hope for the best."

As I listened, my stomach churned. Was Harold serious? The answer was yes. A silence ensued, but I could see in Dr. Hitzig's worried expression that he too realized Harold was sincere. I had hoped, and actually believed up until that dinner conversation, that Harold's talk about meeting with los bandoleros was just that, a lot of talk, pompous talk. *My god*, I suddenly realized, *the man is obsessed.*

"Obviously, I don't have any direct connection with the guerrillas, and furthermore, I don't know of anyone who does," said Dr. Hitzig.

"Surely there's someone," said Harold.

Dr. Hitzig sighed in defeat. "Here's what I suggest," he said. "Why don't you call the local press and give them an interview in which you state your intentions and purpose. Perhaps the rebels will be alerted to your needs and will get in touch with you." He paused. "Harold, I hate to say this, but I believe it would be not only foolish but terribly dangerous for anyone to go alone into the mountains."

When we got back to the hotel that night, the civilized atmosphere in the lobby and the comforts of our modern suite did nothing to ease my growing fear of Harold's plan. I had not been terribly concerned before dinner because I thought Harold was just posturing, as he was prone to do, in an effort to make a point. But this time he wasn't—he was dead serious.

"I agree with the doctor," I told him. "I don't think you should even try to meet the bandoleros."

"I can't write a book unless I know the subject I'm writing about," he said. "That's the purpose of our trip here. I didn't come to Colombia to get hearsay information from a bunch of bureaucrats. I need information. I need hard facts."

"But, Harold," I started to protest.

"Don't argue with me, Grace. What I have to do, I have to do. End of discussion."

I held my tongue, knowing that to squabble with a man so determined would be to no avail. He was like my father when his mind was made up, and I reverted back to the little girl I had been when I was growing, masking my concern with a serene face. I slept fitfully, although not as fitfully as I would in the days and night to come; at one point I awakened to see Harold sitting on the side of the bed muttering to himself.

"I can hear them," he was saying. "I can actually hear them now, their voices, somewhere up there in the mountains. Goddammit, I've got to find a connection to them."

The next morning, with the help of Dr. Hitzig, Harold contacted several members of the local press. "I need someone who speaks English," he insisted. "My name is Harold Robbins. I'm a novelist from the United States that wants to alert los bandoleros to the fact that I'm going up into the mountains to meet with them, to find out what they are about."

"Did you say Harold Robbins?"

"Yes."

"*The Carpetbaggers?*"

"Yes."

The name Harold Robbins was as magic in Bogotá as it was in New York or Hollywood. By afternoon he was at the terrace bar overlooking the grounds and the mountains, giving a lengthy interview to a reporter from the major Bogotá daily newspaper, *El Tiempo*. Harold seemed excited about the prospects of his interview, and when the article ran the following morning, we were hardly out of bed before the telephone rang. Harold answered it.

"Yes, I'm Señor Robbins," he said. He listened for a moment before cupping his hand over the transmitter and whispering excitedly to me: "It's a priest who has some contacts with guerrillas." My heart sank.

The priest was Father Guzman, a learned man of local distinction who headed a parish patronized by relatives of many to the guerrillas, if not by the guerrillas themselves. Both Harold and I liked him instantly, although what he had to say was not what I wanted to hear. He reiterated Dr. Hitzig's concerns about Harold's intention to go unprotected into rebel territory, but with some rather frightening embellishments. He was blunt.

"Señor Robbins, I don't think you will come back alive from such a venture," he said.

"Shit!" responded Harold; had Guzman not been a priest, I'm certain more expletives would have rolled off Harold's tongue. He caught himself up with a deep, disappointed sigh. "I have to find a way to meet with these people, Father. Someway, somehow, I have to go up into the mountains. It's the reason I've come all this way from the United States."

"Señor, don't be foolish," continued Father Guzman. "You should stay in the safety of your hotel and enjoy a holiday. To go into the mountains, even with protection, does not assure your safety. Our country is deeply divided between the vast peasantry and those few powerful people who control the money and wealth of our nation."

"That's the point!" exclaimed Harold. "You've got the starving people on the one hand and the power mongers on the other, and I need to learn about both firsthand. I need to see and feel the lives of the guerrillas. I have to go, regardless of the danger. Regardless!"

Father Guzman shook his head in frustration, sighed, and turned contemplatively away from Harold's searching gaze. He stared into space and shook his head again. He then said rather despondently, "Even if I go with you, Señor, it is not a guarantee of your safety."

"You'll go?" cried Harold. "You'll go with me?"

The priest nodded his head, ever so gently and not very convincingly, as though at any moment he might come to his own senses and abruptly change his mind. Harold did not give him a chance to reconsider.

"Thank god, Father, and thank you! Let's get the hell out of here. Right now, today! Let's get on the road before nightfall!"

With Harold's constant prodding, they left, to where I had no idea; just somewhere "up in the mountains." It happened so quickly I hardly had time to say goodbye.

"Don't worry, Tiger," said Harold. "I'm gonna check these guys out, ask a few pertinent questions, and then get my ass out of there and back to you in nothing flat."

And he was gone, with Father Guzman trailing in his wake.

From the suite in the hotel the view of the Andes, which had looked so beautiful when we arrived, now took on an ominous appearance. For the first time since I had made that fateful decision to go to Hollywood with Harold, I was suddenly alone. The Hitzigs tried to fill the void, and to the best of their ability they did, but having constant company in your lover's absence doesn't replace the lover. Harold was gone, and God only knew where he was. Time and again, I buried my head in a pillow and cried my eyes out. This was no longer the stuff of fiction; this was real.

Compared to most Colombians, the Hitzig family lived a life of luxury. They seldom left me alone and I ate out with them daily, at select, upscale restaurants, but even their relative affluence could not overcome the quality of some of the foodstuff on the Colombian market. I could not stomach Colombian food, beef, pork, lamb, or fowl. One night Mrs. Hitzig even cooked a special chicken dinner for me in an effort to lift me out of my doldrums, but it did not suffice. I needed Harold, and without him the food, regardless of whose kitchen it came from, was inedible. My imagination ran rampant; with news of guerrilla activities constantly in the Bogotá press I dreamed that he would be shot, or hanged, or worse. It was a terrible experience for me, and then one day, quite out of the blue, he and Father Guzman returned in a flood of enthusiasm. What had seemed an eternity had been four days.

There was no question Harold was glad to see me, and I think he was as happy as I that he had returned in one piece. He gave me a grand and passionate kiss and then wrapped his arms around Father Guzman. They had left as distant acquaintances, but now they returned as something more than friends—they were bosom buddies, having shared one of those intimate male experiences, like two warriors returning from combat. There was even a slight role reversal. The irreverent Harold was slightly more reverent, at least for the time being, and the reverent priest was—well, let me say that he was a little unpriestly in his exuberance.

They had made almost immediate contact with the guerrillas, who had taken them in as friends rather than enemies, allowing Harold to ask any questions he wanted. Harold was full of zest for the success of his research, while Father Guzman's gusto came for the fact Harold had somehow helped reunite two warring brothers who represented different factions of the revolutionary movement.

"It was wonderful!" exalted Father Guzman. "These two boys who have been at odds for years—now they are bothers again because of Harold, and they have joined forces." His happiness seemed to vividly unmask his own personal political conviction, which favored the guerrillas.

Later, Harold used the reconciliation incident as a subplot when he finally sat down and wrote what became *The Adventurers*.

When at last Father Guzman bade us goodbye, still glowing from his experience and his newfound friendship, Harold threw his arms around me and excitedly shouted, "It's time to play, Tiger!" I agreed, and we played everywhere in Bogotá for the next two weeks. Harold was Harold again.

Long before Colombia became a prime scene of combat in the drug wars, the country was most noted for its precious and semiprecious gems, foremost among the first being Andean emeralds. I had left the Cinderella-syndrome behind in New York, what with three fur coats, a diamond ring, a new car, and sundry other material items I had never really expected to have in my entire lifetime, but now Harold resuscitated the fairy tale.

"Today I'm going to get you a Colombian emerald ring," he said one morning when we woke up.

"Oh, Harold—"

"Now dammit, don't argue with me," he interrupted with determination. Not that I was going to. I had learned that when Harold's mind was made up, nothing was going to change it. Then he added, "The emerald is my birthstone, Tiger, and I plan to find something for myself also."

"Whatever you say," I answered happily, and with that we were off to see some of the most beautiful jewelry in South America.

This Cinderella was reborn, as she would be time and again during the next couple of decades, and Harold—well, Harold always was and always would be a carpetbagger. This time the northerner had come far, far south in search of political and economic advantage, and it would eventually pay off handsomely. He was a carpetbagger, yes, but he wasn't a scalawag. He never failed to leave vast riches in his wake when he left, no matter where he went to gain advantage.

The ring he gave me was a treasure, as are my memories of those weeks in Bogotá. The stone was beautiful, set in gold; how much it cost, I don't know. If

I had not realized it before, however, I realized it now: Harold, grinning all the while, threw money around as if indeed it did grow on trees. For himself, he settled on a very masculine ring with a highly polished but not faceted convex cabochon. It was gorgeous.

"Let's go play somewhere else," said Harold.

"Like where?" I asked.

"How about Cartagena," he said. "I hear it's great."

We had a final dinner with the Hitzigs, who agreed enthusiastically with Harold's choice.

"It's a romantic city," said the doctor, and his wife nodded her vigorous approval.

The next afternoon we left Bogotá, the Andes Mountains, and los bandoleros. It was one of the happiest days of my life; a new adventure lay before us. I was madly in love with Harold and he responded in kind. I had a new emerald ring, but he didn't have to give it to me to prove his love.

In contrast to the modernity of Bogotá, Cartagena was an old Caribbean seaport, established in the New World by the Spanish in the sixteenth century. It was well after dark when we got off the plane; we had stayed up late the night before and we were both tired. Getting to the hotel was a slow process, but it was a charming drive through narrow cobblestone streets flanked by the shadows of antiquated stone and brick buildings. By the time we got to our suite, Harold's four days with los bandoleros and three weeks of play-time were beginning to show on both of us.

We turned on the light and what appeared to be an exquisite Colombian surprise was awaiting us. The bed was blanketed with fresh flowers, from side to side and from end to end, petals upon petals, as if the bed was a pond and the flowers were floating on it. It was lovely and the scent had an aphrodisiacal effect. We were too tired to eat, but not too tired to make love. We quickly undressed, tossed our clothes, and dove into the pond of flowers. He made love to me like never before. There was no foreplay, just wild, never ending thrusting, flowers flying everywhere. The next morning we paid the piper heavily for following the unthinking instinct of our desire. We had not been alone in our pool of pleasure; we had not been remotely alone. The flowers were haven to hundreds of blood-sucking mosquitoes.

"Damn!" moaned Harold, scratching his body. "What a way to go! The only thing that hasn't been bitten is my cock!" We laughed, but it wasn't as funny as we made it out to be. We itched and scratched for days, comforting each other like two monkeys picking fleas.

Eventually, to forget our discomfort, we decided to explore the city rather than hang around the hotel pampering our wounds. It was a wise choice; Cartagena was a rich cache of surprises.

By day the shadows of the buildings I had seen during the night en route from the airport to the hotel turned into an antiquated New World city of wondrous intrigue. A former seventeenth century sanctuary for buccaneers, Cartagena was nicknamed the Jeweled City because pirates had often dumped their stolen treasure in the shallow harbor for later retrieval.

The Thieves Market was a colorful plaza where goods of all kinds were traded or sold.

"I'm hungry," said Harold. "Let's try some of the native fare. After all, when in Rome . . ."

I looked around. Most of the food in the marketplace was definitely of the peasant variety, the main entrée generally being a stew concocted of vegetables and chicken, kept heated on the spot in gas-fired cauldrons. The chickens had been precooked and lay in large pieces on greasy old newspapers. I had lost my appetite for the refined dishes in Bogotá during Harold's trek to the mountains, but suddenly the street cuisine in Cartagena, regardless of the squalid conditions in which it was presented, looked appetizing. I, too, was hungry and nodded my agreement with enthusiasm.

We ordered two bowls of *cocido con pollo*. I still vividly remember watching the woman ladle out the soupy vegetables—carrots and corn and potatoes—and then grabbing some cooked chicken in her bare hands, ripping it into strips, and plunking the pieces into our broth. It smelled wonderful, but I was concerned, if only slightly, about the lack of sanitation.

"Hey, don't worry about it," laughed Harold. "When in Rome . . ."

I rationalized: if Harold could survive four days up in the Andes, sharing food with the guerillas under even more primitive conditions, then I could at least partake of a bowl of stew in the public plaza of Cartagena. We dug in, and much to my surprise, the stew was excellent.

That afternoon we boarded a plane for New York. Harold was in good spirits, making passing sexual innuendos about our lovemaking of the night before. "You're great, Tiger! Did you know that? The best piece of ass in the whole world!"

Normally, I appreciated Harold's fixation with my body and my sex, but for some reason, as we got airborne, his words stopped registering with me as expressions of love. Something was wrong, but I couldn't put my finger on it. An hour into the flight I began to grow queasy, and then I experienced cramps—deep, painful, stomach cramps.

"What's wrong, Tiger?" asked Harold.

"I don't know," I told him. "I don't feel well."

The cramps and the pain increased in direct proportion to the long hours of the flight. It became apparent that I was really ill, but with what I didn't know, nor did Harold. The only remedy the flight attendant had to offer was an aspirin. I thought I was going to faint, and then I thought I was going to die. No matter what Harold did to comfort me, it failed. By the time we landed in New York, I was virtually delirious.

I don't remember getting into a taxi, but I did, apparently telling Harold all would be okay if I could just get to our apartment and into bed. Harold encouraged the taxi drive to race through the Manhattan streets; as soon as we got to our apartment, I flopped down on our bed and curled up into a ball in an effort to stop the pain. It didn't work; I was all but screaming in agony. Harold got on the telephone, desperately calling the New York branch of the Hitzig medical family.

"No, not to the hospital," I vaguely remember hearing him say. "She's too sick. You've got to come to the apartment, Bill. Now!"

The instant Dr. Hitzig saw me he diagnosed paratyphoid fever, an acute intestinal disease. He concocted a shot, not only to kill the bacteria but also to put me to sleep. Three things I remember in vague disorder: Bill saying, "I'm going to give you my own special Molotov cocktail, Grace," and I think he actually laughed; and then I saw the huge emerald sparkling on my finger and I thought, *If I'm going to die, please bury me with my ring*; and finally I know I saw a huge hypodermic needle sort of flash in the air, and before I could protest I was out of it.

Through the night my fever subsided. When I woke up the next morning, I was a new person, except for the pain left in my stomach by the cramps. Bill, still there, told me that paratyphoid fever is a milder form of typhoid.

"You either contracted it from contaminated water, contaminated food, or from insect bites," he said.

Harold looked at me. "It must have been the water," he said.

"How can you say that, Harold?" I asked. "The bugs in our bed? That horrible chicken stew!"

"Yeah, but the bugs bit me also, and I ate the chicken like a hungry hyena," he said rather seriously, "I just didn't drink any water."

I stared at him. He grinned slyly, tipped his glass, and took a sip of champagne. "Next time, stick to Dom Pérignon, Tiger!"

7

The Côte d'Azur Beckons

At last, I met the fabled Joseph E. Levine. *The Carpetbaggers* movie had been completed in Hollywood, and Levine, a master showman, scheduled a worldwide press premier at a showcase theater in Manhattan. "Unfortunately, we have to go," said Harold unhappily. "Joe will spend a fortune exploiting the picture, so I suppose I owe it to him." The event was scheduled to take place a week before the film's public release.

The Carpetbaggers was one of his first big budget movies, and in 1964 Joe wasn't quite as flamboyant as he would become after the success of later movies, like *Carnal Knowledge* and *The Graduate*. He was still full of himself, however, with a rapidly ballooning ego.

"What's Joseph E. Levine like?" I asked Harold a few days before the premier.

"Joe?" said Harold. "He's full of exaggerated self-importance, but he always seems to come out on top. He's interesting, you know, for about ten minutes. Most of his movies are terrible, but I like Joe. He epitomizes the American dream; you know, from rags to riches. I respect that, and he's a tough bastard. Besides, he has vision. Sometimes he's right and sometimes he's wrong, but he looks beyond the closed door. He's a risk taker."

Not to be outdone by Joe, Harold planned to follow up the premier of *The Carpetbaggers* by throwing a huge gala publicity dinner at Four Seasons restaurant. It was an evening gown and black tie affair.

We sat with Levine and his lovely wife, Rosalie, at the screening. I was not terribly impressed by Joe, a burly, gruff, forceful man who liked to give orders; he reminded me of a well-dressed politician with a big cigar in his mouth. Each statement he made seemed memorized from a public relations memorandum. Harold was the only person who didn't pay much attention to his commands. Rosalie, however, was wonderful, not at all taken in by the glamour of show biz. In that respect, she was like Harold, who also liked her. She had once been a singer with Rudy Vallee's band in Boston.

It wasn't a secret that Harold had become jaded to motion pictures during his years at Universal Pictures, but his contempt was more than I had realized. He complained that a two-hour movie did not have enough time to properly translate his novels to the screen.

"They always cut the shit out of the story," he said. "One time when Louie B. Mayer complained to David Selznick that he thought *Gone with the Wind* was too long, Selznick said, 'How long is good?'"

"Well, that's my fucking attitude," Harold commented. "They should spend as much time as the story requires, but they never do. Someday television might be able to do it."

Never Love a Stranger and *A Stone for Danny Fisher*, Harold's first and third novels, had been translated to the screen pre-Levine (and therefore pre-me) and he had been terribly disappointed with both of the movies. "Hollywood productions are put together by committee, and a committee will always fuck up any good story," he said frequently.

At *The Carpetbaggers* premier we sat front and center with the Levines. Fifteen minutes after the screening began, Harold wanted to leave the theater, and had it not been for me he would have. At one point I actually threw my leg over his knee to keep him down in his seat, nervously watching Joe out of the corner of my eye. Harold was unbearably restless, and it was apparent, at least to me, that he didn't think much of the movie. Finally, he said bluntly and embarrassingly above a whisper, "This movie is a piece of shit!" I ignored him, and if the Levines heard his utterance, they didn't show any displeasure. Every few minutes he shifted his weight and started to stand up, but I kept my leg anchored over his. He grunted his displeasure, but then relaxed back into his seat. He gave me a dirty look a couple of times, but retuned his expression with a hard, knowing stare and a sweet smile.

I thought the movie was a good and typical big-budget melodrama, an entertaining diversion from the daily gruel of life. Starring George Peppard, Alan Ladd, Elizabeth Ashley, and Carroll Baker, the movie had its own drive, although the characters seemed far removed from those Harold had depicted in his novel. But Harold?—it seemed the only thing he liked about movies was the large fees his stories had begun to command. When the curtain finally fell and the lights came up, Harold gave Joe a disappointed stare. I dug my fingernails into his arm, smiled ever so sweetly, leaned in toward him, and said through clenched teeth, "Don't say a word!"

His party at the Four Seasons was an affair that became legendary in showbiz annals. I was not privy to his planning, so I was as surprised as everyone else at some of the antics. Harold had four beautiful models present, each bejeweled and dressed in floor-length furs. He placed them at specific tables, introducing each one as Miss Jones. "Have you met Miss Jones? May she sit at your table?" Believe me, no one turned down one of the Miss Joneses. They were gorgeous women. Harold seated one at Cornelius Ryan's table and another at Irving Wallace's.

When everyone was seated, Harold gave a cue to the orchestra, which went into a lively rendition of "Have You Met Miss Jones?"—a popular song that year. With that, the four models stood up at their respective tables and dropped their furs from their shoulders. They wore nothing underneath, except flesh and a few expensive jewels. The girls, as they had been instructed to do, dined and drank away the evening as though there was absolutely nothing unusual about their attire. None of them was asked to leave.

A few weeks later, after I had recovered totally from paratyphoid, we drove out to Long Island one Sunday afternoon, where my parents had invited us to dinner again at their home. En route, I had hunger pains as if I hadn't eaten in days.

"Let's stop and have a hotdog," I said.

"But Grace, we're going to your parents for dinner darling. Remember? Your mother will have enough wonderful food to feed an army."

"But I'm hungry now," I told him. "I want a hotdog."

"Are you crazy?" said Harold. "You know how much food your mother cooks up."

"I want a hotdog, Harold," I repeated sternly, "and I want it now."

"You don't even like hotdogs," he said.

"Dammit, I want a hotdog!"

Harold stopped arguing with me. A Howard Johnson's loomed ahead on the opposite side of the highway. He had to make an exit and drive to an overpass before we could get on the proper side of the road.

We parked and went inside. I stuffed my face with a hotdog—onions, mustards, relish, the works.

Harold watched me in silence, obviously thinking hard. "You don't like hotdogs, Grace," he finally repeated.

"I like this one," I said, relishing every bite of it, considering in fact that it was probably the best hotdog I had ever eaten in my entire life.

"Yeah, and I think you'd better see Dr. Pearl first thing tomorrow."

"Why would I want to see Dr. Pearl?" I asked, still stuffing my face. "I feel fine. Besides, she's a gynecologist." At that instant the revelation suddenly dawned on me. I stopped in midchew and stared at Harold.

He grinned. "Like I said before, Tiger, you fucking hate hotdogs."

We said nothing about my condition to my parents that evening at dinner. I devoured my usual amount of my mother's delicious Italian food as if I'd had nothing beforehand, and tried to avoid Harold's continuous but secret grin. Again to my mother's delight, Harold asked for a second plate, and later for sauce to take home. The next day I made an appointment at the doctor's office.

Dr. Pearl was a European Jew from Vienna who had survived the Holocaust as an inmate in a Nazi concentration camp. During the last year of the war she had secretly attended to pregnant prisoners, nursing them along in hopes the Allies would liberate them before their delivery dates. She was elderly by the time I met her, but she was an excellent gynecologist.

"Grace," she said with a thin smile, "if you didn't know it with certainty beforehand, I now confirm that you are pregnant."

My immediate happiness was abruptly quelled; I saw a look of consternation on Dr. Pearl's face.

"What is it, Doctor?" I thought back to my bout with paratyphoid and the pain it had caused, to the dreadful insects and the sickening chicken stew in Colombia. I wondered aloud if that experience had done my body any damage.

"No, but you have a weak uterus," she said.

"What does that mean? How weak?" I asked. I felt like I had just been diagnosed with terminal cancer.

"Let me put you at ease," said Dr. Pearl. "I can save your baby."

She explained that she had developed a chemical formula while working in the concentration camp during the war, one that she had used on inmates to strengthen their wombs.

"Let's begin," I told her.

After my first shot, I rushed home to confirm to Harold what he already knew. He was exhilarated, and began to make plans willy-nilly (although I felt he had thought them out beforehand), pacing back and forth across the living room floor.

"Listen," he said, "the baby should be born in France, where they have great state-of-the-art prenatal care. We'll rent a villa! I'll write my book there. We'll have your parents fly over when the baby comes!"

I was taken by surprise at his suggestion, although it sounded like a wonderful idea, particularly when I considered we were both still married to people other than each other, both of whom lived in the New York area. Where

Harold's knowledge of French obstetrics came from I didn't know or question, at least not at the time. I later decided it came strictly from his very fertile imagination.

Although Harold usually had preconceived ideas about what he and those around him wanted to do, in those days he was more diplomatic about it than he was in later years. He was still forceful, yes, but he always tried to manipulate you into thinking that whatever *he* wanted to do was your idea. Rare was the time when I argued with him, because I generally agreed with his plans. I was usually game for anything; I just wanted to be with Harold.

"Yes," he continued, almost in a soliloquy as if I weren't present, still pacing back and forth, "the South of France. It's a great idea." He turned to me, like a bull, ready to charge if I waved a red flag.

"It's all right with me, Harold," I repeated. "I'd love to go to France. It's been one of my lifelong dreams."

"Terrific!" he cried enthusiastically, and then he embraced me in a loving and tender hug. "You know, Tiger," he said in my ear, "sometimes you come up with some of the greatest ideas."

Now that my pregnancy was a confirmed fact, I began to think seriously about the future. Because of Harold's experience with Yvonne, and his daughter Caryn, I began to hope our baby would be a girl, although I didn't know what Harold's preference was. I mentioned my thinking to him.

"You know, Harold, I know how much you love Caryn and how much you've missed out on by not being able to spend more time with her," I said, and then added hesitantly, "I hope our baby is a girl."

"Me too," said Harold with enthusiasm. "Boys with famous fathers never turn out right. They always have problems living in their father's shadow. I hope it's a girl also." He then added confidently, "And it will be, Tiger."

I had to finish my injections before we departed, so we had a few more weeks. One day while Harold and I were walking in the streets of Greenwich Village a small, wiry black man with bulging eyes and a lot of energy emerged from a small restaurant just as we approached the doorway.

"Jimmy!" cried Harold.

The man turned, recognized Harold, and smiled broadly.

"Hello, Harold—how's my man?"

"Meet Grace," said Harold. "Grace, meet Jimmy."

The man took my hand and kissed it charmingly. "My pleasure, Miss Grace," he said. He smiled widely, but it seemed fake, exaggerated, as if he found it hard to smile.

He was James Baldwin. After the introduction I recognized him, not that I had read his books, but because he had been on the cover of *Time* magazine the year before regarding his activities in the civil rights movement. More recently he had celebrated the success of his famous essay, "The Fire Next Time."

I see that you keep topping the best seller list, Robbins," said Jimmy.

"You're not doing so bad yourself," answered Harold.

They talked for a few moments, about nothing in particular, just writer talk, and Baldwin began to shiver noticeably. As usual, Harold was wearing his favorite sheepskin sport coat. We were on the cusp of winter and the day was chilly. Jimmy, however, was wearing an open shirt and a pullover sweater. After a few moments Harold said, "Jimmy, my god, aren't you freezing to death? Where's you fucking jacket? Did you leave it in that restaurant?"

"Man," said Baldwin, "I don't have a jacket."

"Come on, Jimmy. You don't have a fucking jacket? With winter blowing in? It's already cold for god's sake! Look at you, you're fucking shivering your ass off!"

"Listen, Robbins," said Baldwin, "if I were making your kind of money, I'd have a warm jacket, but I'm barely getting enough royalties to take care of my family."

"What family?" asked Harold, knowing Jimmy was gay and that he certainly did not have a woman or children to provide for.

"Man," continued Baldwin, "I got brothers, sisters, uncles, aunts, and cousins I've never even met that I gotta take care of. I got lawyers and accountants and publicists and agents that think they own me. And after Uncle Sam's portion, there's not much left."

"Dammit, I won't hear of you being cold this winter, Jimmy," said Harold. He ripped off his sheepskin and placed it on Baldwin's shoulders. Jimmy tried to refuse the gift, but Harold ignored him.

"When are you going to France this year?" asked Harold.

Harold explained to me that Jimmy was an authentic exile, or "half-exile," in the tradition of Hemingway, Fitzgerald, Dos Passos, and so many other American writers, splitting his time each year between the United States and France, primarily Paris.

"If you get to the South of France, look us up, Jimmy. We're leaving in just a few days."

"I will," said Baldwin. "Where will you be?"

"We don't know yet," Harold told him. "But you'll find us."

"I'll do my best," said Jimmy.

We left, with James Baldwin wearing Harold's favorite sheepskin jacket and with Harold wearing an open shirt. I loved him for that, and so did James Baldwin.

Harold wanted to see Caryn before we left for Europe. He called Yvonne from our apartment. Although I did not intend to eavesdrop, it was apparent from his end of the conversation that his relationship with Caryn's mother was stretched to the limit of affability. His friendliness with her was cold at best and he had to cajole her into letting Caryn visit us. He was almost begging, which was extraordinary for Harold; when he hung up, he was angry.

"She's tough, Yvonne is," he said. "Mean and tough. Mean and tough and manipulative."

Caryn was eight years old. She was a cute child, but her neuroses were many and apparent. She was a classic case of being the injured party in a parental breakup. Harold was crazy about her and did his best to please her, which only served to aggravate her problems. He went overboard, catering to her every need and demand. She adored him, but like any child in her position, she had already learned to manipulate him. She stayed with us for a weekend; I tried to make it as pleasant for her as I possibly could, but she remained distant, remote. It was obvious she was unstable for her age, but then what could Harold do about it? Under the circumstances I suspected he could do nothing more than what he was doing. When he left to return Caryn to her mother, he said, "Just watch; Yvonne will be calling me with a rash of complaints the minute I get back."

He was right. After dropping Caryn off, he had hardly returned to our apartment when Yvonne called. She was dissatisfied about this, about that, but it was evident to me that her real problem was jealousy; she was jealous of Harold's lifestyle, which of course included me. I made no comment, but Harold showed a different persona when he spoke to Yvonne; I rationalized it away; he had to be overly nice, I suspected, if he wanted a continuing relationship with his daughter.

There was one more woman in Harold's life he felt I should meet, one I had assumed was dead.

"We'd better go up to Blanche's place for dinner," he said out of the blue.

"Your mother? I thought she was—"

"My foster mother," he interrupted.

A few nights later we were in a taxi en route to Blanche's home in upper Manhattan. Harold was unusually quiet, even glum.

"Darling, is there something wrong with you?" I asked.

"No," he said, "except Ruth is going to be there."

"Ruth?"

"My foster sister."

"I think that's nice," I said.

"She's full of it. Don't believe a word she tells you," said Harold. "Don't believe a fucking word either of them tells you, Ruth or Blanche."

We rode on in silence. I was hoping Harold would explain more thoroughly what he was talking about, but he didn't. I stared off into space, my thoughts confused.

Blanche was an elderly lady, very nice, very distant, and very cold. Her home was a stylishly appointed abode that was as cold as she was. Ruth was a plain woman, a couple of years younger than Harold. The minute I was alone with her, Ruth pulled me aside and said, "Don't believe a word Harold tells you."

I was taken aback and didn't know how to respond. "What do you mean?" I asked.

"Harold was reared in a normal Jewish home just like millions of other Jewish boys, but he just won't accept the reality of it."

Again I was at a loss for words. Before I could mutter my confusion, Ruth continued, "Has he told you about his first wife?"

"Lillian?"

"No, the Chinese girl," she said, rather snidely.

"No, he hasn't."

"He will, but don't believe a word of it. She never existed. Lillian was his high school sweetheart and the only woman he was ever married to, and then you came along."

Was I supposed to suddenly defend myself? I didn't know, but it made no difference whether I wanted to or not, for Ruth was going to get in every word she possibly could until we rejoined Harold and Blanche.

"He always lived in a world of fantasy," she continued, "ever since we were little kids. He was writing stories when he was eight years old."

"How do you know that?" I said. "He wasn't adopted until he was almost twelve."

Her face screwed up. She looked at me. "Harold wasn't adopted," she said.

Later, when I was alone in the kitchen with Blanche, she repeated Ruth's curt dictum, "Don't believe anything Harold tells you."

"Oh, and why not?" I asked. By this time I had decided I would stick up for Harold, if necessary, but I didn't really care one way or the other about Harold's background. I was determined that I wasn't going to let either of them, Blanche or Ruth, criticize Harold behind his back. It seemed unfair.

"Just don't believe anything he says," Blanche repeated, and, perhaps seeing my reaction, she let it go at that, without any further embellishment. She perked up with a smile. "I'm serving Harold's favorite meal," she said as if to change the subject.

"Oh? What is it?"

"You'll see," said Blanche.

'I can't wait,"

A few minutes later, when I was alone a moment in the dining room with Harold, he said, "Remember, don't believe a word either of them tells you."

Again, I didn't know what to say.

Finally, we sat down for dinner. I thought it was strange; Blanche, Ruth, and Harold hardly spoke to each other.

Dinner was a huge bowl of thick lima bean soup. "This is Harold's favorite," Blanche repeated.

The soup was good, tasty, although I did not find it to be great, and I was certainly surprised it was Harold's favorite. I watched him lap it down though, like a hungry puppy, and then he was ready to go home.

Before we left, however, I quietly asked Blanche for the recipe of Harold's favorite soup. She nodded and I followed her to the kitchen, where she wrote down the recipe, handed it to me, and said again, "Don't believe anything he says. He has a fantastic imagination. Always did."

When we returned to the living room, Harold and I left, quite as suddenly and deliberately as the subject of visiting Blanche had come up to begin with.

"Thanks, Blanche," said Harold with little enthusiasm. He gave her a perfunctory hug. "The soup was delicious." He turned to Ruth. "Nice to see you, kid."

On the way home Harold was again silent, as if lost in thought. I decided it was best not to renew the subject of his foster mother and foster sister, although I was curious about the Chinese wife who Ruth said never existed.

A couple of days later, I thought, *Well, if lima bean soup is Harold's favorite, I'll make it for him.*

When Harold returned that evening from Paul Gitlin's office, I had a glass of wine and a bowl of steaming lima bean soup waiting for him. It had taken hours to make it and I was quite pleased with myself.

"Look what I've prepared for you, Harold," I said with a hint of deserved pride.

He took one look at it, and said, "What's this shit?"

"Lima bean soup," I responded. "Blanche said it was your favorite meal."

"Forget what Blanche said." I thought he was angry, but then he looked at me and smiled. "I appreciate what you've done, but Tiger, darling, I fucking hate lima bean soup!"

I put the soup aside and made sandwiches. We dined; it wasn't a feast, but it was apparently better than lima bean soup.

"Blanche and Ruth have good intentions," he said, "but don't believe anything they say."

"I won't," I said, but I was curious as to why they would make stories up regarding Harold. Maybe the wine influenced me, but as we sat talking, eating, and drinking, my curiosity warmed up. At last, sufficiently uninhibited, I asked, "Did you have a wife before Lillian?"

"Muriel Ling," said Harold nonchalantly.

"Muriel?"

"An oriental girl," he continued. "She was in the chorus line at Billy Rose's Diamond Horseshoe, where I used to hang out when I was a rich food broker."

"And you married her?"

"Oh, yeah," he said. "She was a terrific girl. I was crazy about her. She was exotic as all get out." He took a bite of sandwich.

I paused my inquisition, feeble as it was, but I was still curious. Finally, I said, "Well?"

"Well, what?" asked Harold.

"What happened to Muriel Ling?"

"She died," he said. "We were only married a month. Her father was an eccentric painter in San Francisco, very famous. He gave her a parrot as a wedding gift." He shrugged and took another bite of sandwich.

"How did she die?"

"The fucking parrot bit her, and she got an infectious disease," he said. "It was a real tragedy."

"I would think so," I commented vaguely, trying to sort the story out.

"Some fucking parrot," said Harold, and he poured more wine.

I quizzed him no more. Furthermore, I believed him. Why would Harold make up a story like that?

I finished my injections with Dr. Pearl, and then we were airborne again, this time eastward, to Europe. We had no way of predicting it at the time, but as the airplane lifted off the runway and jetted out over the Atlantic blue, we were embarking on the best year of our many years together. As we settled into our seats, I looked at Harold and leaned my head against his shoulder. He smiled shyly, gently reached out his hand, and lovingly caressed my belly. We were now a threesome.

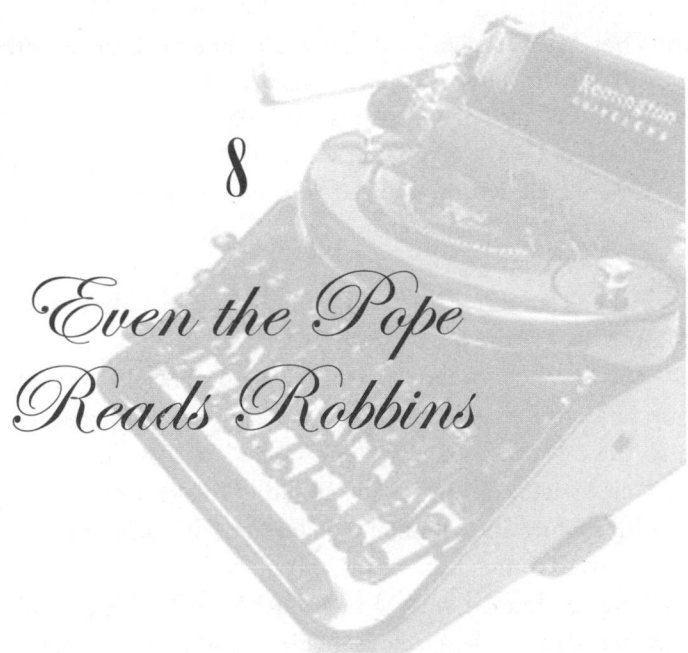

8

Even the Pope Reads Robbins

*I*t was January 1964, and the French Riviera was a welcome respite from the biting cold of Manhattan. We took a gorgeous suite at the extravagant Hotel Beaulieu sur Mer, not far from Monte Carlo. The baby was not due until July, so we had time to stake out our French claim on the Côte d'Azur. It was wonderfully romantic; the hills were scented with herbs, the harbors filled with yachts. I could not help but recall how this area had been the residence of so many American expatriate writers in years past, from Hemingway to Fitzgerald, famous writers who in their lifetimes had not collectively sold as many copies of their books as Harold's *The Carpetbaggers* had.

Those first days were a heady, adjusting experience, as if anyone ever needed to adjust to the South of France. We made mad, passionate love; dined at the finest restaurants; drank the best champagne; and devoured with zest the world famous cuisine, particularly the endless varieties of seafood that came together in one wonderful dish that epitomizes Provençal gastronomy—bouillabaisse.

While I rested and sunbathed by day, Harold scoured the countryside and villages, looking for a villa to rent. He wanted to get to work on *The Adventurers*, the book his publisher was waiting for back in New York, waiting rather anxiously I might have thought, since they had advanced Harold an unprecedented half-million dollars for a work of which he had not yet written a word.

Harold eventually knew every realtor on the coast. At night, after a day of sun and search, we would start play anew, just the two of us, enjoying our life together. We were living a dreamy fairy book existence, without a worry in the world. We did not seek new friends; at the time we were so much into each other, and Harold of course, was essentially a loner. He just didn't seem to need friends. "All I want is you," he would tell me, and I would grow warm all over.

One day he returned to the hotel earlier than usual.

"I've found a villa!"

"Where?" I asked.

"In Le Cannet, a little village in the hills just above Cannes," he exclaimed. "Come on. I want you to see it!"

We drove down the coastal highway in Harold's rented car (he had not yet purchased the first of what was to become our European fleet), and then up into the hills, to a sleepy, picturesque village overlooking the Mediterranean. The views were breathtaking and the village was charming, just what one would conjure in a moment of luscious imagination. No wonder so many artists lived in the area.

I was enthralled when I saw our new villa. First of all, it was impressive, Mediterranean-style, spacious, made of stone and native wood, and only a five-minute walk from the village proper. It was shaded in a variety of cool, soft pastels, fully furnished, with little porcelain birds hanging from the living room ceiling. Cannes, the famous resort, was farther below but in full view, with its fabulous beachfront boulevard de la Croisette and the famous Hotel Carlton.

Harold had already cased the entire area and as we stood in the driveway looking down on the village, he pointed out specific landmarks. It was a classic Harold Robbins production.

"See that building?" he said.

"Yes."

"It's a branch of Barclay's Bank, and that one over there is a branch of Credit Suisse Lyonaisse."

"Convenient."

"And just below that," he continued, "is a *charcuterie* that the locals say is the best in the area."

I laughed to myself. It was so typical of Harold to first find what he considered the most important adjuncts to our home: a bank for his money and a deli for his tummy.

He turned back to the villa. "Do you like it?"

"I love it!"

"You've got great taste, Grace. I love your sense of style. You've made one hell of a choice!"

I was unbelievably happy. We had a new home; we were in the South of France; I was pregnant; and I was terribly in love.

The charcuterie was an excellent replacement for Reuben's in New York, Harold's favorite deli. Its specialty was *langue en gelée* (tongue in aspic) and it became my favorite choice on the menu, although during the next few months I consumed enough of its wonderful salads to feed a batch of rabbits. For the first time I was introduced to bottled water. It seemed peculiar that one had to order fresh water in a bottle

Another food novelty I thoroughly relished was the croissant that today is commonplace in every little coffee shop in America, which gives one a pretty good idea of our constantly shrinking world—but I had neither seen nor tasted one until Harold and I moved to France. I was the first person, however, to import Riguad scented candles into the States, although unfortunately not for retail. I sent them to friends. I fell in love with the concept and filled our villa with candles that produced various bouquets, depending on my mood.

After we moved into the villa, Harold went to the nearby Hotel Carlton seeking information about local obstetricians. We didn't know a soul, except for a few realtors, so it was logical to seek help from the concierge. The French have always placed writers on a pedestal, therefore it wasn't difficult for Harold to get what he considered the soundest of advice; they loved him at the Carlton.

"Ah, you want Dr. Guilleman," the concierge recommended with marked enthusiasm. "He's the best doctor, the best at delivering babies, the best at everything!"

This Dr. Pierre Guilleman became our first friend in France, although I hasten to add that for me he was always a distant friend and one with some rather weird quirks.

My first examination was memorable. Harold and I went down to Dr. Guilleman's office, a pleasant apartment on the famous and colorful rue D'Antibes, in Cannes. The doctor seemed more interested in "the famous American writer" than he was in me, exclaiming to Harold that he had delighted in reading all of his books in translation—an unlikely statement since France was the only European country that held little awe for Harold's particular brand of commercial writing. "It's their fucking lousy translations," Harold complained.

Finally, I was alone with the doctor in his office, on the table, so to say, in that most embarrassing aspect of being pregnant, with my legs spread and my feet in the stirrups, covered haphazardly with a thin sheet. The doctor smiled and then took a look. Exactly what he was looking for, I don't know, but he suddenly lifted his head above the rumpled folds of the sheet, looked me straight in the eye, and said with all the seriousness he could possible muster, "Did you know Errol Flynn?"

My legs clamped shut like the jaws of a vice. "Errol Flynn has been dead for years," I responded, hoping the doctor would realize I was at most a very young teenager when the famous actor met his demise.

Dr. Guilleman gave a casual laugh, and with some effort he spread my legs again. Later, when I told Harold what had transpired, he burst out with his infectious laughter. "Flynn was a womanizer," he said, "and the good doctor associated the old rogue's activities, and rightfully so, with your wonderful pussy!" He laughed again and continued his analysis. "Flynn's women were gorgeous, and so are you, Tiger! That was the doctor's association."

My interpretation was different. Harold was twenty-two-years older than me, and I assumed the doctor thought a famous American writer would surely have known a famous American actor.

Since Harold thought I should have our baby under the guidance of the Lamaze method, a technique invented by the French, Dr. Guilleman assigned to me a midwife, who would also serve as my birthing coach. She was a stern-looking woman but very obliging. She spoke no English, which reduced our immediate method of communication to sign language.

Meanwhile, Harold began writing *The Adventurers*. I saw for the first time how really dedicated and disciplined he was when it came to his work. He cordoned off a niche in the living room with rope, placed his manual typewriter on a desk, and declared the territory off limits. Margot, our housekeeper, laughed out loud when she first saw Harold's makeshift office, but she earnestly respected his wishes.

He worked ten and twelve hours a day, starting in the morning and often working straight through the evening until he was too fatigued to continue, "hunting and pecking" the keys of his typewriter with his index fingers, but almost as rapidly as a professional typist. He was a man consumed. Every time he finished a page, he would rip it out of the carrier, toss it aside, and exclaim, "Voila!" Then he would insert a fresh page and attack it with renewed vigor.

At intervals, I would gather up the strewn pages, place them in order, and peruse them. It was fascinating to see the book unfold, not knowing exactly where Harold was going with the story or what character he would invent next. He let the story unfold as he worked, using neither notes nor outline. Every once in a while, while he continued nonstop typing, he would yell, "How does it read, Tiger?"

"It's great," I always said, and I meant it.

"It's because of you, darling," Harold would say. "You're my muse."

He never asked me to help solve a plot problem, if he had one, nor did he ask my advice of any kind. This was as close to a collaborative effort we would ever have. He just didn't discuss it with me, although it was evident he wanted my approval.

I began French language lessons. Harold had met a handsome young college boy from the local university whom he hired as my tutor. I was hoping that by the time the baby arrived, I would be able to converse in basic French (if only to understand the midwife). Since I already spoke Italian, I was optimistic about quickly gaining a working knowledge of the language. Although it was more difficult than I had anticipated, I was able finally to make myself understood.

Le Cannet and Cannes became our universe; we had little reason to venture beyond the immediate area. While Harold worked, I continued my French and Lemaze lessons, sunbathed on the scrupulously clean Cannes beach, went weekly to a small salon in Le Cannet for my hair, and shopped at the local charcuterie. Occasionally, I drove down to Cannes and shopped in the boutiques.

It was inevitable that we made a few friends. Our lifestyle was simple though not in the least presaging what was in store for us after the baby was born. We dined frequently at a little maman et papa bistro in Le Cannet, where the kitchen stove was placed squarely in the middle of the dining room and you could watch Papa do the cooking, while Maman served. The food was peasant French: fresh sardines, escargots, simple pastas, and always delicious. It became "our" restaurant.

Cannes and Le Cannet were replete with art galleries and the neighborhoods with artists. In my spare time, I wandered through the galleries in search of something different. During the annual art show in Le Cannet, I fell in love with the work of Giselle Balleud. She was the only living student of the great postimpressionist Pierre Bonnard, and when I met her in person, I liked her immediately. With Harold's permission, I bought her entire collection, with the intention of introducing her work in the United States when we returned. (Unfortunately, a year later when I took the Belleud collection to Greg Juarez, a major art dealer in Beverly Hills, he dismissed the work as "too romantic," which of course was the precise reason I admired it. Greg, however, was not in error. Other dealers responded in kind, thus ending my career as an art broker.)

In March, Harold's work was interrupted. He received a call from a German motion picture producer who was interested in translating one of his earlier books into a movie. In contrast to France, Harold's books were popular in Germany and one critic hailed him as the "new humanist," comparing him to John dos Passos and James Farrell, who were two of Harold's favorite American writers.

When the German producer called, Harold smelled money. His attitude toward pictures had not changed, even though Joe Levine's production of

The Carpetbaggers had become a huge box office success. He had little faith in pictures or picture people, no matter where they were from. He was not critical of them as individuals; he just looked at the industry as a different entertainment medium, one essentially incompatible with his books. But motion picture money—now that was something else. We flew to Hamburg to find out what kind of money the German producer was speaking of.

It was dreary in northern Germany, and the deal came to naught. Since we were there, however, we decided to fly east to Berlin. Harold wanted to see the Berlin Wall, and he may have been tinkering with an idea in which it would be the backdrop for a future novel. We flew over the Soviet occupied zone and landed at Tempelhof Airport. We rented a car and check into a hotel.

Although it was 1964, Berlin seemed not to have changed much from photographs I had seen of the city that were taken at the end of the war. It was depressing, and our stay was short. It was one thing to read about Berlin's plight in a newspaper or see fleeting glimpses on television, but to be there in person brought home a reality impossible to achieve vicariously.

We toured the wall. That very morning East German VOPOs had shot a young man to death while he was attempting to escape into West Berlin. They had left his corpse entangled in the wire atop the wall, in full view of passersby on each side, a reminder in the East what was in store for those who sought freedom, and a reminder in the West that freedom was primarily confined to a small enclave of Berlin.

Harold and I stared mutely at the bullet-riddled body. Although I was emotionally devastated by the stark scene, I reached back to my youth, when I had learned to be calm and stoic in the face of tragedy, and held my true feelings within. It wasn't easy, for I was sick to my stomach and wanted to be away from there, not just the wall, but Berlin.

"Let's get the hell out of here," Harold said quietly.

We flew out of Berlin the same day we arrived.

We did not go directly back to Cannes. Over the past few months we had talked many times of visiting Rome, where Harold thought I would "find my roots."

"But I'm Sicilian, Harold, not Italian."

My words always went in one of his ears and out the other. Like most Americans, Harold never understood the cultural differences between Sicily and Italy. According to him. If you had an Italian name, then damn it, you were an Italian.

There was a significant reason we had not ventured to Rome earlier; after all, by air from Nice, it was only three hundred miles, hardly a sixty-minute flight. No, we could not go until Harold had heard from Father Guzman in

Colombia. After their trek into the Andes wilderness, Harold had told the priest that someday we would like to have an audience with the Pope, and once we arrived in France, the two pals had begun to communicate about the intention. I realized, of course, that Father Guzman, wonderful man that he was, was nevertheless a lowly parish priest with little clout, if any, with the Vatican. Harold, on the other hand, was a supreme optimist, always reprimanding me when I pooh-poohed Father Guzman's efforts. I thought Harold was being naïve, but I learned to keep my mouth shut. When Harold was determined, common sense and logic fell to the wayside.

We stayed at the Grand Hotel Plaza in the heart of the historical district. Harold never went second-class, and the Grand was extravagant and emblematic of the city's spirit, laden with sparkling fountains, lush gardens, and antique statuary. It was like going back in time, except for the sumptuousness of our suite. During the day we saw the tourist attractions, the Forum, the Coliseum, fountains galore, roamed up and down the Tiber River; at night we drank and dined in some of Rome's many splendid restaurants, drinking the finest Italian red wines (always a one-glass limit for me) and eating exquisite Italian cuisine.

There was no end of things to do, although we had no particular plans. I was now in my sixth month of pregnancy and prone to growing tired rather quickly. One morning I climbed out of bed convinced that I didn't want to walk another cobblestoned block. "I'm a little tired, Harold. Let's do something different today, something more sedate than following the tourist path."

"That's okay by me," he said, leaning back on his pillow, his arms folded behind his head.

"Do you have any good ideas?" I asked.

"Well," he responded casually. "I hope you're not too pooped to Pope."

My head snapped. "What did you say?"

He grinned. "You heard me."

Evidently Father Guzman had come through after all. I felt terrible that I had doubted his ability and Vatican connections.

By midmorning we were entering a gate that led directly into St. Peter's Square. Something comes over you, regardless of your religious faith, the moment you see St. Peter's Basilica across the huge piazza a lump forms in your throat. To the north of us was the Sistine Chapel and then the Vatican Museums that house the astonishing and priceless treasures of art collected by the Church over the centuries.

"Per square inch, this fucking place has gotta be the richest country in the world," said Harold.

"Harold," I said rather piously, "watch you language."

He went to an information window beside the post office, and soon a priest who spoke English so softly we could hardly hear him was leading us into an area obviously off-limits to tourists, and then into a building that reminded me of heaven itself. We followed him down a long corridor whose walls and ceiling were resplendent with gilded angels, each of their faces different, our footsteps echoing around them. We passed not another soul as we left the corridor and went up a narrow staircase, pausing finally at a huge wooden door. The priest did not knock, so we waited, Harold and I stealing glances at each other, wondering what was next.

Finally the door opened and we were ushered into a huge, ornate office. We suddenly paused in awe, for there before us, at the far end of the room, sitting behind a huge desk like a corporate executive, was none other than Pope Paul VI, dressed in a white cassock and satin skullcap. I became so nervous that I thought I was going to drop my water on the spot. The Pope lifted his arm and motioned for us to come forward. "Please, please," he said in English. "Come in."

I was frozen in place until Harold gently tugged me by the arm and whispered under his breath, "Come on, Tiger. This is the real thing. Don't forget to kiss his fucking ring." Then he patted me on the derriere and edged me forward.

A priest-in-waiting, apparently one of innumerable aids to the Pope, suddenly announced, "Your Holiness, Mr. and Mrs. Harold Robbins." I almost fainted. The Pope smiled broadly, stood up, came out from behind his desk, and extended his right hand. I took it immediately, curtsied as though I had been practicing for a week, and kissed his ring with all the passion I could muster. When I lifted my head and straightened my shoulders, he placed a hand on my tummy and muttered a papal blessing. I was beside myself.

The Pope then turned to Harold and extended his hand again.

"I have read two of your books," said the Pontiff with a twinkle in his eye, "and that's all I'll say about your writing."

Harold laughed, although uneasily. What was said after that, I don't remember. I was in a state, not of shock, but of absolute spontaneous tranquility. The Pope had blessed my baby! There was a moment of small talk, and then we were ushered out, via the same route by which we had entered. Back in the sunlight of St. Peter's Square, still flush from our audience with the Pope, Harold tugged me by an arm and pulled me off my cloud, back down to earth. I looked at him; he had the strangest, most curious expression on his face.

"What is it, Harold?"

"Which two of my books do you think he read?"

9
Villa Grazia

$\mathcal{W}$hen we returned to Le Cannet, Harold began work anew with unmitigated vigor on *The Adventurers*. He would work five or six hours straight, pounding on the keys of his typewriter, and then he would break off for thirty minutes or so, take a walk in the hills and woods, and return again for another stretch of uninterrupted hours.

Time went on, rather slowly it seemed to me, but I didn't care.

No villa seemed complete without a pet. I wanted a cat, but Harold said he was allergic to them. We settled on a dog. We got a beautiful Kerry Blue Terrier from London that seemed to complete our household. We already had a full staff—our chauffeur, René; our butler, Jacque; our cook, Laura; our housekeeper, Margot—and now with a dog so smashing that we actually named him Smasher, the only thing our domicile lacked was a child, and he or she was in the making. It says much for Harold's patience and discipline that Smasher wasn't relegated to a doggie orphanage, for it barked constantly at any and everything, indeed even at nothing. Smasher barked and barked and barked, morning, noon and night, to no end and for no purpose as far as we could determine. It barked at its own shadow.

Smasher was in the midst of a barking spree, when I heard Harold push his typewriter away and go outside. Shortly after, I saw him standing outside our villa, taking in the charming sweep of the village. I was concerned that he had taken a break because Smasher's barking had finally gotten to him. I went outside and joined him, expecting the worst, at least regarding to Smasher's future, whose barks were yet echoing through the house. Harold looked at me and said, "You know, I really like living here in the South of France. How about you?"

"I love it," I said.

"Why don't we buy our own villa?"

"Oh, Harold, that would be wonderful!"

"Then let's do it," he said enthusiastically. "You come up with great ideas, Tiger!"

Again Harold began to look for a house. A few days later we heard about a new villa that was being built on Avenue Victoria, a little higher up in the hills than our present location. Harold decided to check it out. When he returned, he was excited. He wanted me to go back with him and take a look. I was very near the termination of my pregnancy and felt like a cow, but, yes, of course, I wanted to see it.

The construction of the villa was not completed and its steep driveway even less so. We huffed and puffed up a hill, which was not easy for me.

"What do you think?" said Harold, when we arrived at the site.

It was a huge stone villa, just behind the Carlton Hotel, designed in a style that architects call *mas Provençal*. I did not think it was as luxurious as our rented villa, which was Mediterranean style, what Harold called "a real villa villa." The new one, however, was split-level, ranging across the hill in three tiers. Below the structure was a swimming pool and above it was a garden. The view of Cannes and its famous Croisette far below and then beyond to the blue-green waters of the Mediterranean was spectacular, truly breathtaking. I looked around. The structure and the grounds certainly presented a dilettante designer like me with something to work with, and I thought it would be nice if we had our own home when the baby arrived.

I nodded my approval and Harold bought the place. Our lives were on the brink of change, although we didn't know it. He also purchased a small house above the garden, which was owned by a lovely elderly couple. Eventually, the second dwelling was used by our servants, with one wing of it converted into a garage for the fleet of vehicles that Harold began to collect almost immediately. He called the cars "toys." They ranged from a prototype Jensen and Mercedes 380 SL to a four-door Cadillac sedan and a van. That was just the beginning of his fleet. His books were selling like pancakes or French crepes. At one point we could wake up in the morning with the knowledge that ten thousand of his novels would be purchased that very day in stores ranging around the globe from Calcutta to Vancouver, in three-dozen languages. It was mind-boggling, and I could not fault Harold for letting his ego swell a bit. If the number of his readers was a gauge, then his proclamation that "I'm the best novelist in the world" was not far from the truth. He was certainly the most popular.

The new house was soon completed and we moved in, taking Smasher with us. Harold named it Villa Grazia, *grazia* meaning "grace" in Italian. Our property had a history, which we thought was fortuitous. Pierre Bonnard, that same famous postimpressionist who had influenced all the Giselle Belleud paintings we now owned, had once had a studio on the sight of our new villa; it was there he had painted "The View from My Studio in Le Cannet," one of his most renowned works. Years later, when I saw the painting for the first time, it was as though I was back in our villa, viewing the Mediterranean from my bedroom window.

If our new home did not seem like "a real villa villa," it was nevertheless impressive, although less so than some of the other abodes in our neighborhood. Even with Harold making what he called "big money," his prosperity seemed paltry compared to that of many of our wealthy neighbors.

No matter in what direction I looked from our property, I saw an imposing home. To the east was La Douce France, a grand villa owned by a French mogul who had made his fortune in the pharmaceutical industry. He had converted some of his rooms into a complete, state-of-the-art laboratory. Above us and to the west was the Yaki Amour, the magnificent home of Her Highness, the Begum Khan III, the mother of the young Aga Khan IV who had recently inherited from his deceased grandfather the role of Imam, leader of the world's fourteen-million Ismaili Muslims.

With Harold's propensity to base his stories on real events and real people, and with his *idée fixe* on money, power, and sex, the very mention of the name Ali Khan conjured up a glamorous world of fast cars, beautiful women, racehorses, French chateaux—all fascinating fodder for his imagination. Furthermore, the Begum was reputed to have intimate salon gatherings that made those of famous yesteryear notables, such as Gertrude Stein's appear as mere tea parties. How much truth was in the rumors about the Begum's grand soirees, we didn't know, but we were soon to find out, for one day I answered a knock at the door and a courier presented me with an invitation, neatly penned in the Begum's hand.

"Hell, Tiger, let's go see what she's all about," said Harold. For once he shoved his manuscript away and closed shop, if only temporarily.

We hiked up to Yaki Amour from Villa Grazia, following an ancient path that ultimately became an exterior stairway cut into the granite stone of the hillside, with an overview of the Mediterranean that was intoxicating. It was the beginning of a perfect evening, the first of many for us at the Begum's villa, although Harold may have been initially disappointed. The playboy image of the deceased ex-husband of the Begum was not remotely in evidence; rather, the attendees were an eclectic mix of sophisticated world travelers ranging the broad spectrum from art to business, left to right, although in Harold's words "a bit stuffy."

The Begum was a beautiful woman, in her mid-fifties, with an elegance mirrored perfectly by her perfect jewels. As usual, Harold pretended shyness at the Begum's presence observing what was happening more than participating in it. Not that he was reticent, but in those days when Harold engaged in conversation it was more of a question-answer situation than it was a dialogue, with Harold asking all the questions. When we left the Begum's villa and started our downward trek toward home, he said to me, "Now, that was class, Tiger. Maybe not exactly my cup of tea, but real class, nevertheless." In the distance we could hear Smasher barking his head off.

The next time we received an invitation from the Begum, Harold declined and I went alone. Although he was working hard, he wasn't hunched over his typewriter all the time by any means, as he had been when he first went to work on the novel. He would often stop abruptly and take a stroll by himself on one of the many trails in the hills or go to the bank to check his account or drive his new Jensen prototype over to the Carlton Hotel for a quick drink at the bar. I think he was still writing in his mind, even though he wasn't in his office, because he would be very incommunicative.

One day when he was walking on the path above the villa, he veered off toward Mougins, the adjacent village. Had he taken the other prong in the fork, he would have gone to the Begum's mansion. He was gone longer than usual, and I grew concerned. Then I saw him coming back, at a sort of double-time, which was unusual for Harold. He was often supercharged with nervous energy, but he did not usually expend it walking. His movement this time, however, was indicative of something else. I could plainly see he was excited.

I met him at the door as he burst into the house. "You're not going to believe this," he said. "You are not going to fucking believe what just happened!"

"What? Tell me."

"Who do you think I just met?"

"Harold, I haven't the slightest idea."

"Guess," he said with a self-satisfying grin. He was clearly pleased with himself.

"God only knows," I said. "Tell me, Harold. I can't guess who you met."

"How about Pablo Picasso?"

"No."

"Yes!"

Harold had been strolling along the trail, lost in thought, flanked by the forest of trees through which he could catch only glimpses of the sea, when suddenly his path was blocked by a wiry little bald-headed man whom Harold immediately recognized as the master himself. There was a momentary impasse. Lacking a conversational knowledge of French, Harold was going to let the moment pass, as well as Picasso, when suddenly the maestro said "Ecrivan!"

It was one French word Harold definitely understood—writer.

"Yes, yes," he answered excitedly, and the two of them began an effort to converse, world-famous writer and world-famous artist, with Harold attempting to hold forth in what can only be described as his pidgin-French. It was enough, however, for Picasso to understand at least something, and I suspect his English was on par with Harold's French.

"Donnez-moi votre photo, s'il vous plait," said Picasso at last.

As Harold related his story to me, I was thinking how he had surely misunderstood Picasso, and I finally said, "Oh, Harold, you must have confused his words."

"No," cried Harold almost indignantly, "That's exactly what he said. I'm certain of it. Really, Grace. I am!"

Picasso, according to Harold's translation, had asked him for a personal photograph, which seemed strange at best, and I thought most likely a total misinterpretation on Harold's part.

"Are you sure that's what he said?" I asked again.

"Yes," said Harold, "I'm positive. For whatever reason, Pablo Picasso wants my photograph!"

"What else did you talk about?"

"Women," he laughed. "French women versus American women."

I shrugged, dubious. However, just in case Harold's translation of the meeting with Picasso was correct, the next morning we dispatched our butler, Jacques, to the master's studio with a snapshot of Harold in hand. Picasso lived in Mougins, which was virtually walking distance, but his studio was in Vallauris, another nearby village that was populated primarily by craftsmen, mostly potters. When Jacques returned, having left the photo with one of Picasso's servants, we assumed the story had come to its end.

A month had passed when one day we received a telephone call from someone at Picasso's studio, requesting that we send Jacques to pick up Harold's photograph, as if it were consuming too much space. Harold and I looked at each other with a shrug—it was all very mysterious—and again we sent Jacques driving away. When he returned, however, he had more than Harold's photo.

He had a sketch of Harold done in the master's postcubist style, a rendering that resembled a convoluted cartoon character. We were ecstatic.

"My God!" I cried. "A Picasso!"

Not to be outdone, Harold grabbed a French edition of one on his books, inscribed it, and sent Jacques scurrying back to the studio. When he returned, Jacques explained that the signed book was what Picasso had been requesting to begin with that day when he and Harold had fortuitously met on the walking path. "He was most grateful," said Jacques.

"What a trade," exclaimed Harold, "one of my autographed books for an original Picasso!"

10

"Believe Me, Tiger, It's a Girl."

*I*n late July I interrupted Harold's work one of the few times in my life. He looked up from his typewriter with a blank expression on his face. Then, before I said a word, he leaped up; my own expression was all revealing.

"Let's go!" he said.

Moments before, I had experienced the first signal pains preceding childbirth. I knew intuitively it was time to go to the clinic. Harold rushed about as though he thought I was going to deliver at any moment. There was no reason to do so, for I was beginning the first minutes of the most horrifically long forty-eight hours of my entire life.

What French I had learned from my young tutor, which I thought had been considerable, went down the drain once we arrived at Clinique Lutetia. I hardly understood a word of the innumerable commands dictated by my midwife, which annoyed her to no end. Once the pain started, it seemed not to end. I was out of it, in my own French torture chamber. I thought I was going to die; the cramps from my paratyphoid had been child's play compared to this. Minutes became hours and hours ultimately became two long days. It seemed I couldn't deliver my baby regardless.

Dr. Guilleman explained that the baby was not positioned properly, that it was reversed in the womb, feet first rather than head first—the makings of a breach birth. No effort was made to turn the baby around, a normal procedure in the United States.

"So what do we do?" asked Harold.

"It may take a little longer than it usually does," said the doctor, "but eventually the baby will work its way out by its own volition."

"My God," I thought, "is this man crazy? How many babies has he given birth to?" I was having excruciating contractions every few minutes and each one seemed to last forever. It was pure torture—slow, debilitating torture. What few lucid thoughts I remember were absolute damnations of the clinic, the doctor, the midwife, and the Lamaze method. I wasn't even given an aspirin, much less an epidural. The only "saving grace" was that Harold remained at my bedside from the outset, never leaving once, not even for a cup of coffee. For his sake, I tried to put on an air of bravery, stifling my screams whenever I could, but finally it became too overwhelming for me. I was depleted of energy; all I could do was cry. I was afraid, all the more so because I could see that Harold, too, had reached an emotional state whereby he could not hide his own fear regarding the outcome.

Dr. Guilleman checked on me frequently. One time he came into my room and started telling off-color jokes in broken English, as if humor would break the spell of my non-delivery and bring our baby at last into the world. He had picked up Harold's propensity for using expletives and his only words I remember clearly were earthy American vulgarities that seemed totally out of place, particularly coming from his mouth in his thick accent. When Harold said "fuck this" or "fuck that" it meant something; but the doctor, who was trying to be humorous, was only annoying.

After almost forty-eight hours I had not started to dilate. Nevertheless, Dr. Guilleman decided it was time for me to be transferred from my suite to the delivery room. That was okay with me; it gave me some sense of eventual termination, until I discovered I had to walk. It was maddening, but somehow I made it down that long corridor with Harold's aid in absence of a gurney or wheelchair.

"This is fucking ridiculous!" mumbled Harold under his breath. "I'm not gonna let this continue."

When he got me to the delivery room, Harold suddenly took charge. He had a psychic quality and an extraordinary intuition. The room was bathed in brilliant lights, radiating from huge overhead reflectors. One would have thought we were on the Cannes beach at high noon.

"Dim the lights," he said sternly.

"Pardon?" said Dr. Guilleman.

"Just dim the fucking lights, doc," Harold repeated; it was a command, not a request.

The lights were dimmed. Somehow Harold's sixth sense signaled to him what needed to be done. Once the light in the room fell to a shadow, the atmosphere seemed to cool considerably, as though an air conditioner had been placed above me. I began straight away to relax, and then to dilate. Even the pain began to diminish.

I did not feel the baby leave my body, but I know I was finally giving birth when the pain diminished to an empty throb. I remember hearing the doctor exclaimed excitedly, "There, I think I see its head! Yes, yes, the baby has turned itself around!" How many minutes it took to actually deliver, once I started dilating, I don't know, but suddenly I felt empty and relieved, and then I heard a hand slap against flesh and the baby's first bellow that signified life.

"What is it?" I asked weakly.

Harold leaned over me, smiled proudly, and said, "Darling, she has your pussy!"

It was July 23, 1964. The baby was a beautiful little girl, whom we named Adréana Grace Robbins. Her first name had been predetermined months before. Harold and I had been swimming in the Adriatic on a holiday weekend getaway, when he said with impromptu relish, "Hey, let's name the baby Adriana, except instead of an "i" as it would be spelled in Italian, we'll use an "e," for France, her birthplace. We'll spell it A-d-r-é-a-n-a."

"I think that's a beautiful name, Harold, but what if it's a boy?" I asked.

"It won't be," he said. "Believe me, Tiger, it's a girl."

The night following Adréana's birth, although I did not know it until later, Harold went to the Palm Beach Casino in Cannes. He went to a roulette table and placed $25,000 on number 7, for July, and lost. Then he placed $25,000 on number 23, for Adréana's birth date, and lost again. He shrugged.

"I'm sorry you lost," said the croupier as he took Harold's chips.

"What do you mean? I didn't fucking lose!" exclaimed Harold without flinching. "Harold Robbins never loses. Never! Believe me, I'll get it back another day, here, Las Vegas, Monaco. I play to fucking win! I've got a daughter to take care of!"

At the hospital the next day, the nurses drove me crazy. Suddenly they seemed to be everywhere, like busy ants, in contrast to my two days of what I considered lonely labor, with the exception of Harold's presence. They chattered away, without qualms for my personal feelings.

"Ah, nous avons un petit garçon! Tres heures!" said one. "Nous avons une petite fille! Çinq heures!" said another.

I had lost what command I had of French when I entered the hospital, but now with the pain gone and my baby delivered, it all came back. The nurses were comparing my forty-eight-hours of labor to that of other new mothers, saying one had delivered in three hours, another in five hours, as if I were some sort of American misfit in a French clinic. Of course, I didn't give a damn what they thought. Our baby in my arms was all I needed.

We had planned that my parents would come to France upon the baby's arrival. Harold called them after I went to the hospital and made arrangements for them to catch the first flight out of New York. They arrived just hours after Adréana was born; after Harold and me and the hospital staff, they were the first to see her. They were effusive with compliments, not remotely aware of the problems I'd had with the delivery.

"She's beautiful!" exclaimed my mother.

"You bet she is," agreed Harold.

"A girl," said my father. He then added in typical fashion, "You'll have to watch out for the boys when she gets older."

I was delighted with their joy at having a granddaughter, even though my mother, upon reexamining Adréana for the umpteenth time, cried out in Sicilian, "What big feet she has!"

Then she laughed and said, "Try to keep them covered." I didn't care if she thought Adréana had big feet or not. I was in heaven. I had Harold, I had my baby, I had a beautiful home in the South of France, and my parents seemed gloriously happy for the first time in years.

Harold was not content with just having my parents present. He wanted more people, and a week after I went home with Adréana from the clinique new guests began to arrive. The first were Paul Gitlin and his wonderful wife Zelda, who became a dear, fun friend, a woman always full of life and energy. Next came Sylvia and Irving Wallace, who were already vacationing in Cannes. Irving was basking in the success of his third novel, *The Prize*, which had been turned into a successful film starring Paul Newman. Cornelius Ryan made a special trip from the States with his wife Kathryn, taking a break from the grueling task of writing the second book of his World War II trilogy, which had begun with the enormously successful *The Longest Day*. Even Catherine Pitts, who had so graciously covered for me at Grey Advertising when Harold and I had taken off for Hollywood, arrived with her husband and an actress friend, Marianne Marshall. Marianne and I had a good laugh, for I had once cast her in a Polident commercial, qualifying her according to FCC regulations because she had a minuscule removable bridge that could, if necessary, be held in place by denture cream. Harold was full of pomp and a lot of exaggeration, telling everyone that it was he who had finally delivered the baby.

"You're kidding, of course," said Irving skeptically.

"No, not at all," Harold answered with great pride. He turned to me, "Am I darling? Am I kidding? Tell them! Didn't I deliver Adréana?"

"Harold delivered her," I responded, and before the day was over he even had me believing it.

"I have no doubt he did," said Connie Ryan.

"Harold never bullshits about anything," said Paul, biting his lower lip.

"When there's an emergency, Harold always comes through," said someone else.

"I'll drink to that," said Paul.

"You'll drink to anything," said Harold.

With respect to my parents and my Catholic upbringing, Harold decided we would have Adréana baptized in the local parish church. We asked Zelda and Paul to be her godparents, and a few days later our group formed in the small auditorium of what Harold called "the Cannes Cathedral," a nondescript church that was not much larger than one of California's frontier missions. We were in high but respectful spirits until the priest threw a wrench into the plan. He was disconcerted because the Gitlins were Jewish, informing us that he could not perform the baptism without Catholic godparents. He seemed adamant.

"Father," said Harold calmly. "You have no need to worry. Mr. and Mrs. Gitlin have pledged to convert to Catholicism the minute this ceremony is finished."

The priest looked around slowly, from face to face; everyone nodded, solemnly and seriously. He still wasn't convinced.

"Father, may I speak to you in private?" asked Harold.

"If you wish," said the priest.

The two left the parish chamber; when they returned a few minutes later, the priest had a big smile on his face, no doubt convinced our Jewish friends would soon be Catholics.

The ceremony was then performed, but not without a couple of small hitches. Zelda was holding Adréana and the priest was performing the sacred rights when suddenly the baby started crying.

"For God's sake, Zelda," said Paul, "don't you know how to hold a baby?"

"Of course, I do," exclaimed Zelda indignantly.

"Then why in hell is she crying like that?"

"Because she's a baby, that's why!"

"Here, let me hold her."

"Would you shut up, Paul? What on earth do you know about holding babies? Let the priest continue."

Adréana was baptized and Zelda and Paul were recorded as her godparents.

Later, when I asked Harold what he had said to the priest in order to get him to accept Zelda and Paul as the godparents, he responded, "Nothing."

"Come on, Harold," I begged.

"It wasn't what I said," he replied with a laugh, "It was the donation I gave him!"

Back at the villa, we had a wonderful party.

I noticed that Sylvia and Irving Wallace were not partaking of the good tidings. They were quiet and withdrawn, distant for each other. I cornered Harold. "What's wrong with the Wallaces?" I asked.

"Sylvia caught Irving screwing around with another woman," said Harold.

"Oh no."

"Oh yes," he said.

"What happened?"

"Irving got remorseful and confessed his dalliances." He laughed. "Now he's gonna be a poor, miserable bastard for the rest of his natural life. Sylvia will never let him out of her sight again as long as he lives. The man is fucking doomed!"

I could not picture Irving as a "lech," but I didn't dwell on it. I was too happy with the knowledge that nothing like that would ever come between Harold and me.

A few weeks after Adréana's baptism, when all of our guests except my parents had gone their merry ways, Harold went back to work on his novel. To ensure the privacy he needed, he had a hole cut out in the ceiling of a hallway; he secured a folding ladder to the opening and made a makeshift office in the rather large attic of the villa. After breakfast every morning, he would bid us a cheery adieu, climb up the ladder, pull it up after him, and settle in for at least ten hours of work. In the distance, we could hear the muffled clatter of the typewriter keys and the slam of the carriage for the length of the long day.

Although we hired a French nanny, a lovely young woman named Françoise, I spent most of my time with Adréana. I adored my new baby, but in the process of giving her my attention, I was ignoring my parents. It was Harold, however, rather than I, who saw they were getting restless, without much to do except sit around our villa. I knew intuitively that he was trying to come up with something creative for them to do while biding their time.

"Grazia, why don't you take your parents to Sicily to see your mother's family," he suggested one morning, quite out of the blue. "We have Françoise to take care of Adréana, I have my work to do, you could use a break"—he turned to my mother and father—"and I think all of you would enjoy seeing and visiting the old country. Wouldn't you? What do you think?"

"Why, I think it's a wonderful idea, Harold," I said, afraid my parents would be too embarrassed to accept his gift.

I was wrong.

My mother beamed; although my father no longer had relatives in Sicily and felt my mother's family had never approved of him, it was evident he relished the idea also. He had never met my mother's relatives and perhaps he thought he could assuage any hard feelings that might have endured through the years. He believed his shortcomings as a businessman had incurred my mother's family's wrath. The problem was further compounded by a certain Sicilian snobbism. Most of my mother's brothers and male cousins were formally educated, with some of them actually having academic careers; thus they frowned upon my father (he thought), who had bypassed college in his unsuccessful effort to fulfill the American dream of becoming an entrepreneur.

My parents accepted Harold's offer, and I was more than willing to go with them. Harold quickly made the arrangements, and the three of us prepared to embark for Marsala, Sicily, my mother's birthplace. After so many years of absence, she did not want to forewarn her relatives of our coming. She made up various excuses for not calling them in advance, but what she really wanted to do was to surprise them with a dramatic arrival.

We arrived on a Sunday and went straight to her sister Angelina's home. Mother directed the taxi through the streets as if she had never left. Angelina was not home, but everyone in the narrow street apparently realized intuitively who we were without our announcing it. As we waited at the door, talking among ourselves, considering where to go next, heads began to bob in and out of windows and doorways up and down the street; we heard women's voices rattling excitedly in Sicilian, "La sorella d'America! La sorella d'America!"— the sister from America!

"Mamma, they're talking about you!" I whispered excitedly.

"Yes, I know," she said. Suddenly her shoulders grew taut and straight, and with great pride and a thin confident smile she nodded to the myriad half-hidden observers. "Yes, I am Angelina's sister."

In a matter of moments the neighbors began to emerge from their homes, dozens of them, filling the street in front of Angelina's house. They welcomed us with Sicilian greetings, and soon my mother was engaged in conversation as though she had never left her homeland.

"Where is Angelina?" she asked.

"At the cemetery, laying flowers at your mother and father's gravesites," we were informed. "But don't worry, she will soon return."

My father was growing impatient. "Just settle down," said my mother with a sigh. "We will wait."

When Angelina entered the street a few minutes later, she had a bemused expression on her face, undoubtedly wondering why a crowd was gathered at her doorstep. We recognized her before she recognized us, but when she finally focused on my mother, her cautious pace suddenly became a sprint and she rushed to embrace her long absent sister. I could not have been happier for my mother; it had been a full three decades since the two sisters had seen each other. It was like a wonderful scene in a melodrama, except it was real, both sad and glad at the same time. Before I knew it, they were crying, and then I was crying, and then everyone on the street was crying, except for my father.

A joyful reunion on the street became a full-blown party once we got inside Angelina's home. The crowd increased in size and we quickly moved to my mother's brother's house, which was much larger. My Uncle Andrea, who looked like the actor Rossano Brazzi, was the principal of the local high school, but when he saw mother he lost all pretense of a professorial demeanor. He was overwhelmed with happiness and excitement, and he expressed it to all as only a passionate Sicilian can do.

I thanked god for Harold's unflinching generosity. Later when we got to the little hotel he had booked us into through a travel agency in Cannes, it was perfect. It was not only charming, but it was midway between Angelina and Andrea's homes, hardly more than a stone's throw.

One thing Harold couldn't control, however, was the plumbing. For reasons never quite explained to us, the local water taps were dry, no water. In lieu of running water, the hotel delivered to our rooms every morning an abundant supply of locally bottled mineral water, which we used to bathe in—bottles and bottles of it. At first I was hesitant, but the use of carbonated water for my bath soon became a luxury and to this day I still use it on occasion.

It was August and school was in recess, which gave Andrea and Maria Pia, his stately schoolteacher wife, plenty of time to spend with us. There were so many uncles, aunts, and cousins that it was hard for me to keep up with them and their names, although my mother seemed to have no problem at all, even with the younger members of her family whom she had never seen before.

During a luncheon Andrea related a story that had occurred earlier in the day. He had observed a queue of young men curving from his doorstep all the way around the corner and down the intersecting street. He told us he went outside to find out what they were doing, but then he paused without revealing an answer.

"Well, what were they doing?" I finally asked.

Uncle Andrea laughed heartily. "They wanted to know if my sister had returned to Sicily to find a husband for her daughter!"

Then my uncle explained to me the Sicilian tradition of returning to one's homeland with an unmarried daughter in search of a husband, a custom that is still practiced today, which I suppose is a primitive need to wed the virgin daughter before it gets too late.

"I explained to them that you were already married to a famous American writer," he told me with a laugh, "and that you were already the mother of a little *bambina*."

That Andrea called Harold a famous writer was intriguing. I had been careful not to rain on my mother's parade by talking too much about my own good fortune; of course, my parents adored Harold and they could not help but boast a little about him to everyone.

I was aware that Harold was the best-selling, foreign writer of fiction on the Italian mainland, but I now learned it was true also in Sicily. Andrea had majored in English literature, and he kept up with both English and American writers. He had read all of Harold's books, much to my amazement. I was impressed. He explained to me that Italian critics, unlike their American counterparts, did not find fault with what in the States was called Harold's "explicit sex." The Italians took his stories in stride. I was pleased, and could hardly wait to tell Harold how well his books were received in my parents' home country.

At last it was time to sign off on our holiday. My parents were ready to get back to their little house on Long Island, having enjoyed the best vacation of their lives, and I was anxious to return to Adréana and Harold. Before we departed, Uncle Andrea made me promise that I would one day return with both my bambina and Harold Robbins, his literary hero.

"I promise," I told him.

"You promise me for real?" he asked seriously.

"I promise you for real."

Five years would lapse before I fulfilled my promise, but when I did, it would be a spectacular return, even more dramatic than our arrival at Angelina's house. This time, Harold and I would sail into the harbor of Marsala aboard our own private yacht—the ninety-foot *Gracara*.

11

A Blind Masseuse

$\mathcal{O}$ne of the downsides of pregnancy and its aftermath is the addition of unwanted pounds to an already overburdened physique. I was no exception, but the added weight, compounded by the lack of exercise in the last month before Adréana was born, motivated me to get back in shape when I returned to Le Cannet. Harold agreed enthusiastically, knowing I needed something to do in my spare time when I wasn't taking care of our baby. He was still hard at work on *The Adventurers*, and in the final stretch (or what we thought was the final stretch) he was spending more time in his attic office.

I had been terribly dissatisfied with the Lamaze method and the French maternity hospital, but it unfolded that France was the place to be for slimming and beautifying. All the many clinics offered state-of-the-art treatments, including the use of novel beauty products. I began a training regimen.

One of the most effective techniques for losing inches as well as pounds was the paraffin detoxification program. At the time it was unique to France and consisted of hot paraffin wax being poured over the entire nude body. Activating the sweat glands to expel the toxins one accumulates from food, drink, air, and other environmental exposures. It worked, and fast! I began to lose the water weight I had gained during my pregnancy with the very first hot-wax session, and after just a few treatments I could see as well as feel my body's gradual return to its former self, with improvements to my waistline, breasts, and general muscle tone. Not that it was easy; the treatments were time consuming and tedious. But I did it, with Harold's encouragement, over the course of the next few months, while he pushed toward the conclusion of his novel.

Dr. Guilleman, suggested that I have daily massages in conjunction with my wax treatments. Harold agreed, and I began to trek daily to a masseur and physical therapist whom the good doctor recommended. The man was blind and he wore dark sunglasses. I had no qualms about disrobing every morning in his office and reaping the relaxing dividends of his stout hands and fingers, but only after going through a preliminary exercise he had developed for the purpose of first limbering one's body.

"Have you disrobed? Are you now naked?" he would ask me. We spoke in French.

"Yes."

"Then scale the wall."

He was referring to a wooden, lattice-like rack that climbed against a wall from floor to ceiling. At his command I would begin to edge up the trellis, stretching my muscles.

"Climb, climb," he would command, and up and down I world go.

"Are you climbing?" he would ask.

"Yes, I've been to the top and back three times now."

"Do you feel you've stretched your muscles sufficiently?"

"Very sufficiently."

"Good, then lie down on the table."

He was a wonderful masseur, and after my hot-wax treatment and his sixty-minute massage, I always felt great, on a physical high. Harold got a kick out of my daily health reports, and one morning when I was climbing the rack, he popped in unexpectedly to meet my masseur in person.

Thank god for his sense of humor. Neither the masseur nor I heard him come in the front door of the office, and when he crossed the threshold of the workroom itself, he must have had a difficult time holding back his belly laugh. Here I was, stark naked, crawling up and down this rack, while the masseur stood by quizzing me as though he had a real interest in my stretching my muscles. His sunglasses were in one of his hands and his eyes were pinned to my pink derriere, both of them moving with it, up and down, left and right, as I maneuvered through a variety of awkward contortions.

"This guy ain't blind!" Harold suddenly barked in audible New York English. "He's a fucking fake! He's got you crawling up and down that goddamned contraption only so he can watch your ass!" Fortunately Harold then laughed, rather than punching the masseur in the nose.

I climbed down, completely humiliated by what should have been obvious from the beginning. I grabbed my clothes and was fully dressed and in the street almost before the masseur could get his sunglasses back on. Harold followed in my wake, laughing like a hyena. All my blood seemed to have rushed to my embarrassed face, now ready to burst at the seams.

"Hold up, Tiger, hold up," said Harold, catching up with me. His face was suddenly serious. "I've got one question to ask."

"What's that, Harold?" I said. My voice was now filled with a combination of anger, shame, frustration, disgrace, and more than a little mortification at my own naiveté. I looked at him. "Just say it. Just tell me how stupid I am."

"Tiger, baby, baby," said Harold soothingly. "I don't think you're stupid at all."

"You don't?" I said, suddenly relieved. "Then what is it? What's your question?"

"All I want to know is how a girl can get so sunburned in a masseur's studio? Your face is as red as a beet!"

It was—but from embarrassment. Then he took me in his arms. "Hey, baby," he said comfortingly. "Just chalk it up to another fabulous day in the South of France." We laughed all the way back to the villa.

Although Harold was not finished with *The Adventurers*, I could tell that he was getting restless. I knew the story intimately because I had read the pages as they poured out of his manual typewriter like a river. Once he moved to the attic, he had begun dropping ten or fifteen pages at a time through the hole in the ceiling. He was pleased with what he had created this far, but I sensed he wanted a break from the grueling process and from his confinement in the attic alone with his imagination. When we were out for dinner at night, he grew reflective, even lighthearted, and began to speak often of home, which meant the United States.

Slowly he began to wind down from his normal exhausting pace. He took longer breaks and we spent more intimate time with each other. When James Baldwin, whom we had not seen since that winter day when Harold had given him his favorite sheepskin jacket, called one day, Harold was happy to give his typewriter a hiatus. Jimmy was in Cannes and we drove down the hill to meet him at a local bistro.

"How'd you find us?" asked Harold.

"Hell, are you crazy?" said Jimmy. "It's not difficult to find Harold Robbins!"

Unlike Harold's other writer friends, Jimmy was seldom merry. Someone once wrote that he moved about "like a dark cloud" and the description was my precise impression of Jimmy—a dark, brooding cloud on the edge of a storm. Actually, his latest rendering, *The Fire Next Time*, had put him in the very heart of the tempest of the new civil rights movement. The book was his passionate explanation of what it meant to be a Negro in America, and a lot of whites, particularly Southerners, had not appreciated it. Harold, who did not have a prejudiced cell in his body, sympathized with Jimmy and his black colleagues.

Although Jimmy was far more respected by the press than Harold ever was, I could tell he yearned for the type of publicity Harold received, not because he needed to satisfy an overblown ego but because he wanted more book sales. Harold's name was invariably attached to what the press usually called his latest "steamy novel," which prompted a large segment of the public to dash out and buy a copy of the current Robbins bestseller, a commercial phenomenon that Jimmy seldom experienced. Jimmy was regarded as an intellectual, and his books, although highly acclaimed by the critics, generally suffered from low sales, or so he claimed. He lamented that he would be happy "with only a fraction of the number of Harold's books that sold."

In many ways Harold shunned "intellectuals," but with Jimmy he was different. "It's one thing to be an intellectual," said Harold privately, "but it's something else to be an intelligent intellectual, which is what Jimmy Baldwin is."

At the same time of his arrival in Cannes, Jimmy was prepping to write *Going to Meet the Man*, a series of short stories, and he was beset as usual with financial problems. He had suffered a heart attack a few months before and Harold told him he could use our villa to work and recuperate after we returned to the States. I believe it was the first time I heard Harold mention our imminent departure, but it indicated how restless he had become.

"Are you joking, man?" asked Jimmy surprised.

"Do I sound like it?" said Harold.

"But it's your home."

"Do you fucking think I would joke about something like that?" Harold responded. "The place is yours, Jimmy, for as long as we're gone. Furthermore, we'll leave the staff intact, our cook and so forth, and all you'll have to do is write, and . . . "

Harold's voice suddenly trailed off. I think Jimmy thought he was reconsidering his offer. "And what?" he asked.

After a moment of contemplation Harold continued, "There's one thing more."

"And what's that, Harold?" asked Jimmy suspiciously.

"You'll have to take care of Smasher."

"Smasher?"

"Yeah, Smasher."

"Who in hell is Smasher?"

"Our dog."

Jimmy laughed under his breath, pleased. "It's a deal, Harold." He said.

Of course, Harold said nothing about Smasher's barking his head off night and day.

In our communications during the forthcoming winter, while we were in the States and Jimmy was living in our villa, not once did Jimmy mention Smasher's bothersome behavior. Harold attributed Jimmy's silence on the subject to "he's just being grateful, poor guy." When we returned to France during the spring of the next year, however, with Jimmy already gone, Smasher no longer had a problem. He didn't bark at anything, Harold thought maybe Jimmy had cut the dog's vocal chords, but they were intact. I never knew what stroke of magic Jimmy used, but whatever it was, he cured Smasher of his barking addiction.

A few days after we met Jimmy on the beach Harold climbed down from his attic office and said, "Tiger, let's go home for a while. I'll finish *The Adventurers* in the States."

"Whatever you want to do is fine with me, darling," I told him sincerely.

That evening we drove down to Cannes and had dinner by ourselves, maintaining the cool aloofness from others that we had become accustomed to while Harold was working. For the most part we had laid low during our time in France, meeting few people and drawing none into our inner circle, which essentially consisted of just Harold, Adréana, and me. It would be very different in the future, but as we ended our first season on the Riviera, I did not remotely fathom that our next trip abroad would be anything but what we had experienced during our first season. When Harold worked, he needed privacy, and I had done my best to give him that, never bothering him unless he called on me. I had spent most of my time taking care of Adréana, managing the household, and acclimating myself to the culture of the region by visiting the small village of Le Cannet. It had been a wonderful retreat, and as I look back from the vantage point of time, I realize it was one of the foremost gloriously happy periods of my life.

"Well, Tiger," said Harold that night, "we've had a great time. We've made a family for ourselves, a few good friends, bought a villa, some cars, and I'm close to finishing the biggest novel I've ever written."

"Are you pleased with it?"

"Pleased? Hey, the fucking thing's gonna be a blockbuster! The critics will hate it and the readers will love it!"

Nothing more was said about the book. We dined on French cuisine and Dom Pérignon; we talked of the past and the future, nothing about the present. As we were leaving the restaurant, however, Harold said, "Unfortunately, all good things come to an end. It's time to go home for a while, back to the States."

"Yes, I know," I said wistfully.

"Cheer up!" responded Harold. "We'll be back here in no time at all. Dammit, Tiger, we love this place!"

The next morning we took a final stroll along the boulevard de la Croisette. It was a beautiful day. The beach was laden with sunbathers; yachts and sailboats skimmed the glistening waters of the Mediterranean. Suddenly we heard a voice calling from behind us, "Monsieur! Monsieur!"

We turned and looked. A pretty young woman, about twenty, caught up with us. She was breathless but excited.

"Aren't you the famous American writer?" she asked Harold in fractured English.

"Well, I'm a writer," said Harold, "and I'm pretty well known, if that's what you mean."

"Please, monsieur? Would you do me a favor? May I have your autograph?" she asked.

"Of course," said Harold. He smiled, visibly pleased. He glanced at me with a sort of "fame is following us wherever we go" expression. Like anyone, Harold needed and enjoyed being stroked.

The girl handed him a piece of paper and a pen, her face filled with a glowing, expectant smile.

"What's your first name?" asked Harold.

"Lorraine," she said.

"That's a beautiful name. Do you spell it with two *r*'s?"

"Yes, monsieur."

Harold wrote a salutation on the paper, followed by a lengthy note, and then his signature. He grinned enthusiastically, winked at me, and then handed the paper to Lorraine.

She was so excited that I was afraid she was going to faint. She read the note eagerly but slowly. Then something unexpected happened. Her face fell; as well as her smile. I wondered, *What on earth did Harold write in the note?* I glanced at him, but he too was taken aback at her reaction.

"Is there something wrong?" asked Harold.

Lorraine stared at him for a long moment, and then she said, rather despondently, "You are not James Baldwin?"

Harold's laughter could be heard at the far end of the boulevard.

When we were finally ready to leave, Harold mentioned casually that we were going to make a slight detour en route to the States.

"To where?" I asked.

"Look, you've worked hard to get your figure back, Tiger," he said, "and I wanna buy you some clothes that'll show it off."

He never, ever failed to surprise me. We left for New York, via Paris, where Harold took me to virtually every major couturier in the fashion capital of the world. I had never had a designer dress in my life, and frankly, although I had never thought about it, I probably wouldn't have known where to go had I wanted to buy one.

Harold did know. How and why he knew are two questions that have always intrigued me. No matter how much he exaggerated his past concerning his childhood and youth, I had no doubt that he lived in a state of poverty at some point while he was growing up. How he knew details about Parisian couturiers and their designs was beyond me, but he did. Harold observed everything, and as his writing dissected the rich and the powerful, while simultaneously earning him a great deal of money, he began to want many of the same things he gave to his characters for himself, and as an extension, for me.

In Paris, he arranged appointments at Balenciaga, Chanel, Courréges, and the House of Dior, as if with a snap of his fingers. I was suddenly cast into the glamorous world of haute couture like a character in one of his books.

We were treated to a private show at each house. For me, it was like being in a dream or watching some farfetched motion picture unfolding a rags-to-riches story. Except it was real! It was just the two of us and dozens of models coming at us one by one. Each spectacular outfit sending me into a spin.

Harold went berserk in the halls of fashion, choosing for me the most grandiose and elegant wardrobe a girl could possible imagine, although there were a few moments when I thought he was more interested in the models than he was in dressing my body. He chose something from each couturier: casual dresses from Courréges for afternoon soirees; a stylish Chanel suite (perfect for the career girl that I no longer was!); cocktail dresses from Dior; a formal gown from Balenciaga. They were all beautiful, but at some point during the process I thought that our so conspicuous consumption was perhaps going overboard. Not so Harold.

"It's a beautiful outfit," I would say, "but don't you think I have plenty enough already?"

"Shhhh," he would respond in a whisper. "I want you to have it," and he would nod casually to the director of the private showing, much like a bidder at a Sotheby's auction.

At last we were done with purchasing and the glamorous part of haute couture came to an end. I had an exquisite wardrobe, but now each item had to be tailored to fit, a time-consuming and excruciating ritual. It entailed five separate steps, beginning with the initial measurement, followed by four separate fittings. After a half-dozen fittings, standing still and straight as a statue, I began to lose my patience. Apparently, the seamstresses did also, because I began to feel the prick of pins as they hinged fabric up and hinged fabric down, wrapped and unwrapped, overlaid and under-laid the various pleats and folds of the dresses to make them fit me. By the time we were finished with all the selections, several days had come and gone, many seamstresses were exhausted, and I felt like a pincushion.

We made arrangements to have the new wardrobe shipped to New York, had one final dinner of gourmet cuisine and Dom Pérignon at Maxim's Restaurant, and caught the next flight to Idlewild.

12

The Beginning
of a New Year's Tradition

*I*t was October. In New York, autumn had blown in on a chilly breeze and leaves were falling from the trees, a stark contrast to the Indian summer of the Riviera. We checked into a suite at the small but opulent Stanhope Hotel on a stretch of upper Fifth Avenue known as Museum Mile. It was across the street from the Metropolitan Museum of Art. The hotel's atmosphere helped reduce our culture shock after so many months on the Côte d'Azur. Its terrace café was a popular Parisian-style gathering place; its public rooms were appointed with French antiques; and the bedroom in our suite was furnished with Louis XVI reproductions. We felt at home.

The next few days were a whirlwind of activity. I called and met with friends, while Harold attended to business with Paul Gitlin. We went to Long Island to see my folks, wined and dined at Harold's favorite haunts, and got little sleep. Soon we were tired of the hotel suite as well as the weather. Our many months in the temperate climate of the Riviera had spoiled us. The New York winter seemed an unnecessary burden.

"Why don't we go to California for a while?" said Harold. He posed it as a question, but I knew his mind was made up. However, I did not need to be persuaded.

"I would love to," I said, remembering that first wonderful trip that had started us on our odyssey.

"Then let's get the hell out of here!" cried Harold.

Again we stayed at the Beverly Hills Hotel—this time with baby, Adréana, and her nanny. The nanny took morning walks with Adréana in her English pram. One morning she returned, frantic. "There's a man who follows us every morning and I am frightened for the baby." Startled, Harold immediately started making inquiries and found that it was our next door neighbor Howard Hughes, who had told his bodyguard to watch Harold Robbins's baby.

Finally we found a rental on Collina; it was in a quiet, peaceful neighborhood in Beverly Hills, just off the western end of the Sunset Strip, near the Hamburger Hamlet, one of the famous designer hamburger restaurants owned by Marilyn and Harry Lewis, who later became our friends. The house was not comparable to our villa in France, but I didn't expect it to be. My main interest was being with Harold, regardless of the location, and being a good mother to Adréana.

When we moved in, I assumed our lives would pick up where they had left off in Le Cannet, rather cloistered, with little outside interference. Harold staked out a claim in the guesthouse for his office, where he planned to pound out the remaining pages of *The Adventurers* in continual ten and twelve hour stretches.

My designer wardrobe, which had been rerouted to Los Angeles, arrived from Paris. Unfortunately, I didn't have anywhere to wear it. I didn't know a soul in Beverly Hills, although when we occasioned out for dinner, it was evident Harold's growing notoriety had preceded us. He had suddenly become know, far more, it seemed to me, than he had been when we made that first fated journey to Beverly Hills two years before. People were always coming up to speak to him, and usually he had not the foggiest idea who they were. He may have been a perpetual loner, but it was evident he liked being in the limelight, as long as he set the conditions. I was proud of him.

Except for his public recognition when we were out for lunch or dinner, we did try to live in the same mode we had come to appreciate in France, with Harold working and with me taking care of Adréana. I thought it was better for Harold; he was more isolated in the guesthouse than he had been in the attic at the Villa Grazia, where he could hear the baby cry or people converse, no matter how quiet they tried to be. We received several invitations to attend cocktail or dinner parties, but we seldom accepted.

"Right now, I'm only interested in functions where I can charm the press," he said, which he was very good at doing.

When we received an invitation from Corbina Wright, a gossip columnist for one of the Los Angeles dailies, I showed Harold the invitation. He looked at it and nodded.

"We'd better go to this one," he said. "She's got a lot of important friends and a horde of readers. I'd better start prepping the publication of *The Adventurers* by getting my name back in the spotlight."

I was getting a little stir crazy, so I was glad he wanted to go.

Corbina's was a typical "Hollywood party," as I would eventually learn through experience, with a lot of drinking, backslapping, glad-handing, and downright lying. Yet, amid all the brouhaha about nothing, there was a serendipitous occurrence. I met Edana Romney, a formerly successful actress in her native Britain, who had moved to Los Angeles a few years before. She was articulate and warm, the type of person whom you instantly intuit will become a close friend. Edana knew everyone. There was not a person who passed by us at the party or was mentioned in conversation that Edana did not know who they were, usually personally. She was a goldmine of information, both trivial and profound, about any and everything in Los Angeles and especially Beverly Hills.

A few nights later when Harold and I were out for dinner at Scandia on the Sunset Strip, he said contemplatively, "You know, Tiger, you've got all those beautiful clothes from Paris and you haven't had a chance to wear them. I want you to shine out here like a diamond!"

I didn't know what to say. "How would I go about it, Harold? I don't know anyone."

"No, that's not true. You know Edana Romney."

"Well, yes, but—"

"Give her a call and tell her you'd like to have a little get together with some of the local socialites—you know, the crème de la créme of Beverly Hills. She'll help you work up a guest list."

I liked the idea. I wanted to meet some new people; in fact, needed to, since again Harold was working constantly on his novel. "I'll do it," I told him. "I'll call Edana tomorrow and we'll plan a little luncheon at our house."

"No, not our house, not at home." Harold thought for a moment; then his eyes sparkled with an idea. "You'll have it at The Bistro, in their private room upstairs." The Bistro was the hottest, most elegant eatery and watering hole in Beverly Hills, having been started a couple of years before by Kurt Niklas, the former maitre d' at the legendary Romanoff's Restaurant, and Billy Wilder, the famous movie director. It was *the* place for the elite of Beverly Hills. It was a perfect idea.

"That's a brilliant idea, Harold!"

"Hey, it's your ideas as much as mine." He leaned back, staring at me with a smile. "You've got a terrific figure and a beautiful wardrobe and I want my Tiger to start showing off. You've got the most gorgeous ass and breasts in the world and I want these Beverly Hills yentas to know it!"

The next morning I called Edana. She was as thrilled with the idea as I, and she volunteered to help me organize it. We drafted a guest list that included

Betsy (Mrs. Alfred) Bloomingdale, Harriet (Mrs. Arnold) Deutsch, Altovise (Mrs. Sammy) Davis Jr., Jolene (Mrs. George) Schlatter, Sheri (Mrs. Buddy) Hackett, and Ruth (Mrs. Milton) Berle, Rosemary (Mrs. Robert) Stack, Shirley (Mrs. Henry) Fonda, Ginny (Mrs. Henry) Mancini. I knew none of the ladies, so it was a coming out party for me as well as a high tea. I called Kurt Niklas at the Bistro, a European restaurateur who understood precisely what I wanted, reserved the room, and then I had some invitations printed and sent them out.

While all of this was going on, Harold, when he wasn't writing, watched my enthusiasm and excitement with growing pride. In those days I think Harold got more pleasure from pleasing me than from anything else he did. He enjoyed escaping from his office, if just for a few minutes, to get the latest lowdown on how the party planning was progressing. At last the day for the tea party arrived.

From my new wardrobe I chose a Courréges dress, with Harold vigorously nodding his approval, and Chanel shoes. I pulled my hair back and fixed it in place with a Chanel bow. I wore my diamond ring from Tiffany's. Somehow, it seemed symbolic. We had come such a long way since that first trip out of New York, sort of full circle, back to where it all had begun.

When I left for The Bistro, Harold said, "Now the very minute the tea wraps up, let me know how it went." I promised him that I would. "Now don't forget," he said. He was like an excited little boy waiting for his first birthday party to begin; yet he wasn't going.

As I drove to The Bistro on Canon Drive in the heart of Beverly Hills, my own enthusiasm was diming. I was nervous. Would anyone show up? I should have known better; it had been an RSVP invitation and all of the invitees had responded positively. But still, there was that gnawing anxiety . . .

Everyone arrived precisely at the appointed time of 4 p.m., each very fashionably attired. It was an enjoyable affair; I loved the ladies, and some of them became close and dear friends. Each at varying times posed the same question: What's Harold working on now? Who is he writing about this time?"

"Oh, you'll find out soon enough," I told them.

"Can't you give us a hint?"

"I think that would be breaking Harold's confidence in me," I laughed.

"I heard it was about Elizabeth Taylor and Richard Burton."

"You'll know soon enough," I said.

The idea of a high tea, which Harold had drummed up on the spur of the moment, was a first in Beverly Hills, as far as I know. It certainly was at The Bistro, but after my "coming out" it became *de rigueur*, and gradually high teas became popular at fine restaurants and hotels across the city.

The Christmas–New Year holiday season was approaching, and because of our hermit-like existence we had received few social invitations, limited almost exclusively to the women who had attended my high tea at The Bistro. Their laid-back functions were not exactly to Harold's taste; he liked the fast lane and he thought their affairs were generally boring. As the year progressed to its end, I noted that we did not have an invitation to a New Year's Eve party. I enjoyed festive occasions and I knew Harold had never experienced the usual tradition of holiday celebrations during his growing-up years. I had an idea.

"Why don't we have our own New Year's Eve party?" I suggested.

His eyes lit up and I could almost hear his creative gears cranking into action. The problem remained, however, that we had not befriended very many people in Beverly Hills and Hollywood. Who could we invite?

"I've got it!" said Harold. "I'll get Gene to work up a guest list."

He was speaking of Gene Schwamm, a dynamic young publicist Harold had recently retained in his continuing effort to exploit the press. Gene knew almost everyone in Hollywood who was worth knowing, and after a telephone call from Harold, he supplied us with an extensive list of names and addresses of people he thought we'd like to meet. It was too late to order engraved invitations, so I purchased some attractive cards at a local shop and wrote the invitations by hand, one by one, as we decided on whom to invite. Aside from the names of a few movie stars, I hardly recognized a single name on Gene's list.

"Who's Sue Mengers?" I asked.

"She's a big Hollywood talent agent," said Harold, "maybe the most powerful woman in town."

"Should we invite her?"

"Why not? She probably won't come because I'm sure she already has three-dozen must-go invitations, but what the hell. Maybe she'll invite us to one of her parties sometime!"

I went down Gene's list. I wondered: *Do we know what we are doing, inviting all these people we don't even know?* We posted the invitations anyway, to about sixty people, and then waited to see if anyone aside from our few friends showed up. Just in case they all did, we spent lavishly on food and drink, hiring a well-known Beverly Hills catering firm. We need not have been nervous. Without exception, everyone on the list came, plus a few holiday revelers who were not invited.

Sue Mengers lived up to Harold's description of her: "Maybe the most powerful woman in Hollywood." If she wasn't, it wasn't because she didn't think she was. She was short, loud, abrasive, confident, and very funny. She represented several major actors and directors, and she brought along as her guest a new client, a shy and tentative twenty-three-year-old singer from New York, who, like me, was feeling her way around Beverly Hills high society. She had already begun to make a name for herself on Broadway and was just a few years away from doing the same in motion pictures. She was from a working class family in Brooklyn, which gave me an instant empathy with her. Her name was Barbra Streisand.

Although it was simply a conventional, elegant, traditional New Year's party—it nevertheless set a precedent. The name Harold Robbins was indeed magic, and I realized people would come out of the woodwork to attend one of his parties.

That first party set off a chain-reaction of social functions that we sponsored, topped at the end of each year by our soon to be famous (or infamous) New Year's Eve parties. Through the years we had thirteen (a number predisposed to be a bête noir) in a row, each more spectacular and sometimes more outrageous than the one before, until we finally realized we could no longer outdo our ingenuity, and in the late seventies we stopped having them. But during that thirteen-year period the parties became the talk of the town, attended by the most important people in the entertainment industry, always reported by the media, envied by those not invited, crashed by many who weren't, and finally fabled as modern day equivalents of the Zelda and Scott Fitzgerald parties of the Jazz Age. Gene Schwam, who was involved in some way with each of them, probably best summed it up when he reflected, "I would say those parties were to New Year's Eve what the Swifty Lazar parties were to Oscar night. Everyone who was anyone wanted to go."

In retrospect I realize those parties, which through the years Harold began to take credit for having created and planned, were my way of involving myself in Beverly Hills life. While Harold was working, I needed something to do; after the first, almost impromptu New Year's Eve party in 1964, I began to immerse myself in the planning of the next year's blowout. If there was anything I did during my almost three decades with Harold that was independent of him, it was arranging, preparing, and sketching out our parties. At the last moment Harold might throw in his considerably more than two-cents worth—ideas that usually added a few thousand dollars to the party budget but that always gave a touch of novelty to what I had already planned.

For whatever reason our parties became the end-of-the-year social showcase for comedians. Present would be the likes of Bob Newhart (who attended from the beginning and became a good friend of Harold's), Don Rickles, Milton Berle, Red Buttons, Dan Rowan, Dick Martin, and Buddy Hackett, to name a few. Marty Allen once came as the New Year Baby wearing a white satin diaper. The gate-crashers were usually celebrities who, for whatever reason, had not made the guest list, but occasionally I saw a lucky individual wandering through the crowd whom no one knew.

"If they were so fucking clever as to find a way in," said Harold, "then the hell with it. Let them stay and enjoy themselves!"

One time our security guard called from the front gate, saying there was a young man who wanted to come to the party but that his name was not on the list. "Claims he's some kind of sports figure or something," said the guard.

"What's his name?" I asked.

"Spitz, Mark Spitz."

"By all means," I told the guard. "Let him in!"

Mark Spitz had just won seven gold medals at the summer Olympics and his name and photograph had been plastered on the cover of every magazine in the country—yet our security guard didn't recognize him.

Another time a young female intruder arrived barefooted and wrapped in an Indian blanket. The guard let her in because he *did* recognize her. She was Mia Farrow, recently married to Frank Sinatra, and they lived in the neighborhood. The newlyweds had had a spat, and Mia, dashing out into the night, saw our lights and heard our guests and thought her spirits might be lifted. She appeared very unhappy, but after I gave her a grand tour of our home, amid all the holiday revelers, she cheered up considerably. When she left, she seemed transformed, and I thought, *There's a reason for these holiday parties after all!*

Success often breeds lethargy and indolence, especially among writers. Harold was never afflicted with writer's block, but he made it clear that he did not particularly enjoy the process of writing. His goal was the finished book; when that occurred he could gloat and be happy for a few weeks. He agreed with Kurt Vonnegut, Jr. who once told a symposium of collegiate, would-be writers that if they enjoyed writing they probably should consider another field. Writing was not easy, as Harold often said, even for the most talented writers. He lamented that no one but the writer himself could do the work, that there were few people, if any, a writer could call upon, even for moral support. But Harold didn't have a problem with inspiration; he always had a story brewing in his mind. His problem was success itself. It is difficult under any circumstances to lock oneself away from the world and go through the grueling task of writing a book, but as Harold said, "When you have a million dollars in the bank, it's not as difficult."

"Grace is my muse," Harold often claimed, but the truth is I could not motivate him to work when he didn't want to, nor did I try to. It took Paul Gitlin to do that. Paul was more than a muse; he was a driving force and the only person who could actually force Harold to sit at his typewriter. He did it with threats of impending bankruptcy.

When Paul showed up on our doorstep alone, I came to realize it was to prod Harold along on his present project. There are some legendary stories about Paul locking Harold alone in a hotel room and not letting him out or even giving him something to eat and drink until he had written a given number of pages and shoved them over the transom or under the door. I've always doubted the validity of those stories; if they occurred it was before my time with Harold. Nevertheless, Paul could be persuasive. He tried to instill fear: "Robbins, if you don't get on the stick, you're not going to have a dime left in the bank come this time next year. You'll have to sell the villa in France."

Usually Harold responded with something like, "Paul, will you fucking shut up? Robbins always comes through!"

By the time I met Paul, Harold's personality had come to dominate the duo, although they still seemed to be alter egos. Over the years Paul seemed to grow more like Harold—purposefully, I think—picking up his habits and quirks, cursing when Harold cursed, drinking when Harold drank, until some people, upon meeting them for the first time, didn't know which was Robbins and which was Gitlin. Paul was bombastic, but his bark was far worse than his bite, and Harold had no qualms about telling him to shut up when he grew tired of Paul's yelping; furthermore, when Harold gave a command, Paul followed it, like a dog obeying his master. And why not? Paul had helped make Harold rich, beginning with *The Carpetbaggers*, but in turn Harold's books had made Paul thousands of dollars richer also, with many thousands more to come, and Paul knew it. He was a lawyer-agent with several houses in his stable, but Harold Robbins was the one who drew the stud fees.

Paul enjoyed having fun as much as Harold, and when he arrived on our doorstep with his wife Zelda, it was usually party time rather than business time. That's what happened after the turn of the year, following our first New Year's Eve party.

Paul and Zelda were our houseguests and we were enjoying cocktails on the terrace. "Let's go to Vegas and do some gambling," said Harold out of the blue.

"Let's go," said Paul.

"Okay by me," said Zelda, who was game for anything.

They didn't need my approval. I was as eager to go as anyone, even more so perhaps, for something mystical and romantic had been playing secretly in my subconscious mind for several months.

While Harold called the airport and made hotel arrangements in Las Vegas, I packed our bags. Actually, I over packed. I'm not certain I had a plan at the time, but for safety's sake I placed in my suitcase several new negligees drawn from my extensive designer wardrobe, along with a variety of jewelry and hairpieces and the usual summer dresses and outfits. It did not take me long, and before I knew it we were in a taxi speeding through the streets to the airport and then we were airborne for the forty-minute flight to the desert gambling mecca. When the lights of Las Vegas glimmered through the portholes, Harold looked at me and said, "What do you think, Tiger?"

"I don't know what to think, darling, having never been there," I responded coyly. "All I know about Las Vegas is that lots of people get married there."

"Only the ones who are too broke to gamble," said Harold. Everyone laughed, except me.

In the midsixties, Las Vegas had come a long way since Bugsy Siegel had built the then lavish Flamingo Hotel in 1941 with mob money. It seemed ironic that Howard Hughes, who had been the prototype for Harold's protagonist in *The Carpetbaggers*, was at the very moment we landed trying to take over the gambling industry after having discarded his aircraft and motion picture empires. One of the few hotels on the strip he had not purchased was the garish, new, 700-room Caesar's Palace, where Harold had made our reservations. The dynamic and public Hughes that Harold had used in his composite character of Jonas Cord was now ensconced like a hermit just down the street in the Desert Inn.

I don't think any of us thought about Hughes as we debarked from the taxi in the crowded circular driveway at Caesar's, amidst the sparkling lights and flowing fountains. Harold was in a gambling mood. After checking us in at the desk, he took off immediately for the tables, telling me in a roundabout way that I should take care of the luggage. "Tiger, I know you want to freshen up, so why don't you go to the suite with the bellman and join me later in the casino." Before I could answer, he was gone.

I went to the suite. When we had left Los Angeles—even before we left, when I was packing—I had a vague idea of doing something dramatic, although I did not have an exact plan. Now I began to organize one. Whether it would work or not, I didn't know, but the result would be telling, regardless. Adréana was over a year old now and Harold and I had been together for two years. Maybe the time had come . . .

Zelda and Paul had given little attention to my comment about Las Vegas marriages, but I wasn't sure about Harold. He was an astute observer and few if any words ever went in one of his ears and out the other, regardless of his often-deadpan expression. Our respective divorces had been finalized months before. Perhaps it was time to make our relationship and family legitimate.

I looked at my image in the mirror. I was in the youthful prime of my womanhood, very attractive, even if I said so myself, and I was with a man whom I loved and who not only proclaimed his undying love for me but had also joined me in producing a child. Well, why shouldn't we be married? What had begun as a nebulous idea drawn from my subconscious desires suddenly became a conscious agenda, although I did not know exactly how to implement it.

With a little imagination any one of the several negligees I had packed would make do as a wedding dress. I chose a long white one, not as shear as some of the others. For sure, when I put it on, it was sexy and lush with sensuality, enticing and pretending to virginity, a perfect wedding gown. I topped it off with one of the hairpieces—a wreath of white flowers. I took a deep breath, expelled it with a hopeful sigh, and exited the suite.

The elevator door opened and I was plunged into the noisy bedlam of a Vegas casino. There were yells and hurrahs for momentary victories. Slot machine arms were pumping up and down and ringing bells were announcing jackpots. Roulette wheels were spinning and dice were rattling. It was packed. I knew instantly I had done well with my choice of dress and accessories; as I wove between the table and down the aisles looking for Harold, not once was I exempted from the gaze of others. My only fear was Harold's response when he saw me. Would he say, "Grace, are you walking in your sleep? What the fuck are you doing in a nightgown?"

Harold was with the high rollers at a baccarat table. A crowd was gathered around, including Zelda and Paul, looking over his shoulder. I did not know if he was in a good mood or not until he suddenly shouted, "Banco!" My heart fluttered like a bird's wing and my shoulders lifted a notch—he was winning! Yet, that fact presented a quandary in my mind. Would he be so obsessed with the game as to ignore me? Should I wait, or continue? I chose the latter, not by design as much as by instinct. I maneuvered myself to where, if Harold reacted like all the other men whom I had passed en route, at the very least he would glance at me. I made my move and sort of floated, gossamer-like, by the baccarat table. I watched from the corner of my eye. Paul saw me first, then Zelda. Their expressions were a bit disconcerted, to say the least, as if they were saying simultaneously, "Grace, what on earth are you doing in that outfit? Are you crazy? Harold is going to flip!" Before I could really digest their reaction, Harold looked at me. He didn't stare a hole through me at all; he simply gestured for me to join them. I edged my way through the crowd, my heart beating fast, my stomach turning a little.

"Hey, Tiger!" he exclaimed; then he gave me the once over, his eyes sparkling mischievously. Even with the sound and the fury of the gaming going on about us, there seemed to be a moment of silence. Harold grew serious. "Are you sure this is what you want to do?" he asked.

I didn't say anything; I didn't have to. He knew instinctively what I wanted, and had known since my casual remark on the airplane. I just stared at him, my eyes sparkling, and then he said with a burst of enthusiasm, "Well, then by God, let's do it!" which was the closest he ever came to asking, "Will you marry me?" He took me in his arms, kissed me passionately in front of the baccarat world, and then turned to Zelda and Paul. "Let's go!" he shouted. "Grace and I are gonna get married!" As we took off, almost running, he added as an afterthought but with a laugh, "Fasten your seatbelts. We may be in for a bumpy ride!" He was trying to be funny, and was, but also in his uncanny way he was being perceptive before the fact, although no one realized it at the time, including him.

Suddenly, we were in the midst of a whirlwind. Things were happening so quickly that it all became a blur. Somehow, Paul had the foresight to buy a couple of bottles of champagne and before I knew it we were hopping into a taxi in the carriageway of Caesar's. "Take us to the nearest marriage chapel!" cried Harold to the cabbie, and off into the night we drove, tires squealing, at one o'clock in the morning.

Las Vegas seemed to have as many marriage chapels as it had casinos, which on the surface seemed incongruous. In the final analysis, however, each promoted gambling, one with money, the other with love. Nothing could have been further from my mind than failure at marriage as our taxi negotiated through the honking traffic on the bright, neon-lit strip of highway that was flanked on each side by gaudy and garish hotels and casinos.

Paul was babbling nonsense, Zelda was screeching her excitement, and Harold was popping open a bottle of champagne. Then we were drinking the bubbly, as well as inadvertently splashing it, and talking silly, high-spirited talk that no one would later remember. Soon we were off the beaten path, on a less well-lit street with a small, white chapel looming in the near distance. It was the moment of truth.

The taxi pulled up to the curb and before we were actually out of the vehicle, a tall, funereal-looking man in a black suit and thin necktie, was framed in the doorway of the chapel, bearing greetings and good tidings. A short, plump little woman in a blue lace dress joined him. "Welcome, welcome," they intoned in unison as we climbed out of the taxi.

"We wanna get hitched!" barked Harold.

"Sir," said the tall man with a hint of affected solemnity, "we are here to accommodate you."

We entered the chapel in a fit of laughter, following the minister and his wife down a small aisle to a dais. There was an arbor of fake ficus trees and plastic roses and tulips in tacky vinyl pots and a tawdry carpet worn thin by a thousand midnight weddings. It was a far cry from the splendid auditorium and appointments of St. Patrick's Cathedral where Tom and I had timidly muttered our vows so long ago in a formal ceremony. If I had any last minute doubts, however, they were quickly overcome when I realized the pomp and circumstance of my first marriage had done nothing to ensure its success.

I'm sure there was a pre-wedding consultation, but I don't remember it. I don't even know how Harold got our marriage license. What I do remember is prerecorded organ music suddenly issuing from a sound system. It was Mendelssohn's time-honored wedding march, belching tinny chords, but it served to bring us down to earth, if anyone besides me was up on a cloud to begin with. Harold and I were "getting married, getting married, getting married" was the refrain in my mind, and with that sudden, dawning reality I began to shake like a person suffering a breakdown and started to cry. Harold took my arm and squeezed me hard between the elbow and the shoulder, an unsuccessful effort to calm me down. Then he pulled me close as we stood before the tall minister and his short wife; on the periphery I could vaguely discern Zelda and Paul, standing aside as witnesses. As the ritual began, Harold was rather solemn for one of the few times in his life; Paul, if I recall, was still sipping champagne (as well as recording the event on a portable tape recorder); tears were flowing silently from Zelda's eyes; the minister was uttering his well-rehearsed phrases; his wife was trying to stay awake; and I was bawling, uncontrollably.

The minister was unfazed. "Do you take this man—"

"Yes, yes!" I wailed, unable to stem my tears.

"And do you take this woman—"

"I do," said Harold, and I bawled even more.

"Then I pronounce you man and wife. You may now kiss the—"

I didn't wait for him to finish. I wailed again and locked my arms around Harold as if we were topping out at the greatest height of a roller coaster ride. Harold bellowed laughter; the minister smiled; his wife opened her eyes; Zelda and Paul clapped with glee; and I bawled and bawled and bawled.

"Let's get the hell out of here, Mrs. Robbins!" cried Harold, and with that, we were gone.

Part Two

The Middle

> *"From his luxurious yachts in the south of France to his lavish jet-set parties, Harold was King. He was larger-than-life."*
>
> —Jackie Collins, *New York Times* bestselling author of *Drop Dead Beautiful*

13

Let Them Eat Cake

I had been enormously happy before our marriage, but if happiness can be measured, mine now tipped the scales. I was not only deliriously blissful being Mrs. Harold Robbins, but I was also absolutely content. And Harold was too, or so it seemed. Although many people had assumed we were married before we actually were, Harold now made a *big issue* out of introducing me as Mrs. Harold Robbins. "Isn't my wife the most gorgeous creature you've ever laid eyes on?" he would say, quickly adding, "and she's the best goddamned lay this side of Eden." I had no reason to doubt the sincerity of his words; Harold's passion for sex, *my* sex, that is *me,* had not diminished one iota. He was as ravenous as ever.

After we got back to Los Angeles from Vegas, we had hardly unpacked our bags before we began to make plans to return to France. To Paul's chagrin, Harold told him he was going to finish *The Adventurers* in Cannes. Paul shrugged, knowing there was nothing he could do to get Harold to finish the book any sooner. Paul and Zelda flew back to New York, and Harold and I repacked our bags. Before we left Los Angeles, however, Harold had some unfinished business to take care of, namely a meeting with Joseph E. Levine at Embassy Pictures.

"I wanna sell him *The Adventurers*," said Harold.

"But you haven't finished it," I told him.

"So what?"

Joe had now produced three of Harold's books into successful box office movies and he was chomping at the bit for more material. There had been much talk and publicity about a six-picture deal Harold and Joe had entered into (no doubt with Paul Gitlin as the intermediary), but I think it really boiled down to a "right of first refusal," whereby Joe had the first shot at optioning or buying Harold's forthcoming books. Joe had just come off of a good year, having reaped huge dividends from *The Carpetbaggers* and Vittorio De Sica's *Marriage Italian Style*, with Sophia Loren. *The Carpetbaggers* movie, although most of the critics, including Harold, had panned it, had already become one of the top twenty-five grossing pictures of all time.

After Harold met with Joe, he told me what happened with relish.

When he arrived at Joe's office (I believe it was on the Paramount lot but I'm not certain), they decided to take a walk, away from prying eyes and perked ears. Harold hated meetings in the atmosphere of a business office.

"How's your new project coming along?" asked Joe with genuine interest.

"A little behind schedule," said Harold. "They're anxiously awaiting it back in New York."

"What's it about?"

"It's a big, big book that begins in Latin America and shifts to Paris and other places," Harold responded. "It will make one hell of a good movie if it's told in its entirety."

"What's the storyline?"

Harold took his time telling Joe the story, teasing him, getting him into the characters, especially the Latin protagonist superficially patterned after Rubirosa, the Latin playboy politician who had garnered so many gossipy headlines in the late fifties and early sixties, particularly for *his* marriages to American multi-millionaire heiresses Doris Duke and Barbara Hutton. When Harold thought he had the producer sufficiently excited, he concluded his narrative.

"What's it gonna be called?" asked Joe.

"The Adventurers."

"That's a great title, Harold."

"Damn right it is!"

"I want it," said Joe. "I'll buy it."

"Good, but it's gonna cost you a million dollars."

Joe did not flinch, but he was silent a moment. Then he repeated Harold's price, "A million dollars?"

"Actually, over a million, Joe," added Harold. "A million three." They walked on in silence.

"Why the extra three-hundred thousand?" Joe finally asked.

"Because sometime in the near future some producer, probably you, is gonna pay a million bucks to get a good property. So, I want a million-plus. Besides, I'll write the screenplay for you."

Joe tossed it around in his mind, muttering, "A million dollars, a million dollars. That's a lot of money for a book that hasn't been published, Harold. For that matter, a million is a lot of money for any story."

"Think of it this way," said Harold, "if you spread the payments over a few years, you won't be alive to make them and I won't be alive to accept them."

They walked full circle back to Joe's office in silence. Joe stopped and stared off into space, thinking. Harold said, "You could hear the gears clanking and the engine revving in his mind."

A million dollars would be a precedent setting price for a book-screenplay deal, and perhaps the unsettling silence seemed noisy because Joe was negotiating for a novel not yet published and much less written. But he was a decision maker, an aspect of his character that Harold admired.

"Joe," Harold finally said, "you can take it or leave it. There are plenty of producers out there, and I've never written a novel that didn't become a best seller.

That was enough for Levine. "Okay," he said, "it's a deal."

When Harold came home to tell me what had happened, he was elated. Joe wanted the movie to go into production as soon as the book was published, which was tentatively scheduled for the spring season of 1966. In time, Harold would meet his publication date, but Joe wouldn't meet his production date. Before *The Adventurers* ever got to the silver screen, Joe produced another fifteen or so movies. Harold didn't care; Joseph E. Levine always paid his bills.

"Let's go see Verita," Harold said one morning just before leaving for France. I did not have to ask who Verita was. Although I had never met her, I felt as though I knew her already. Her name had surfaced in our conversations a hundred times or more, and I was curious.

Verita Thompson had been a friend of Harold's for many years, and she was undoubtedly one of those few people in that select group of finger counting. We drove to her penthouse apartment overlooking the Pacific Ocean in Santa Monica. I looked forward to meeting her. Most of Harold's friends I had met so far had been men, and I was curious about his female acquaintances.

"She's a character," said Harold as we parked the car.

I didn't know what to expect, but I was certainly not disappointed. Verita *was* a character. She was a tiny spitfire of Mexican-Irish descent who had been born in the Southwest and had once been Miss Arizona. She was a few years older than me, but younger than Harold. She wasn't prone to bragging or revealing her personal life, so Harold told her story for her. Beginning in 1942, and until his death in 1956, she had been the on and off mistress of Humphrey Bogart. Subsequently she married Walter Thompson (who was out of town on that first visit), a motion picture producer at Universal Pictures. In the late fifties Walter and Harold had formed a production partnership in an effort to make their own films. Walter had wanted to make Harold's *79 Park Avenue*, and although Harold agreed, he put a twist in the package—he had wanted to make the picture with an all-black cast. MGM approved the screenplay idea, but balked when Harold broached the black cast. The powers at MGM wanted white actors. Harold, stubborn as ever, had stuck to his guns and the potential production had gone down the drain.

"He's hardheaded," said Verita. "When he makes up his mind about something, you can't change it. He'll manipulate the hell out of you, but in the end it usually turns out okay."

I realized that Verita knew as much about Harold as anyone I had met. She had been privy to many of Harold's romances, including his affair with Yvonne, and she was Caryn's godmother.

"Boy, you like them young," said Verita to Harold after giving me a cursory inspection.

"And why not?" said Harold with a laugh. "We only live once."

I didn't know exactly how to take Verita's statement, but I learned quickly that she could be as blunt as Harold. I did not expect it at the time, but she became one of my closest friends.

While Verita was busy in her kitchen, Harold explained to me his days at Universal and how he had met and befriended Walter Thompson and so many other motion picture people. "You see," he said, "I was vice president in charge of production." At that moment Verita reentered the room, obviously overhearing his comments.

"Oh god, Harold," she said with a sarcastic laugh. "You were never vice president of anything, except your imagination!"

"Of course, I was," said Harold confidently.

"You know, Harold, you're full of shit," answered Verita bluntly.

"I love you anyway," said Harold.

"Don't believe a word he says," Verita said to me.

Harold turned the conversation away from movies, but it was the first time in my experience that anyone had ever questioned *his* résumé, his biography, directly in front of him—a biography that I heard him tell without deviation a thousand subsequent times. Of course, I didn't give it a second thought; I didn't care, but Verita's statement reminded me of Blanche and Ruth Rubin's comments that night at Harold's stepmother's home when we had lima bean soup.

The happy days of 1970, here on our yacht "Gracara." We really were in love.

(Photo courtesy of Mirrorpix/Lebrecht Music & Arts. Reprinted with permission.)

Poolside at Villa Gracia in the south of France. Harold is playing with our daughter, Adréana. This photo was taken for *Life Magazine* in 1967. *(Photo courtesy of Getty Images. Reprinted with permission.)*

Harold pulling off another publicity stunt to promote his new book
Goodbye Janette (1970) with all the mothers of Adréana's 6th birthday party.

(Photo courtesy of Mirrorpix/Lebrecht Music & Arts. Reprinted with permission.)

The **Celebrity Pictorial**

THE PHOTO MAGAZINE OF SOCIETY

Vol. 5, No. 7   *Single Copy: Two Dollars*   May, 1977

My surprise 40th birthday party (1977) at "My Place" Disco in Beverly Hills.
Wish you could see the four very hunky men carrying me!

Greeting George Barry, owner of Faberge, at one of our parties.
Larry Flynt is in the upper right corner.

(Photo courtesy of Image Collect. Reprinted with Permission.)

New Years Eve (1975) at our home in Beverly Hills, CA.
Actress Shelly Winters decided to be a gondolier in a tiny boat
filled with fruit for decor . . . it was a floating cornucopia
made all the more abundant with Shelly in it!

HAPPY TIMES...

THE *Celebrity* PICTORIAL

PEOPLE / SOCIALS

CLUBS / RESORTS

Vol. 3, No. 1   *Single Copy: One Dollar*   Nov., '74

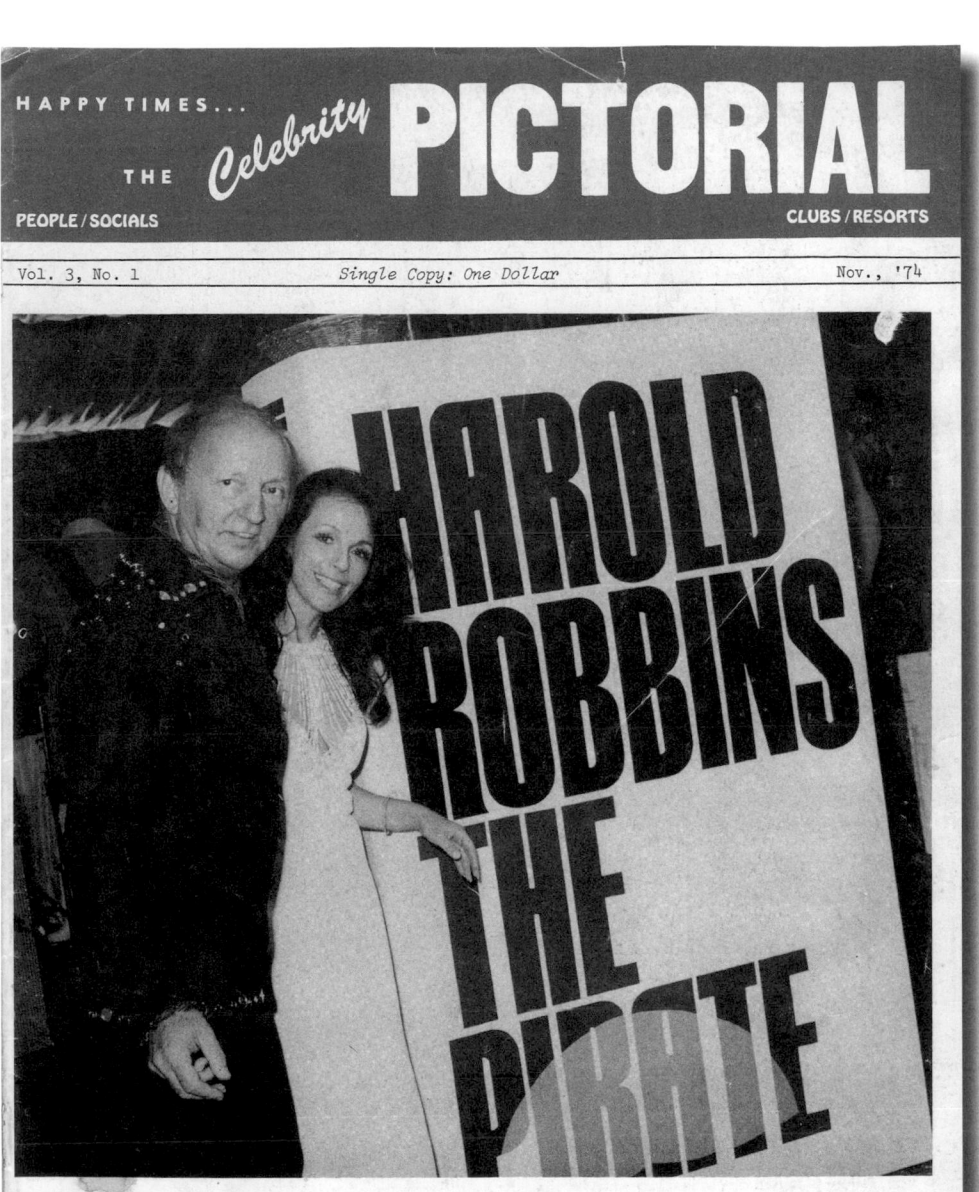

GRACE AND HAROLD ROBBINS

Their fantastic Hollywood party!

Our 1974 "Out of Season" New Years Arabian themed party
on Universal's back-lot. Who has a New Years party in October?

We greeted 1977 at "Gatsbys"—a popular place owned by our friends, the Rosens. This would be our last News Years event. The parties became too much work!

(Photo courtesy of Image Collect. Reprinted with Permission.)

"Don't believe a word he says."

Later that evening Verita told me in a moment of privacy, "Harold is what I would call a rounder. He's crazy and sometimes cantankerous, but he's got a heart of gold and an imagination as big as the sky. When he wants to do something, no matter how nutty—well, he's gonna do it, regardless. He's hardworking, but he likes to have fun, a lot of fun. Sometimes he has a roving eye. But don't they all? I wouldn't worry about that because it's obvious he's crazy about you. Down deep he's a good guy, always loyal and generous to his friends. And that macho barroom stuff? It's mostly show. He's basically as harmless as a fly, but don't ever cross him. He can do a Jekyll and Hyde act pretty fast."

Again, I took her comments in stride, sort of letting her words go in one ear and out the other. I felt I already knew Harold pretty well, but in the course of time I found out that Verita knew him much better than I. She was right on all counts.

By May we were ensconced again in Villa Grazia. For the next few years, before Adréana began school in the US, we divided our lives between Beverly Hills in the fall and winter and Le Cannet in the spring and summer. We always arrived in time for the Cannes Film Festival, which, as Harold said, "was a *real* festival, a combination of work and play for the movie folk."

For me it seemed all play. I was aware that Harold was already tinkering in his mind with the idea for his next book, although he admitted that his mind was not yet made up. He always had three or four ideas fermenting, but he was talking more and more about the final novel of his Hollywood Trilogy. As a consequence of the film festival that year, he did not go to work immediately on *The Adventurers*.

We partook of the activities and festivities, a whirlwind of events, from screenings to parties, but mostly parties, many of them at Villa Grazia. Our home took on the aura of a convention hotel, and often I did not know whom the delegates were, nor did Harold.

"Who's the couple sleeping in the guest bedroom?" Harold was apt to say when we got up in the morning, or "Who's the guy that's crashed on the couch?"

I was as often in the dark as he was.

"Well, check the swimming pool and make sure no one has drowned," he would say with a wry laugh but also with an ounce of truth.

"I've already done so. Nothing there but a couple of sharks. "

"What species? Agent or lawyer?" Harold would laugh, and then add, "Let's go party, Tiger!"

I was not astute enough at the time to realize Harold was at a stage in his career where he was beginning to seek excuses to avoid sitting at his typewriter until it was absolutely necessary.

In those years I loved the Cannes Film Festival. It was always exciting, so sexy and daring. The beaches were crowded with beautiful young women and handsome men, although none of them were stars; the latter had learned long before that the paparazzi and the multitude of fans would devour them if they made an impromptu public appearance without security. We always had guests at our villa (people whom we actually knew), and the hotels were packed, from the Majestic to the Carlton. It was the only place in the world where the entire international film community converged at the same time, and it was exciting.

Most people don't realize that only thirty films, sometimes less, are in the actual festival competition, while over 600 are screened. "The American studios don't seek competition," Harold explained. "They think the Palme d'Or [the festival's equivalent to the best picture Oscar] is a death wish, and it usually is. The competition is really for new, young directors to showcase their talents."

That was and is probably true, but the festival always opened with a blockbuster, noncompetitive American movie to set the stage, and the showcase was always glamorous. After we got our yacht a few years later, we hardly went to any screenings, but our parties were par excellence, and, like our New Year's Eve affairs in Beverly Hills, an invitation was much sought after.

The most memorable festival was in 1972, when pornographic movies were first given a category. They were not screened at the Palais, the main auditorium, but in a theater on the rue d'Antibes, a block north of the Croisette. There were several movie people Harold wanted to talk with that year; and rather than running them down at the various hotels that were packed to the gills, he simply got tickets to the triple X screenings, the most talked about of which was *Behind the Green Door*, featuring the former Ivory Snow model Marilyn Chambers.

I was not averse to seeing a porn flick, but I protested, "Harold, no one you want to see will be at those screenings."

He laughed at me. "Believe me, Tiger, all of the people I want to see will all be at the porn house!"

As usual, he was right, and the producers he was speaking of were some of the most important people in the motion picture industry. It was at the *Green Door* screening that I met Sammy Davis, Jr. for the first time, although his wife Altovise and I had been friendly since my high tea at The Bistro in Beverly Hills.

"So you are Mrs. Robbins," said Sammy with a twinkle in his eye.

"I am she, Mr. Davis," I responded.

"Well, Mrs. Robbins," said Sammy. "Have you served as a model for any of the characters and sexual escapades in Harold's books?"

"Oh, you'll never know, will you?" I said with a sly smile.

"Never say never," Sammy responded.

For Harold and me, the film festival was a party. I don't think Harold ever attempted to do any serious motion picture business; he used its social activities to meet new people, particularly beautiful young women. I was not jealous, because I assumed his flirtations were no more serious than mine had been with Sammy Davis, Jr.

A few years later when Daniel Petrie directed the film version of *The Betsy*, Harold had high hopes that at least one of his novels would be properly adapted to the screen, primarily because Laurence Olivier was the star. After we saw the festival screening, we had a huge, wild party on our yacht attended by at least two hundred people, some invited and some not. The next morning Harold said, "Dan Petrie should have filmed our party. It was a helluva lot better than the fuckin' movie and a lot less expensive!"

Finally, when our first film festival concluded, Harold went back to work in his office in the attic at Villa Grazia, but not at his usual non-stop pace. He spent a great deal of time with Adréana and me, and with me in particular, especially at night.

All of our friends thought Harold and I made a heavenly match, and I could not have disagreed with them. My Cinderella existence continued at full speed, but I did not ignore Harold's needs. I did everything I could to make his life pleasant and conditions tolerant when he worked.

He did not write twenty-four hours a day, however, and private parties at home became a ritual part of our lives; I sensed they gave Harold a feeling of family and tradition, something he's never had before he met me. During all our years together, no matter where we were, I tried to make every holiday festival: Easter, Halloween, Thanksgiving, Christmas, and, of course, New Year's Eve.

For Adréana's first birthday Harold masterminded the entire event, although I had trouble finding party favors, hats, and even paper plates. The French love a good time, but time-honored American standards, that is to say commercial standards, didn't seem to exist there in the sixties. Later, I made a point to collect what staples I needed for all holidays that we would spend in Europe and I stored them in a huge treasure chest.

That first birthday party still stands out in my memory, although we always tried to have something grand and special for Adréana. It was held at Villa

Grazia and Adréana's guests were the children and grandchildren of our servants and their families. Harold ordered a huge multi-tiered cake that looked like it was designed for a wedding reception. It was made of chocolate, vanilla, and French créme. "Nothing but the best for our daughter," said Harold proudly.

When it came time to cut and eat the cake, the waiters were appalled when Harold denied them, giving the children knives and forks. In fact, he wouldn't let anyone cut the cake. It was centered on a huge table and he lined up the children in a circle on the table around the cake; when he gave them the go ahead, they dug into the huge frost-covered delight with their bare hands. Adréana hardly knew what was going on, but she, too, was on the table with small fists of birthday cake. It was like a scene from a Little Rascals film, hilarious and wonderful.

During the last week of July, Harold climbed down from his attic office with a grin on his face. "I've typed my last word in this place," he said. "I've finished *The Adventurers*." He seemed relieved and relaxed for the first time since Adréana's birthday party. I was happy for him, although I did not realize how literal "my last words in this place" were. I knew we would be coming back to France after a sojourn in the United States, and I assumed Harold would again work in the villa, if not in the attic.

"I'm so pleased for you, darling," I told him.

"Let's go celebrate," he said.

We went to Cannes for lunch. While we were walking along the boulevard de la Croisette, we heard a newspaper boy hawking the daily. He was saying something about Porfirio Rubirosa. We bought the paper, and there on the front page was the story of Rubirosa's untimely death. He had wrecked his Ferrari while driving at high speed in Paris's Bois de Boulogne.

"Shit, that's just my luck," muttered Harold as he glossed over the story. He was visibly upset.

"What's wrong?" I asked.

"I killed off Dax in the same way, in a high-speed accident in his sports car."

Dax was his Rubirosa-like main character. It was an extraordinary coincidence, a case of fiction imitating life.

"I'll have to change the ending before I turn the book in," said Harold. "I don't want people to think I'm fuckin' copyin' life!"

He did not make the change in France. We whooped it up for a couple of months, did some traveling, and then flew to New York, where once more we checked into the Stanhope Hotel. Again autumn was vying with winter. Harold quickly rewrote the end of *The Adventurers* and dispatched the typescript to his editor at Simon & Schuster. It was then he presented me with a Fred of Beverly Hills jewelry box. It would become an "end of the book" ritual. After each finished novel he would buy me jewelry. This gift from Fred's consisted of the most beautiful bracelets, a trio of three different types of gold. I loved each and every one of them. As I did every time he finished a book!

In a way, he said, it was like getting rid of a disease. All that remained for him to do now was approve the galleys (which he usually did without reviewing them) and participate in the promotion blitz when the book came out, which was a time consuming chore that he disliked. In that respect he compared himself to a motion picture producer, director, and star all rolled into one; he had a public following and it was necessary to meet their needs and demands, if only briefly. Aside from the publicity tours, however, once a book was published Harold considered it out of his hands, the control now transferred to the advertising department of the publisher. He was concentrating already on what he would write next.

After typing the last word of *The Adventurers* Harold had called Paul Gitlin. They were both eager to meet with the powers at Simon & Schuster, since *The Adventurers* was the final volume of a three book deal. Paul, aware that Harold no longer cared to meet on his publisher's turf, arranged a meeting in our suite at the Stanhope. "They're making tons of money on my hard work, so they can come to me," was Harold's attitude.

As we settled into the Stanhope, Harold's latest manuscript was now in the hands of his editor, Cynthia White, his publisher, Leon Shimkin, and the other powers at Trident-Simon & Schuster. They could do with *The Adventurers* what they wanted to as far as Harold was concerned; he was ready to pitch them his idea for his next book, and Paul was prepared to negotiate it.

I did not stick around for the wrangling, although Harold had no qualms with my presence. I dressed Adréana and we crossed Fifth Avenue and went to the Metropolitan Museum of Art. My interest in postimpressionist paintings had grown since Harold had purchased the Giselle Belleud collection for me. Later, we strolled through the park, all the way to the Great Lawn, and then circled back and crossed again to the Stanhope.

When we returned to the suite, the Simon & Schuster-Trident Press envoys had come and gone. Harold and Paul were in high spirits, drinking scotch. I knew without having to ask that Harold's new project had been approved and that he had another magnificently rich paycheck in hand.

The new book would be *The Inheritors*. Somewhere between France and the United States, Harold had decided definitely to write the final volume of his Hollywood Trilogy or The Age of the Tycoons. The first volume had been *The Dream Merchants*, his second novel, portraying the early years of the movie industry, from its golden years in the 1930s, all of it gleaned from Harold's research as well as myriad stories told him by old-timers he met during his years of employment with Universal Pictures. *The Carpetbaggers* had been the second volume, reverting back to the 1920s and then taking the industry history into the 1940s and the aftermath of World War II. *The Inheritors* would again review the motion picture industry, propelling it into the age of television, although I don't believe Harold knew how the story would unfold when he pitched the idea to S&S.

"That's why it's called creative writing," he often said. "If you already know exactly how it's gonna come out, what all the characters are gonna do, then why the fuck kill yourself repeating it?"

When Harold pontificated like that, Paul always nodded as if he understood exactly what Harold meant. Yet in Harold's absence I heard Paul say many times, "The guy is a natural born storyteller. I don't know how his mind works, but in the end something astonishingly creative always comes out of it."

Compared to our laid-back lives in Le Cannet, New York was like being in another world. It was full of kinetic energy, bright lights, and pulsating electricity. Adréana, of course, was not the only daughter in Harold's life; he wanted to see Caryn. He called Yvonne one midday, and after the usual bickering he arranged to pick up Caryn at Yvonne's apartment at Seventy-Fourth and Madison Avenue. He hung up.

"God, that woman's tough," sighed Harold.

"Yes, but you have to put up with it," I commented, "for Caryn's sake. What are you going to do with her?"

"I'll take her to Rumpelmayer's on Central Park South for an ice cream sundae," he said.

Adréana and I stayed at the Stanhope, while Harold took a taxi to Yvonne's. It was November 9, 1965—the day the lights went out.

The sun set over the Eastern United States that afternoon at 4:44 p.m. and the demand for electricity began its usual surge. An array of lights, millions of them, from fluorescent to neon, suddenly blinked out across the Manhattan skyline. By that time Harold and Caryn were enjoying the delights of the ice cream parlor. Adréana and I were lolling about in the Stanhope, when at precisely 5:27 p.m. something went terribly awry. The power grid, from New York City to Canada, suddenly went dead.

At first I thought the hotel had experienced a temporary power failure, but when I looked out a window I saw nothing but a cold, black night on the streets below. The Metropolitan Museum was a dark shadow; Central Park was a murky lake of nothingness. It was eerie. All of Manhattan—indeed, much of the Eastern seaboard—was in a void of darkness. I was frightened, stuck high up in the Stanhope with my baby daughter.

Harold and Caryn finished their sundaes and entered the street. The traffic lights were out and massive car jams were forming on every thoroughfare in the city. It was fruitless to try to catch a taxi, so they hotfooted it back to Yvonne's, which was no mean feat, being several long blocks away. The elevators, of course, were out, so Harold had to climb twenty flights—"Count them," he said later. "Twenty fucking flights!"—of dark stairways, firmly holding Caryn's hand, before he finally returned her to her mother. He later said he thought he was going to have a heart attack. From Yvonne's he trekked back to the Stanhope, and again climbed several flights—"Count them! Thirteen fucking flights!"—to reach our suite. When he arrived, he was exhausted and breathless. His heavy smoking was catching up with him, but I was never happier to see anyone in my life. I threw myself in his arms.

"Hey, baby," he whispered between gasps, "don't worry, don't worry. The electricity will come back on and all will be well. But, hey, let's do it the dark!" He grabbed me and we hit the floor laughing.

Later, people made light of the blackout, but for thousands it was a harrowing experience. Many people were killed. I remember reading about one man who had fallen several floors to his death. His corpse was found the next day at the bottom of an elevator shaft, one hand still clutching a candle.

14

Cruising the Mediterranean

We returned to our rented home in Beverly Hills at the beginning of the Christmas holidays. We lazed about for a few days without really doing anything, except to partake of the laidback lifestyle of Southern California. We wined and dined at The Bistro, Chasen's, and Scandia, but our life seemed lackadaisical and aimless.

"Do you want to have another New Year's Eve party?" I asked.

Harold's eyes lit up. "Yeah, yeah! Let's do it. A party and a good fuck are two great ways to start a new year! Call Gene Schwam to help you.

I began planning, sans Harold's input. He had other things in mind concerning his creative life, none of which concerned his next novel, a novel not yet begun. He paced a great deal and often stared into space, thinking constantly, silently, while smoking one cigarette after another.

"Harold," I said hesitantly, "don't you think you should begin your new novel?"

"Fuck 'em. I'm gonna do something else first."

He explained that he had decided to start his own motion picture production company in an effort to bring to fruition his idea of the "televised novel." He mentioned sundry other projects too, but they seemed, at least to me, a bit murky, like purchasing the film rights to an entire series of French detective novels. "They'll make a great TV series."

I never advised Harold concerning his professional life, never once in twenty-eight years, but I was curious nevertheless about his television project.

"Do you have a storyline for your television project?" I asked meekly.

"No, but don't worry about it," he said authoritatively. "Robbins always comes up with something, but first I'm gonna structure the company."

End of discussion. I planned our party and Harold planned his company, Harco Productions, or, as the trade papers called it, The HR Company.

Sixty people had attended our first New Year's Eve party; for the second go round we invited three times as many. They all came, to the person, celebrities and non-celebrities alike, plus a lot of gatecrashers. As usual, Harold performed as much as a guest as he did a host, wandering about, observing, taking in the conversations of others, sometimes cornering people he deemed important, pushing the envelope but with a laugh, and flirting more than I thought he should have. The fact is Harold was the showcase item; people came because it was *his* party, and it wasn't just because he was the world's number one bestselling writer. As Larry Flynt, the controversial publisher, a good friend, once said, "Harold had an indefinable allure, something beyond description. Here was this nondescript fellow whom you wouldn't think people would give a second glance, but they did! They couldn't help it; he was captivating. And it wasn't just women; he had the same effect on men."

The next morning, after starting the new day with his favorite pastime, me, Harold coughed unmercifully, lit a cigarette, and said enthusiastically, "That was a terrific party last night, Tiger. Let's make it an annual event!"

Thus began an era in our lives whereby one year seemed to fuse into the next, and we separated them by recalling our social events and the publication of Harold's books.

The Adventurers came out in the spring to poor reviews and rich sales. It did not come as a surprise that Harold dedicated the book to me, but I was pleased nevertheless. It read: To my wife Grace who made so many things possible, of which this book is the least.

Trident Press (Simon & Schuster) saddled Harold with a brief but exhausting promotional tour that included a dozen cities. I stayed in Beverly Hills with Adréana, making it the first time Harold and I were away from each other for any length of time. But he was adorable, even in his absence. He called me from every airport, upon landing and before taking off, and two or three times a day from his hotel.

"I miss you and love you," he would begin, and follow up with a litany of complaints regarding his tour. He did not like the talk show circuit, which had blossomed with NBC's *Today Show* and flourished in various facsimiles at every television station across the country. It was an inexpensive way to promote a book, but he grumbled that writers didn't receive the talent fees given to guests who were professional entertainers.

I had to bite my tongue to keep from laughing. Here was a man earning a half-million dollars minimum per book, and he was complaining about not receiving a $150 talent fee for the opportunity to promote said book. Harold was not cheap, but he wanted a fair playing field. "I'm an entertainer too!" he lamented.

When he returned from his whirlwind publicity tour, *The Adventurers* had climbed to the number two spot on *The New York Times* best seller list, behind Jacqueline Susann's *Valley of the Dolls*. Harold had known Jacqueline for years, having first met her in the late thirties when they both patronized Billy Rose's famous Manhattan nightclub, The Diamond Horseshoe. In Manhattan he had introduced me to her at '21' and I liked her. She had spunk.

After he returned from his publicity junket, I asked him if he knew anything about *Valley*, and he said, "Grace, there's a lot of difference between chicken shit and chicken salad." In truth it was not a well-written book, but it was gossipy and fun, very titillating. Harold got a kick out of a piece in the *New York Times* written by Gloria Steinem in which she said "compared to Jacqueline Susann, Harold Robbins writes like Proust."

If *The Carpetbaggers* had thrust Harold into the limelight of fame, *The Adventurers*, regardless of the reviews, made him a celebrity. It was a sprawling, lusty novel, packed full of his favorite themes—money, power, and sex—and now everyone wanted to meet the author who created its myriad characters and convoluted plots. Even though we had an unlisted number, the telephone rang off the wall.

"Dammit, I can't work here," said Harold. "I just can't."

"Then get an office," I suggested, "and don't tell anyone you have it." "By god, I will!"

One of the bungalows at the Beverly Hills Hotel became his temporary office, although he wasn't really working. I think he spent more time wandering around the swimming pool, eyeing the pretty sunbathers and socializing in the Polo Lounge, than he did at his typewriter. I didn't mind; Harold had worked hard for the best part of the last two years and he deserved a break.

In late April, as we were prepping for a return to France, Jacqueline Susann and her husband, Irving Mansfield, came to town. They stayed at the Beverly Hills Hotel. When they discovered Harold was working there and often wandering by the pool to check out the glamorous women in bikinis, they decided to pull a prank on him. Irving dashed off to a bookstore and bought forty copies of *The Valley of the Dolls*.

Later, when Harold took one of his numerous strolls around the pool,

everyone at poolside was reading a copy of Jackie's book. Harold wasn't easily fooled. He went to the front desk and confirmed that the Mansfields were
registered. I thought the prank was funny, but Harold was irked. Perhaps it was
because Jackie and Irving would go to bookstores and cover up *The Adventurers*
with copies of *Valley of the Dolls*. Whatever, a couple of weeks later Harold lost
the bad taste in his mouth when *The Adventurers* overtook *Valley* and became
number one on the *Times* best seller list. (Harold seldom held a grudge against
anyone, and when Jackie died of cancer in 1974, he dedicated his next book to
her and to his friend Cornelius Ryan, who had also died of cancer.)

When we returned to Le Cannet, Harold held true to his words about
never writing in the villa attic again. He wanted an office at the Carlton Hotel,
so in typical Harold Robbins fashion he put together a consortium of investors
and made a bid to buy the place. Both proposals failed and Harold became a
tenant at the Carlton instead.

He hired a cute young secretary who came to work in a miniskirt with a
bikini underneath. He was not working on *The Inheritors*; he was dictating
the screenplay of *The Adventurers* he had promised Joe Levine. He would lie
on his office couch like a Freudian client and ramble through the story aloud.
Unfortunately, the screenplay format was something Harold never mastered.

I often joined him at the Carlton's Restaurant de Plage, an exclusive
beachfront bistro that was a favorite of ours. While we lunched, his young
secretary hit the beach for a couple of hours of sunbathing. What a job!

One day in a moment of levity, Harold called Joe Levine in Hollywood.

"How's the screenplay coming along?" asked Joe anxiously.

"You know," said Harold, "there's a problem with the book that I never
explained to you."

"What's that?"

"For starters, Hollywood producers and directors have fucked up every
book that I've ever written, including you."

"That's your opinion," responded Joe testily. "*The Carpetbaggers* is one of
the largest grossing movies of all time and *Where Love Has Gone* was a hell of a
lot more than a minor success. People made a bunch of money on those films,
Harold—including *you*."

"I'm not talking about quantity of money," said Harold. "I'm talking about
quality of film."

"Well, we can't change anything now. That's history," said Joe. "So what's
the problem with *The Adventurers* that you never told me about?"

"I purposely wrote the book in a fashion that makes it impossible to
translate to the screen."

"You *what?*" exclaimed Joe. "You mean I spent over a million dollars for—"

"That's right, Joe. For a book that doesn't have a movie story," said Harold.

"But dammit I've read the book. It's a great story!"

"Better read it again," Harold told him.

He hung up and had a good laugh. He said Joe was on the verge of a coronary. The next day Joe called back, told Harold to go to hell, and demanded the screenplay ASAP.

Before summer was over, Harold finished a 350-page scenario. Translated into movie time, it would have run longer than *Gone with the Wind*. When the movie finally went into production in late 1968, Joe hired new writers and used Harold's screenplay as a broad outline for the final scenario.

When we returned to the States in the fall, Harold was pleased to note that over six million copies of *The Adventurers* had been sold, and book sales were still going strong. We did not dwell in New York, although Harold took time to meet with Leon Shimkin, his mentor at Trident Press-Simon & Schuster. Leon wanted to know the status of *The Inheritors*, for which he had shelled out a $500,000 advance. "Don't worry about it, Leon. It's coming along just fine," said Harold impatiently.

The truth is Harold was still more interested in pursuing his concept of a book-length novel for television, what he now had begun to call "a visualized novel." He spoke frequently of the vast television audience as opposed to his number of readers, even though the latter was in the millions. He had a mathematical mind and the television numbers fascinated him. It was the concept, however, more than the subject matter, for he had not yet come up with a storyline for *his* television project. When he finally did, it was a spur of the moment thing, based upon necessity, like so many other ideas that came to his mind.

We returned to Beverly Hills and Harold immediately opened an office under the Harco banner at the famous 9000 Building on Sunset Boulevard. He was a loner, yes, but he didn't like to be totally alone, except when he was working.

"I need someone to run the office," he said.

I had no idea what he was talking about, since as far as I could see there was nothing to run. Surely, he wasn't talking about me?

"No, of course not, darling. You've gotta take care of Adréana," he answered. "I need, you know, someone I can trust, like a true friend, a lifelong friend, a buddy."

A buddy? Harold didn't have any buddies that I knew of. He could still count his trusted friends on the fingers of one hand. He made acquaintances, not friends.

Ray Crossett was another select member of Harold's inner sanctum. More than any other person he was responsible for Harold writing his first book,

Never Love a Stranger. It was he, tired of hearing Harold's complaints about the stories he was buying for Universal, who had challenged Harold with the $100 bet to write something better.

Ray was a balding gentleman of medium height. He had wonderful manners and always dressed stylishly. He adored Harold.

Harold persuaded Ray to become vice president in charge of production at Harco. Later, I thought the name Harco should have been Harpo, as in Marx, because the activities of the company, as far as Harold's involvement was concerned, seemed to be one crazy, comedic party. I think Ray was the only person who ever worked for the company who took it seriously.

I would call Harold at his office, but he was always busy. He would return my call, but usually much later. Once, when I really needed to speak with him about something, I demanded of the person who answered the telephone to put Harold on the line. Whoever the person was, he failed to put me on hold; while he was trying to disengage Harold from whatever he was doing, the noise of a hell-raising party in progress registered on the line. It sounded like an orgy.

At last Harold came on. "Yeah, yeah," he said brusquely. "Who's calling?"

"Your wife, Harold."

"Who?"

With so much noise in the background I wasn't surprised he couldn't understand me. I raised my voice. "It's Grace, Harold."

"Hey, darling!" said Harold, suddenly affecting a new, kinder voice. "What's up, baby?"

"I think the question is, 'What's up with you?' It sounds like you're having a party."

"A party? Oh, noooo!" said Harold. "We're in the midst of a casting session."

Casting what? I thought. Harco had no projects to cast, except in Harold's imagination. I didn't challenge him, however; you just did not challenge Harold Robbins. I accepted his BS in stride.

Harold was not anti-social, but he did not like conventional sit-down dinners or staid, quiet parties where you could hear the tinkle of cocktail glasses echoing from another room. Like the characters in his books, he was action oriented; he did not partake of small talk, yet he avoided deep, intellectual conversations also. He hated pompous people—he reserved that trait for himself—and he always grew restless when he was confined with a group of people whom he didn't really know or care about.

After the success of *The Adventurers* we began receiving hundreds of invitations to social affairs. Harold would select the ones he thought were important and then he would dispatch *me* to represent him. It wasn't that he was uninterested; he just didn't want to attend himself. In fact, he would wait restlessly for my report on how the function went, and then quiz me on who was there, what they were wearing, and so forth. (Of course I needed escorts. George Hamilton was one of them and Henry Berger who later married Anita Louise. Also George Gradow who married Barbi Benton—who are very good friends today.)

A sit-down dinner I attended as Harold's emissary prompted a whirlwind of activity that resulted in Harold making hundreds of thousands of dollars with hardly writing a word. I was seated next to Lew Wasserman of MCA-Universal, the largest producer of television products for the three major networks.

Perhaps the rumors were true regarding Wasserman's godfather-like qualities at the studio, but to me he could not have been nicer or more charming. Halfway through the dinner he asked me, "What's Harold up to, Grace? Is he working on anything we might be interested in at MCA-Universal? We're looking for television projects."

I told Lew about Harold's concept of the "visualized novel" he was always talking about. "Rather than the conventional format, Harold wants to carry forward with a continuing story, week after week, chapter after chapter, until the novel is finished."

Lew nodded with an inscrutable expression, but he obviously tossed Harold's idea around in his head because a few minutes later he said with interest, "What's Harold's television novel about?"

"Oh, you'd have to get Harold to explain it to you, Lew," I said, chiefly because I knew Harold didn't have a story, just a concept.

"Why don't you ask him to give me a call at the studio tomorrow," he said.

When I arrived home, Harold was waiting as usual for me to give him a report on the dinner party—who was there, who sat with whom, what did they talk about? I told him about my conversation with Lew Wasserman.

"Very interesting," he said, mulling over my words. "I'll call Lew first thing in the morning."

"By the way," I said, "have you come up with a storyline yet? That's what he seemed to be interested in."

"No, but I'll come up with something," said Harold confidently.

Two days later Harold was in-flight to New York, where Wasserman had arranged for him to meet with Leonard Goldensen, president of ABC, in his thirty-fifth floor office at the network's headquarters. Also scheduled to be present were ABC's programming executives whose expertise could determine the feasibility of financing Harold's "television novel" at Universal. Most important was the story; they wanted to know what the project was about. Harold had managed to talk around his storyline with Lew Wasserman because he didn't have one, but the moment of truth was arriving fast.

Paul Gitlin and his associate Gene Winick went to the meeting in New York with him. Before they arrived at ABC headquarters, Paul said, "What are you going to pitch them?"

"I don't know," said Harold.

Paul was taken aback. "You don't know?" he responded. "Jesus, Harold, this is a golden opportunity and you're not prepared for it."

"Dammit," said Harold testily, "just let me handle it."

Indeed, the ABC contingent was interested in the concept (which ultimately would become the first television mini-series), and after Harold's initial explanation, they asked him what the storyline was.

The headlines in the morning newspapers Harold had read on his flight were blistered with doom regarding a global banking crisis related to the shortage of gold that was supposed to back up paper money. According to Winick, Harold stood up and walked over to a picture window overlooking Manhattan and the Hudson River. He could see Central Park and beyond, all the way to the Seventy-Ninth Street Boat Basin, where the yachts were moored. (Remember, I was there the day before I met Harold.)

"Well," said Harold after taking in the view, "it opens with a boat coming up a river," and he winged it from there, developing a story as he went along, making up a few idiosyncratic characters that belonged to an international banking family, spicing the story with exotic European locations. By the time he concluded, Harold apparently had the executives watering at the mouth. They would finance it, they said, if MCA-Universal could cast a marquee star with the potential of bringing an instant audience to the television screen. It would be called "*Harold Robbins': The Survivors.*"

Harold didn't go to the 9000 Building upon his return to California. He didn't have time for office antics. He burst into our home, laughing and catching his breath. "Tiger, baby, hold the phones for me!" he barked excitedly. "I don't want to speak with anyone!" He went straight to his guesthouse office, locked himself in, and knocked out a one-page synopsis that he had courier-delivered to Lew Wasserman at MCA-Universal. It was the most valuable page he had ever written.

Harold never wrote another word for the series, but he became one of the highest paid writers in television history—$250,000 per episode. "About fifty thousand dollars a word," he beamed. His share of the overall budget was in the millions, and *The Survivors* would be one of the most expensive and lavish television dramas to date. MCA-Universal set up a production schedule for the South of France the following year.

Although ABC wanted a name star for *The Survivors*, casting was not for Harold. Lew Wasserman and Company were the geniuses in that field. Yet he was concerned about it; his profits from the project, which were still potential, counted on it. After writing his one page synopsis, he returned to his office at the 9000 Building, probably because he had more fun there. After all, aside from managing our abode I was a serious mother, a fundraiser for charities, and his constant envoy at social functions. Off to the office one morning he said in passing, "I think I'll ask Lew to cast Lana Turner."

My face fell. Was he out of his mind? The years had not diminished Lana's ire toward Harold's "profiting at her expense" with *Where Love Has* Gone; time and again we heard reliable rumors that when Harold's name was mentioned in Lana's presence, she always retorted, "God, how I hate that man!"

"Surely you're kidding," I said.

"Not at all," he responded, undeterred. "I'm gonna call Lew the minute I get to the office."

He did, and MCA-Universal's response to his suggestion was positive. Lana's career had not been sidetracked by the Stompanato episode, and now at forty-eight, she was a screen legend and still absolutely gorgeous. She had recently married for the sixth time, a man ten years her junior. It so happened that he was Harold's connection.

Robert Eaton was a handsome but failed actor who wanted to be a producer. Lana had set him up in an office in the 9000 Building. Harold befriended him, suggesting that if Robert could help Harold deliver Lana to the starring role of *The Survivors*, then Harold in turn would see to it that Eaton got a lucrative position on the production team. Talk about crazy Hollywood machinations!

But would it work? Eaton arranged a meeting between Harold and Lana at one of the LA country clubs. Although Lana said later that she "didn't want to even shake the man's hand," Harold nevertheless prevailed, as he so often did, persuading her to take the role.

Harold's ability to turn an enemy into a friend was amazing. He even planned a bash for Lana and one of her future costars. His invitation read in part: "If you are interested in broads, booze, and the better things in life, why not join Lana Turner and George Hamilton, stars of the new ABC-Universal Television show, *Harold Robbins' The Survivors*, at an old-fashioned cocktail party upstairs at The Bistro." Including George Hamilton (whom I adored) as a guest of honor was a surprise to Universal, for the party was really programmed for Lana.

"Do you think she'll come?" I asked Harold.

"Of course she'll come," he responded confidently. "Who would miss a Harold Robbins's party?"

He was right. Lana came. She was absolutely gorgeous in a black, chiffon, strapless dress with an array of black ostrich feathers across her famous bosom. Harold made a big fuss over her, and one would have thought they were lifelong friends.

Thus far, it had been a good year. Harold had written one page and made an extraordinary amount of money. We left for France.

I did not think we could improve our lifestyle, but I was wrong. One glorious morning Harold said, "Let's do something different today."

"Okay, let's do."

"The question is what?" he mulled.

"How about hiring a yacht."

"Hey, that's a great idea, Tiger!"

Boats had always been one of my great passions and I was hoping Harold would enjoy exploring the Cannes harbor and the offshore islands. As we cruised about, I recognized that he was thoroughly relaxed, more so than he ever was at the villa or at the house in Beverly Hills, where people were always dropping by unexpectedly and the telephone rang off the hook. It was a wonderful day of cruising, romantic with the breeze and the glistening water. Adréana loved it. When the day was done and we stepped off the boat, Harold and I looked at each other and said simultaneously, "I wish we had our own yacht."

The next day we began looking. In a matter of days Harold purchased a luxurious ninety-foot yacht with a polished teakwood deck—the final item on my Cinderella wish list.

"What shall we name it?" I asked excitedly.

"The *Gracara*!" exclaimed Harold.

"The what?"

"The *Gracara*—*Gra* for Grace, *Car* for Caryn, and *A* for Adréana."

The yacht was superb. We moored it in the new Cannes harbor, Port Canto, and began to spend as much time on the boat as we did at the villa. We had a fulltime crew that included a skilled captain, a deck hand, and a gourmet chef.

Paul Gitlin told his version of how we acquired the *Gracara* to *The New Yorker* magazine. "I remember Harold wanted it so badly," Paul related to the reporter. "I said, 'Well, you finish the book, there'll be cash flow.' And he did *The Inheritors* in five, six months. The book was in his mind, but there was no incentive to start writing. But for a yacht? He sat down and wrote a book."

In those days I often wondered why people, particularly close friends, took liberties in revealing what they called the truth of our lives as well as our lifestyle. There were wild adventures aplenty, without having to embellish them. Paul's story was not remotely true.

By 1967–68, when we purchased the *Gracara*, Harold was totally confident of his work and his track record indicated nothing but future success. We had plenty of money, even before the publication of *The Inheritors*. Harold knew I loved boats and he simply found a craft he thought I'd like, and in typical *Robbins* fashion, bought it. As far as writing *The Inheritors* five or six months, which had been his modus operandi before *The Adventurers*, he spent two years on it, and as far as I can recall he was under absolutely no pressure at all.

As time went on, the number of people who claimed to have intimate knowledge of our lives fascinated me. We read their quotes in the papers; we saw them speak on television. Sometimes they were people we had never met. Harold's introversion kept him at safe distance from most people, particularly men, unless he was interested in using them as a prototype in one of his books. "I'm interested in money, power, and sex," he said repeatedly, "perhaps in reverse order. The same things my readers are interested in. I'm not interested in the average person; his financial circumstances are unfortunately boring."

The *Gracara* gave a new flavor and meaning to our lives that is hard to describe, allowing us a certain freedom that was otherwise hard to attain. If we wanted to get away, we simply told the captain to sail out of the harbor and to go in whatever direction we pointed. We had wardrobes on the yacht, so we didn't have to pack our bags. Hotel reservations were a thing of the past. When we wanted something to eat, we told the chef what we wanted, and then we were served at a table always reserved in our name. We were truly footloose and fancy free; if we wanted to escape, we simply didn't tell anyone where we were going, and often, we didn't know ourselves. We quickly became spoiled, including Adréana, who was a great little sailor at the age of three.

We didn't have to sail away, however, to enjoy the *Gracara*. Even when she was moored we spent a great deal of time onboard, always with carefree abandon. Everyday seemed like a holiday. When we were moored in Cannes, we continued to sleep at the villa, but we were up early, took a light breakfast, and then drove down the hill to Port Canto.

Sometimes we would cruise to St. Tropez or Monaco for a few days. We sailed to Greece, North Africa, the Italian Riviera, and even through the Suez Canal to the Arabian Sea and Iran. Sailing on the open sea, making love on the top deck, and resuming our love making after lunch in our state room, was the best way to get from port to port. Most of the time we would enjoy a sumptuous lunch on the *Gracara*, but if we went between the islands, to

Île Sainte-Marguerite and Sainte Honoré, we would disembark and lunch at Frederique's, a wonderful fresh-seafood restaurant, where Harold delighted in *langoustine*, a small Mediterranean lobster.

Frederique's was a charming outdoor eatery with minstrels wandering the terrace; rustic compared to our favorite places in Cannes. One of the minstrels was an elderly lady, rather shabbily dressed, who played a toy mandolin. Harold always tipped the musicians exceedingly, particularly the old woman; then we discovered she was a wealthy landlady in Cannes, who owned several upscale apartment buildings.

The next time we went to Frederique's Harold tipped the musicians but not the old woman. She wanted to know why.

"You're a wonderful minstrel," Harold told her, "but I've learned about you. I don't tip rich people."

She left, incensed. Harold thought her masquerade was hilarious, however, and I expected him to use her character in one of his novels, but he never did.

Often we would cruise to Antibes, a lovely town with one of the most beautiful hotels in the world, the Eden Roc. We would people watch, while enjoying the over-abundant buffet lunch. Seldom did we fail to run into a celebrity Harold knew or who knew Harold. Harold enjoyed overhearing whispered comments: "See that man over there? He's Harold Robbins." He tried to pooh-pooh it, but he was beginning to enjoy his fame.

Antibes is on a rocky coastline, absent a beach. The Eden Roc had a swimming pool sunk into the rocks where we would sunbathe after lunch. In the late afternoon, if we didn't have guests, we would go back to the *Gracara* for love-making and a siesta on the upper deck before sailing off at dusk into the Mediterranean sunset, which out of Antibes or Cannes is one of the most glorious on earth. When I see a sunset today, I never fail to think of those passionate times when we were on the upper deck of the *Gracara*, sipping *pastis* and watching day fall into night.

At an alfresco disco in Antibes one night, a waiter whispered to us that a couple had recognized Harold as the famous American writer. Could they possibly be introduced to us? The waiter gestured subtly toward a table stationed across the dance floor. The pair was staring at us, all smiles. The man was a slick-looking Arab, immaculately attired, a few years older than I, and the woman, who appeared to be my age, was exotically beautiful, of Anglo-Saxon extraction with jet-black hair.

"Who are they?" asked Harold cautiously.

"Mr. and Mrs. Khashoggi," whispered the waiter.

Harold's chin dropped. "Adnan Khashoggi?"

The waiter nodded.

"By all means!" exulted Harold. "Bring them over!"

The waiter brought them over and Soraya and Adnan Khashoggi became two of our closest friends.

Adnan was a short, well-groomed, pleasant-looking man with a tiny mustache. He had a sweet disposition and impeccable manners, and was certainly not a man one would have pegged as an international arms dealer. Already he was being called "the richest man in the world," and he once complained to Harold that his monthly American Express bill always exceeded $1,000,000. He was a Saudi Arabian with extremely close ties to the Saudi royal family (his father had been King Faisal's official palace doctor), and he had transformed his connections into a world of wealth—in real estate, in banking, in public works, and, of course, in guns and other weaponry. He was a character right up Harold's literary alley.

Soraya was exquisite, a world-class beauty of Black-Irish lineage, born in London. She was petite, with blue eyes and a pale complexion; her figure belied the fact she had given birth to five children. She was the only woman I've ever met who looked as beautiful without makeup as she did with it. We became like sisters, intimate confidantes in a friendship that endured for years.

In many ways, however, the Khashoggis were polarized personalities. It didn't happen often, but when they fought it was war. Usually Soraya was full of energy, fiery with enthusiasm, while Adnan was calm and complacent. One time Soraya joked to me that Adnan spent all of his energy on his daily toilette.

"What do you mean?" I asked innocently.

"He's a perfectionist," she answered. "He spends hours and hours preparing himself for the day. I've never met a man cleaner than Adnan. Look at him. Not a strand of hair out of place. He even combs his pubic hairs!"

After we met them in Antibes the Khashoggis joined us on the *Gracara*. Adnan did not have a yacht and Harold wanted to show him what the good life was all about. He ordered the captain to rev up the engines to thirty knots, which was about top speed.

Adnan was impressed, but Harold was not. He wanted more speed. He motioned for the captain to give the ship full throttle, which he reluctantly did, revving and revving until—kaboom!—both engines blew out simultaneously.

"Damn!" said Harold.

"Nice boat, Harold," smiled Adnan.

We were out of commission for a few days while the engines were overhauled, then we cruised to St. Tropez. I had not mentioned to Harold how stupid I thought he had been to blow the engines; later I was glad I hadn't because I did something almost as bad.

On the beach at St. Tropez I saw a gypsy guitar troupe perform. They were so incredible that I invited them to come aboard the *Gracara* and entertain Harold and our guests at a party. They brought their father who was a famous flamenco dancer. I didn't take into consideration that the harsh tapping that gives flamenco dancing its volcanic rhythm was produced by metal studs embedded in the soles of their boots. The dancer demolished the teakwood deck. The music was so good, however, that no one realized the damage being done as he performed.

Later, when our pissed-off captain surveyed the deck, Harold remained mum, as I had done when he blew out the two engines on our yacht. The Gypsy trio, went on to great fame. They became the world-renowned Gypsy Kings.

After spending time on the *Gracara*, Adnan Khashoggi became obsessed with getting his own yacht. When he did, it was a splendid craft, far grander than the *Gracara*. He named it after his oldest son Mohammad. Unfortunately, Adnan's luck was worse than ours. Harold blew a couple of engines and I let the flamenco dancer ruin the deck, but Adnan's yacht sank. While it was being refurbished in the port of St. Jean Cap Ferrat, a worker accidentally left a blowtorch flaring when he took a lunch break. The *Mohammad* caught fire, and although firefighters rushed to the scene and extinguished the flames, the craft took on too much water from the hoses, capsized, and went the way of the deep.

"Damn!" exclaimed Adnan.

"It was a nice boat, Adnan," said Harold, biting his tongue.

Adnan was hardly fazed by the incident, which to most people would have been a tragedy. He just bought another yacht, this one grander than the first; in fact, it was the largest in the world. The décor was spectacular, and the fixtures in the bathrooms were real gold. Almost every fabric was made from pure silk. He named it the *Nabila*, after his only daughter.

Harold used to call the *Gracara* a floating hotel; well, the *Nabila* was a floating city. It had everything, including a mini-infirmary with a dental chair, a beauty salon, even a discothèque. The only reason one ever had to leave the Nabila was out of sheer curiosity, to explore the new ports where the yacht dropped its anchor.

When the Khashoggi yacht was moored in Cannes harbor, Soraya and I talked to each other every day; and as couples, the Khashoggi and Robbins families alternated back and forth from the *Nabila* to the *Gracara*. We had wonderful times together, and Adnan took an interest in Harold's future. He actually lectured him about the importance of self-promotion, which Harold thought he was already pretty good at doing.

"If you want to be seen, you have to be heard," said Adnan. He took a gold coin out of his pocket and tossed it on the carpet. It made no sound. Then he extracted another gold coin and threw it hard on the marble floor of the *Nabila*. It echoed throughout the yacht as it spun itself out on the hard surface. "Understand what I mean?" asked Adnan.

Harold understood.

For Adréana's fourth birthday party, Harold took over the planning. He often lamented that in a country prized for its cuisine, as France was, no one had ever heard of barbeque. He decided to introduce it. He set up an elaborate barbeque grill on the terrace of Villa Grazia. We invited every child we could find, all of the neighborhood children, kids visiting at the Carlton Hotel, and kids of yacht people we had met, including the Khashoggi children, and Caryn, Harold's oldest daughter. (Yvonne had allowed Caryn to visit us after much pleading from Harold.)

Harold planned Adréana's birthday party like one of his books—meticulously. He had problems, however, because he had to start from scratch. No one had the foods he wanted. He bought a side of beef at our local butcher, demonstrating to him how to hang a beef carcass in his cooler, rather than laying it out in the French custom. Harold insisted that beef tenderized better when it was hanging. I thought he was going to a great deal of trouble for hamburgers and hotdogs, but typically I remained mum.

Another day he was frustrated because he couldn't find American-style wieners in Cannes. "Leave it to the fucking French," he said with a laugh. "They prepare the finest cuisine in the world, but when it comes to a hotdog, they throw their hands up in the air." Determined that French cuisine and culture would not defeat him, he called Bertie Meadows in London.

England was high on Harold's list of favorite places, his books sold in Britain second only to the United States. When we did cross the channel, almost always for a book promotion, the number one stop was the 21 Club, Bertram Meadows's four-story mansion restaurant at 8 Chesterfield Gardens in the Mayfair district. Harold was essentially a meat and potatoes man, and Bertie's club (unrelated to 21 in New York) purportedly had the best steaks, lobsters, bangers, and cocktails in town. The club's reputation for Harold (and for Adnan Khashoggi, too) was enhanced by the fact that Bertie and his brother Harry also had a clandestine gambling casino in an upstairs room.

"I need a case of sausages, Bertie," said Harold into the telephone. A pause followed, then Harold said testily, "Where do you think I am? I'm in fucking Cannes. If I were in fucking London, I'd be at your fucking joint talking to you in person, not calling you on the fucking telephone!"

Bertie accommodated him. The next morning he air freighted a case of bangers from Great Britain to France. Finally, with the appropriate food in the cooler, we had the party. Harold came bare-chested, wearing an apron on which was written, "Kiss the Chef." As he flipped the burgers and turned the bangers on the grill, the children gathered around, curious indeed. Few had ever seen Harold's American-style cooking before. Mohammed, the Khashoggi's son who was about eight years old, suddenly said, "Mr. Robbins, you are a good cooker." Harold laughed at his observation, and everyone began to pick it up, "Mr. Robbins . . . good cooker."

15

Guess Who's Coming to Stay

few days after Adréana's party, Harold began writing *The Inheritors*, although he didn't work twelve grueling hours a day as he had when writing *The Adventurers*. He would force himself to write a few hours, just enough. He then would venture to other activities, mostly social but sometimes solitary. He had other projects to think about, too, although he did not have a hands-on involvement with them. When we returned to California after our season in Cannes, he grinned and told a reporter, "I'm the only man in show business in a position to bankrupt two studios and a television network in a single year." He was referring to a two-picture, big-screen deal he had renegotiated with Joe Levine for production at Paramount and the forthcoming Survivors television production by Universal for ABC. "The thought of bankrupting them all is exciting," he continued, tongue in cheek, "but with luck, they will be successful and I'll be forced to do this for the rest of my life."

In November *Life* magazine did a huge spread on Harold, including a full-page, close-up photograph of him wearing a Beatles cap on the beach in Cannes. A bikini-clad sunbather was reflected in his sunglasses. The caption read: "The World's Best Paid Writer, the man who turns sex and adventure into cash." Harold gloated.

I was not privy to our financial books, primarily because we didn't keep any. Harold kept everything in his head, but he informed *Life*: "By the end of this year, *The Adventurers* will have made two million in royalties alone." The article pointed out that Harold had earned more money on one book "than

Shakespeare, Dickens, Thoreau, Whitman and probably the Bronte sisters made all together in their lifetimes." It was heady stuff, particularly with the knowledge it was true.

We settled into a larger, grander house at 905 North Beverly Drive in the upscale flats of Beverly Hills, and across the street from the Beverly Hills Hotel. It was a beautiful house that had once belonged to screen legend Gloria Swanson. It was large, elaborate, and lent itself to entertainment, although for the time being Harold said he was not in a mood for parties. 'While I get some work done, our social life will have to be satisfied with the ghosts of Norma Desmond and Joe Kennedy," he laughed.

He had hardly typed the first word, however, when Joe Levine called from Italy. I could hear Harold arguing with the producer from another room. Joe wanted Harold to come to Rome, although Harold was against it. The first image that came to my mind was one of Brigitte Bardot taking diction lessons from Harold in her boudoir. As the conversation continued, I tuned it out. When he hung up, I braced myself for the news of Joe's latest request.

"What did Joe want?" I asked.

"He wanted to know what the hell *I'm* doing here in Beverly Hills, while he's in Rome shooting *The Adventurers*."

"He wants you to go to Italy?"

"I'm afraid so."

"What does he need you for?"

"To advise the writers on the script. What else?"

"Well, what did you tell him?"

"What do you think I told him? *I* told him no, but no doesn't work with Joe. He's persistent."

"Are you going?"

"Yeah," said Harold sheepishly, feigning guilt, and watching what he perceived to be my rising jealousy. Then he grinned. "Pack your bags, Tiger! We're catching the first flight out of here!"

I was thrilled and distressed simultaneously. "But Harold," I argued, "I've got Adréana to think of!"

"Oh yeah? What do you think we've got a fuckin' nanny for?" he asked; then he answered the question himself: "For just this type of emergency!"

From Rome International Airport we went straight to a soundstage at the famous Cinecittá Studios as per Joe's instruction to Harold. The company was filming a love scene between Bekim Fehmiu and Candice Bergen, the film's stars. Even a novice such as myself could foresee a movie catastrophe in the making.

Fehmiu was a young Yugoslavian actor who apparently saw his golden opportunity in the role of Dax Xenos, the story's hero. Unfortunately, he wanted to hog the scene, which is very difficult to do when a man and a woman are supposed to be making love. He kept looking at the camera before and after he kissed Candice, as if he were demonstrating for a voyeur. Lewis Gilbert, the director, was beside himself with frustration and growing anger. Joe Levine paced back and forth counting the dollars expended every time the scene was reshot. Two-dozen takes had already been filmed and Fehmiu still would not follow Gilbert's direction.

We watched this tragicomedy in the making for a few moments, and then Harold shrugged and whispered to me, "See why I hate motion pictures? There's nothing wrong with the script; it's the goddamned actor! Not only can he not act, he's not Dax! And not only is he not Dax, he's a fucking ham!"

Harold was right. Fehmiu was as far removed from the character Harold had developed in the novel as an actor could be. Whatever talent Fehmiu had, it wasn't suited for Dax.

After Harold and Joe had a private téte-á-téte, Harold and I went to our hotel. Harold had become jaded to movies long before and now he laughed the fiasco off. "Geezus! Joe gets a terrific international cast—Candice, Ernie Borgnine, Olivia de Havilland, Leigh Taylor-Young, Jaclyn Smith, Rossano Brazzi, Charles Aznavour—and then he hires this unknown to play the lead. It doesn't make sense, but that's show business!"

We learned later that the wife of one of Joe's producers had been enamored of Fehmiu's good looks when she saw him on European television. "That's Dax!" she reportedly said, and her husband persuaded Joe to cast him. Fehmiu was a handsome young man, all right, but as Harold said, "Dax, he ain't!"

We were in Rome a week and for the most part it was a holiday feast. Our first trip to the Eternal City had been wonderful, but this time I didn't have to throw-up like before. I could do whatever I wanted, without worry. We went to the studio every day, where Harold hung around the set just to satisfy Joe Levine and make what he called "a little pocket change." I often went with him, but having already experienced the boredom of shooting film when I was in the advertising business, I did not stay on the set. The Robbins name carried enough clout that I had freedom of movement throughout the studio, which was busy with several productions.

When I learned that Marcello Mastroianni was filming on an adjacent stage, I asked one of the Italian production assistants if I could meet him. He took me to the stage and left me waiting in the wings. Mastroianni was sitting in a canvas chair, his name printed on the back. When the assistant bent over to speak to him—mentioning quite loudly "Mrs. Robbins would like to meet you"—he rocketed out of his chair as if he were in flight to the moon, and brought his chair for me to sit in. He was all but gushing in his broken English.

"Mrs. Robbins! How wonderful of you to come by! I'm a great admirer of your husband!"

"Why, thank you!" I responded, gushing no less than he was, and feeling flattered by his attention. "The admiration is reciprocal."

"This movie I'm making," he said, "it is very different than what I've done in the past."

"Oh? Is it not a love story?"

"That, yes. But its emphasis is on dancing, which I know Mr. Robbins will appreciate."

I hadn't the slightest idea why Harold would appreciate a movie that emphasized dancing, but I didn't argue the point.

"It's about Rudolph Valentino, you see, and I had to learn the tango," Mastroianni continued, affecting a Valentino air and doing a stiff little tango move for my benefit.

"You've learned it marvelously," I responded.

"Yes, and after all these years, admiring your husband so much, I can now say I am trying to do what he, of course, does best."

I was totally in the fog until I suddenly realized Marcello was speaking not of Harold Robbins but of Jerome Robbins, the famous Broadway choreographer. I did not disappoint him by revealing my true identity, and later when I told Harold what had happened, he roared with laughter and did a little tango jig that had all of the wonderful makings of a Charlie Chaplin caricature, although I'm not certain Harold realized it.

One day Frederick Lowe, the famous composer of *My Fair Lady,* telephoned us at the hotel, suggesting we take in the Italian stage production of his play. Harold had known Fritzi for years, and after conferring with me, he accepted the invitation as a courtesy. When he hung up, he said, "How in the fuck can they do a play about the proper pronunciation of English in Italian?"

We went. It was a stylish production with lavish costumes and expensive sets equal to the Broadway production. Harold could put his knowledge of Italian into a thimble, so he bugged me throughout the performance, asking what was going on and who was saying what. My favorite scene was the climax of the first act, when Eliza Doolittle has finally commanded proper English—in this case Italian—and demonstrates her newfound expertise by singing "The Rain in Spain." In Italian the lyrics had been rewritten as "In Spagna S'e banata la campagna," which translates to "In Spain, the countryside is wet." Although much of the poetry of the lyrics was lost in translation, I thought the production was nevertheless marvelous. The "gn" sound in Italian, as in filet mignon, is wonderful, and it was used repetitiously in the *play—Spagna, bagnata, campagna—*to great effect.

The innovation that made the play really different from the New York and London productions was the use of the Alfie-technique of making asides to the audience that Michael Caine had used so effectively in the movie, *Alfie*. In the Italian *My Fair Lady* an actor would simply stop his or her performance, turn to the audience, and comment: "Can you imagine? We have this professor and this beautiful girl. She loves him so much, and yet he's mean to her!" Then the actor would step back into character and the performance would continue.

Each time this happened Harold poked me in the ribs and whispered, "What the fuck is going on?" To compound his confusion, the audience started participating, talking back to the actors when they made their asides. I thought it was hysterical, but Harold didn't like *My Fair Lady* in Italian any better than he had liked *The Carpetbaggers* in English.

"What the fuck are they doing now?" he would ask with exasperation. "What's the audience talking for? What the fuck is going on?"

The next day I gave Fritzi a glowing, thumbs-up review of the production, but when I told him about the asides, he grew furious. "Leave it to the Italians to ham up my play!" he exclaimed. "They'll do it every time!" He went on and on, demeaning everything Italian he could think of; then he abruptly stopped in midsentence, apparently remembering I was Sicilian. He blushed and said, "But I suppose one had to be there to really appreciate it."

Lewis Gilbert finally wrapped the love scene on the Cinecittá set after sixty-plus takes, a foreboding of things to come. Harold took the production problems in stride, salivating over his paycheck for doing little or nothing. I was beginning to think he was there for the sole purpose of keeping Joe Levine's sanity in check. The company moved next to Monte Argentario, a picturesque peninsula northwest of Rome.

The next major scene was to be shot in a villa in Porto Santo Stefano, a small town which at the time was virtually untouched by tourism. It was a pleasant village but not luxurious; families and young people strolled in the evening along the long waterfront just as earlier generations had done in the past. It was like going back in time, to a less complicated era.

The villa the movie company's location scouts secured for the scene was of a different order. It was magnificent in both scale and grandeur. The owner was Contessa Lilli Girini, a lovely woman, who, according to local rumors, had once been the mistress of the local Mafia chieftain. Upon her lover's death the Contessa had inherited the villa, along with a small fortune. She evidently lived a sumptuous and full life.

The first thing we saw upon entering the villa was a vast collection of various pairs of men and women, sculpted in plaster of Paris each pair engaged in some form of erotic position. They were everywhere, standing against the walls, lying on the floor, hanging from the ceiling. I felt as though I had entered an ancient Roman den of iniquity, which is exactly what Harold had intended when he wrote the infamous orgy scene in his book. Now they were going to film it, with Charles Aznavour playing the role of Marcel Campion, the wanton and licentious sex-monger artist who sponsored the orgy in his studio. Harold was delighted with the props and further pleased because Contessa Girini thought the hedonistic display was a welcome addition to her otherwise splendidly furnished palazzo.

Our stay in Porto Santo Stefano was longer than expected because the scene, complicated to begin with, required innumerable camera setups and had to be shot twice, one for a liberal European audience and one for a prudish American audience. For the film cut that would be distributed in the States the actors were partially dressed and their lovemaking was tepid at best. On the other hand the European version exposed a great deal of flesh and was much closer to raw sex.

Harold got on famously with the Contessa. She was a gracious hostess, and when it was time to leave she offered Harold the use of her villa if he ever chose to write in Italy.

"I may take you up on that," Harold told her.

"Please do," she responded with a warm, sensuous smile.

"I will."

Yeah, over my dead body, I thought.

Every day I called Beverly Hills to check on Adréana; although there were no problems, I was eager to get back to her. Harold agreed, since he didn't think he was really doing anything to expedite the production.

We flew to Paris, had a final gourmet dinner and Dom Pérignon at Maxim's, and caught the next flight to Los Angeles International. Harold, too, was anxious to see Adréana, but most importantly he wanted to get started on *The Inheritors*.

The weather in Southern California was primarily of two sorts, summer and Indian summer; thus Beverly Hills was much as we had left it three weeks before. Adréana had hardly missed us, if at all.

Harold had barely finished the first sentence on his manual typewriter when he received a call from New York. Leon Shimkin, now the general manager of Simon & Schuster, was en route to the West Coast. He wanted to drop by our home and say hello.

"Hello, my ass!" said Harold as he hung up. "The bastard wants to come by and take inventory of his half-million dollar investment."

Shimkin was a colorful character, one of the founding fathers of the modern publishing industry. It had been at Shimkin's request that Dale Carnegie put his lectures together and write *How to Win Friends and Influence People*, which became Simon & Schuster's all-time best seller.

Harold was quick to point out, "I don't think Leon ever read Carnegie's fucking book. If he did, he didn't put it to practice, or if he tried them, they didn't work." On the other hand Harold admired Shimkin for his risk taking. It was he, after all, who had entered into the first agreement with Paul Gitlin on Harold's unfinished manuscript of *The Carpetbaggers*, and who had subsequently created Trident Press for Harold's hardback editions when his staid S&S partners didn't want their imprint on Harold's books. It was Shimkin again who had provided the necessary go ahead to issue Harold some of the largest checks to date in the history of publishing.

Being aware of some, if not all, of those facts, I thought Harold was a little too caustic with his remarks about Mr. Shimkin, but then Harold had a built-in distrust of publishers that I never quite understood. One thing was certain, he hated to be disturbed and pressured by them.

"If Leon comes before lunch, maybe we can have a decent conversation," he said. "If he comes after lunch, it'll be a waste of time, since Leon won't remember having been here."

He was referring to Leon's propensity for vodka martinis, a habit apparently well known by those who had contact with him, from writers and agents to employees of the companies Leon was involved with.

The next morning a red-eyed man who appeared to be many years Harold's senior and who was otherwise nondescript arrived at our doorstep at 11 a.m. sharp. He carried a cold thermos in which he said was distilled water.

"Mrs. Robbins, it's my pleasure to at last meet you. I'm Leon Shimkin. How do you do, my dear? Is Harold available? And, oh yes, may I possibly have an empty glass? I need to clear my throat with distilled water."

I called Harold in the guesthouse; he came up to the main house, not too quickly I might add, and greeted Leon with the cold curtness of an undertaker. "Hello, Leon. Come on back to the office and I'll show you where I work." He winked at me, for Shimkin already was filling his glass with "distilled water."

"I would love to see it, Harold," he said, after drinking and clearing his throat.

Harold led him to the guesthouse, where Leon immediately went behind the desk and glared down at the sheet of paper in the carriage. "Harold, you've stopped here in midsentence. Can you explain that?"

"Yeah, the fucking typewriter jammed, Leon."

"Well, do you know how you're going to finish the sentence? I mean, do you know what's coming next?"

"I haven't the slightest fucking idea, Leon."

"You mean you don't know what you're going to write next?"

"No, I don't, Leon, but the fucking typewriter does!"

Harold's assessment of Leon was correct. By noon he was slurring his words, by one o'clock, he was weaving in his tracks; by two o'clock—his "distilled water" thermos empty—he was gone. Whether his excursion into Robbins Land had met with his satisfaction, I never knew. Nor did Harold, but then as Harold frequently remarked, "I don't give a shit."

In December Harold took a break from his work for the Christmas and New Year's holidays. He wanted Caryn with us, so he called Yvonne. I heard him arguing with her on the telephone, but since it was par for the course, I didn't pay much attention to his words. After he hung up, he said, "Yvonne's coming out with Caryn."

I looked at him. "What do you mean?"

"She won't let Caryn visit us unless she comes with her."

He grinned; I didn't.

"Caryn always tells her how much fun we have," he continued. "So I guess Yvonne wants to partake."

"Oh, come on, Harold!" I said. "Yvonne is going to stay with us?"

He nodded and shrugged. For "What else could I say? That's the way Yvonne is. Selfish."

For once I wanted to be selfish myself, but I went along with Harold's wishes, as I always had. After Caryn's visit in France, she had gone back to Yvonne with so many tales about our storied life, the people whom she had met, the crazy things we did, the parties we threw, the fun she had, all the good times, that Yvonne decided she wasn't going to be shortchanged this time by staying at home. If Harold wanted to see his first daughter during the holidays, he would have to have her mother in the mix also. The major problem, at least for me, was that I felt Harold was looking forward to Yvonne's visit as much as he was Caryn's. Nevertheless, I sucked in my pride and determined I would be a great hostess, regardless of the circumstances.

I didn't like Yvonne Russell-Farrow. She was a few years older than me, fairly attractive, spoiled to no end, and a complete bitch. Yvonne was arrogant, jealous, greedy, selfish, and she hated me with a passion. Why, I never knew, because she had broken off with Harold years before I came into his life.

She and Caryn stayed through Christmas, and for me Yvonne was misery incarnate, although somehow I maintained my composure and tried to do everything I could to accommodate her. I even got her a couple of dates, and I had a dinner party in her honor, none of which she appreciated. It finally dawned on me that she wanted people to think *she* was Mrs. Harold Robbins, or at the very least his mistress.

And Harold thought it was a scream. More than once I could have killed him. When we joined a young screenwriter (a woman naturally) for dinner at The Bistro, Harold pointed to Yvonne, then me, and finally to the attractive young writer—in that order—while telling the maître d' with glee that "Life is great, Jimmy! I'm with my ex-mistress, my wife, and my future mistress. Now how do you like them apples?" He then roared with laughter, although none of the rest of us did, with the possible exception of the writer. I thought, "That bastard! He thinks he has it all," but of course I kept my thoughts to myself. I did not argue with Harold, reprimand him, or challenge him; I acted the same way I had with my father when I was growing up, taking my humiliations with a calm, inscrutable expression, sometimes with a thin but grudging smile.

On the afternoon of the dinner party I gave Yvonne, she complained that she didn't have anything to wear. We were about the same size, so I took one of my couturier dresses from my closet, one I had not worn, and offered it to her. She became indignant.

"I would never wear a hand-me-down!" she cried with fire in her eyes. "I don't take leftovers!"

When she showed up in a beautiful new dress that night, looking like a million dollars, I knew Harold somehow had managed to get it for her. Again, I said nothing. But when she and Caryn left to go back to New York, I finally released my steam. I told Harold, "Never again. Never, never, never! End of discussion!"

Harold laughed, but he never invited Yvonne back. Gradually I began to feel sorry for Yvonne, and ultimately I regretted my animosity. Her life came to a tragic conclusion. She went to Latin America for cosmetic surgery; something went awry during the procedure; and she died on the table in the plastic surgeon's operating room.

16

Ominous Drumbeats

*T*he next year was extraordinary. We had our New Year's Eve party to usher in another year, and Harold commented the next morning "it was the best we've ever had." I didn't know if he was talking about the sex we had before he got out of bed or the party the night before.

Harold finished *The Inheritors*, and we took off for New York, where we experienced a heady moment in Times Square. A huge, blinking, neon billboard promoting his books lit up with the words "The World of Harold Robbins." Then an image of each book scrolled across, with the titles in bold color: *Never Love a Stranger*, *The Dream Merchants*, *A Stone for Danny Fisher*, *79 Park Avenue*, *Never Leave Me*, *Stiletto*, *The Carpetbaggers*, *Where Love Has Gone*, *The Adventurers*, and finally the forthcoming *The Inheritors*.

"Look at that," Harold excitedly, gazing up at the sign. "Can you believe it?"

I looked at him. He grew silent, his eyes fixed. What his true thoughts were, I don't know, but he didn't make light of the advertisement, as he was prone to do. He just stared, contemplatively, perhaps thinking of the long climb that had brought him to where he was, standing now on the summit of success. I threw my arms around him. "I'm so proud of you!" I cried.

His work to date was impressive for any writer, commercial or literary, and yet, Harold had not written half of the books he would complete in his lifetime.

When *The Inheritors* was published, it was another success; it hit the best seller list overnight. Harold dedicated the book to Paul Gitlin, but in an afterward he thanked Herbert M. Alexander, the one man at Simon & Schuster he held in high regard. He closed the afterward with brief paragraph: "And to my wife, Grace, without whose love, patience, and forbearing this would never have been written at all—turn down the sheets, lover. I'm coming home." How could I not be in love with this man?

The sixties and seventies were wonderful, even fantastic, years for Harold and me, but faint drumbeats of distress began to signal that all wasn't well in paradise. Feeling secure in my relationship, I did not recognize them at first, but in retrospect they were clearly there, and getting louder.

Harold did not drink alcohol when he was working, but he used cocaine to stay up the long hours. I questioned his use of the drug, but he flagged me away. "It's nothing, baby," he said casually. "It keeps my energy level on a high plateau. It's nothing to worry about. A lot of writers use it. Conan Doyle advocated it."

I shrugged. Drugs had become commonplace, not only in Hollywood and Beverly Hills, but in Europe, too. It was not unusual at all to see people of high station or celebrity status snorting cocaine at parties Yet I wondered if Harold had advanced to a new stage? Was his use of cocaine only confined to work?

The drumbeat grew louder when Harold appeared live on *The Tonight Show Starring Johnny Carson* before we left on our annual trek to France. The flood of morning and evening talk shows were marvelous free venues for writers to promote their books. Even though he still complained about not being paid for his appearances, he seldom passed up an opportunity to increase the sale of his books.

Harold's appearance showcased one of the few faux pas he ever committed regarding publicity. Once he was on stage it took him but a few moments to realize Johnny had not read *The Inheritors*; he hadn't even glossed over the dust jacket. If the average viewer didn't recognize it, I did: Harold was outraged. He considered talk show appearances to be work, not fun, a necessary part of the grueling schedule he entered into upon publication.

He became annoyed at Johnny's social pitter-patter, none of which was relevant to *The Inheritors*. As the interview continued, I saw an invisible steam rising about Harold, a boiler ready to explode. Suddenly he stood, looked sharply at Carson, and said, "Johnny, I'll tell you what. Read the book and I'll come back another time and we'll discuss it." With that he walked off the stage. Johnny was flabbergasted, and then he was livid.

The behavior was so unlike Harold's that I wondered if substance use had checked his natural charm. The press picked up the story and the gossip columns and scandal sheets had a field day with it. Harold wasn't embarrassed, but he realized Carson was too big and too important to be treated on the air in what NBC thought was "a shabby manner." He tried to low key it, commenting, "I wasn't there to waste my time on small talk, but maybe it would have been better had I excused myself during a commercial."

Maybe? It wasn't just that he walked out on Johnny Carson; he walked out on ten million viewers.

"I'll make up for it," shrugged Harold.

"Sure you will."

But he was determined to make amends with Johnny sometime in the future, although he had no specific plan. We went back to France and picked up where we had left off the year before. During a weekend cruise to Antibes, someone told me that Carson was staying at the Eden Roc; he was in town on a tennis holiday.

"Great," said Harold, "we'll have him over for cocktails on the *Gracara*."

"Yeah, you wish," I said skeptically.

He jotted down an invitation inviting Johnny for four o'clock cocktails and dispatched it to the hotel.

I don't think Harold really expected Johnny to show up after the hullabaloo concerning his rude departure from the show, and God knows I didn't. At three o'clock Harold said, "I guess we should dress up a little, huh?"

"Dress up for what?"

"For Johnny Carson."

"Harold, have you lost your mind?"

We dressed anyway, just in case. At precisely four o'clock, I saw a man meandering up the pier, checking the yachts. His walk, his very gestures were inimical—it was Johnny Carson, looking for the *Gracara*. I think I realized then, for the first time, that it was difficult for anyone to turn down a Harold Robbins invitation. He was at the height of his fame and a sought after commodity.

He gave Johnny what he called "the *Gracara* yacht treatment" and the wounds were healed, if any had really existed. Cocktails and lunch or dinner on the *Gracara* worked like a magic potion when it came to disposing of old riffs and making new friends. For sure it cured Johnny's hostility, for he came back again the next day.

The television production of *The Survivors* had started, though Harold had cautious expectations for it. He had never been a hands-on producer, but he'd been on enough sets to understand the potential foibles of remote location filming. "Get a bunch of sensitive artistes together and you've got a cauldron boiling trouble," he said.

Universal had decided to shoot all of the exterior scenes for the production in the South of France and a few of interior scenes at a studio in Nice, a few miles up the coast from Cannes. Although Harold's only writing contribution to the series had been his one-page synopsis, for which he was paid handsomely, he was immensely interested in the show's success. If it had a long run, he would make millions.

"If this thing takes off, we'll be in high cotton, Tiger," he said enthusiastically. "The world of Harold Robbins will transform into the universe of Harold Robbins!"

ABC Television had signed on for twenty-six segments; and true to Harold's vision MCA-Universal anticipated one of the most lavish productions ever assembled. (At the time, *The Survivors* was the most expensive series in television history.) Before filming had hardly started, however, we picked up rumors in Cannes that things in Nice were not going too well.

Harold moaned. "Shit, we'd better go over there and throw them a cocktail party. I want this production to have every chance possible for success!"

Cocktail parties, it seemed, had become Harold's solution for every conceivable problem.

Big productions, whether for television or the big screen, are complicated at best. The problems with The *Survivors* began with the scripts, always late, and ended with the bad blood that ran between one of the producers and Lana Turner. It didn't help that Lana and her husband Robert Eaton were no longer speaking to each other, even though they were living in the same hotel. Harold was aware of the Turner-Eaton estrangement and the script shortcomings, but neither of us was privy to the fighting that had been taking place behind the scenes between Lana and William Frye, the producer.

Harold made telephone arrangements for a party at the popular and famous Hotel Negresco, and we trekked to Nice like two innocent puppies, with Harold confident he could resolve any problems among cast and crew. My interest was seeing Lana again. Before the party I wondered aloud if she would actually come to the affair, realizing that Harold's optimism about having buried the hatchet with her was perhaps one-sided.

"Oh, she'll come," he said nonchalantly. "You can bank on it. She came to the bash at The Bistro, didn't she?"

She did come, as did the other stars, George Hamilton, Rossano Brazzi, Jan Michael Vincent, and Diana Muldaur. It was a typical Robbins bash, and, as usual, Lana was fabulously gorgeous. Although she kept a safe distance from Harold, she was gracious and kind to me, which I appreciated.

"You know, Grace," she said, "my life has been one of continual emergencies, many of my own making. One thing I've learned: it's best to let bygones be bygones. Yesterday's enemy may very well be today's friend and savior. It's just the nature of our business."

Under the glitz and glitter, however, there lay an air of doom, not just with Lana, with the entire company. Late in the evening Harold cornered me.

"All is not well," he said. He had a concerned expression on his face. "Was Lana nice to you?"

"Very," I said. "What's the problem?"

"Fisticuffs. Seems she literally slapped Frye's face this morning, and Frye had the audacity to slap her back," said Harold. He forced a laugh, but it was not in good humor.

"What does it all mean?" I asked, "What will happen now?"

"For one, it means Frye has a one-way ticket back to the states."

"And two?"

"Who knows?" he said. "They'll have to bring in a new producer with all the shit that entails, which is a lot of shit. Let's get the hell out of here before they blame their problems on me."

We did. (Years later we discovered that Lana started the fight to stop production to finally get even with Harold.)

Our French holiday flew by and at last Harold said woefully, "It's time to return to the adult world, Tiger. Time to make some money." Business was business, and Harold had a new story idea to pitch his publisher. I noticed he didn't say it was time to *write* a new book, just time to *pitch* its idea.

Leon Shimkin had gained control of Simon & Schuster, so putting a new deal together with a large advance was not a problem. Harold and Paul Gitlin met with the powers that were and a contract was drafted, signed, and a check issued. It was Harold's largest publishing deal to date: a one million dollars advance, spread over four payments. We were rich again.

The new book would be *The Betsy*, a saga of the ruthless competition in the automobile industry. Henry Ford II was the distant prototype for one of the main characters, although we later heard that Lee Iacocca and John DeLorean laid claim to the same privilege. Apparently Iacocca and DeLorean had heard or read Harold's oft repeated quote, "I never met a celebrity I couldn't turn into a best seller." Harold later commented about DeLorean, who became caught up in a scandal that ruined his reputation, "Damned lucky that I didn't pattern a character after him, the poor bastard."

Ford, whom Harold had known for years, was the real prototype. In fact, we always had a new Ford Town Car "on loan" from Henry, a "freebie," as Harold would say, "one of the perks of fame"; it was replaced annually with a beautifully furnished top-of-the-line car that Ford thought would render publicity dividends when Harold drove it. He seldom did; Harold was a Rolls Royce man and a sports car buff. When *The Betsy* was published two years later, the automobile tycoon's largesse was abruptly terminated. He sent someone from the Ford motor company to pick up the car and we never heard from Henry Ford again.

"Why did they take the Ford?" I asked.

Harold grinned. "Henry read the book."

But that was two years later.

After signing the contract for *The Betsy*, with a pocket full of money, Harold, as usual, was not ready to go to work immediately. We left New York for Beverly Hills. "It's party time," said Harold.

Meanwhile, *The Survivors* began its brief run on television. I was excited, but Harold wasn't. When the title credit rolled on the tube, I felt a shiver run up my spine: *Harold Robbins's The Survivors*. My enthusiasm was short lived; the series ran for fifteen disappointing weeks, hardly adhering to Harold's concept of a "visualized novel." It was preceded on Monday night by a nondescript show called *New People*—"Christ, what a lousy lead-in!" screeched Harold— and it had to compete with CBS's popular hits *Mayberry RFD* and *The Doris Day Show* and NBC's *Rowan and Martin's Laugh In*. The sets and costumes were sumptuous, but as Harold lamented, "You can spend all the money in the world, but if you don't have a fucking story, you're doomed. I gave them a hell of a storyline, but they just didn't develop it." He paused in thought, and then added, "I feel sorry for Lana though."

The minute we arrived in Beverly Hills in September, people began saying to me, "I can't wait for your New Year's Eve party this year!" We tried not to let anyone down, but the invitation list grew so large that our home in Beverly Hills couldn't accommodate our guests. We moved the party to the elegant Crystal Ballroom at the Beverly Hills Hotel, where the red velvet drapes and sparkling chandeliers blended perfectly with the holiday spirit.

As another year began, something happened that would change our relationship forever and ultimately destroy it—the drums were getting louder. Harold was anxious to get started on The *Betsy*. The project would require a great deal of research, much of it in Detroit. Times had changed since that first season in Le Cannet so many years before when Harold had written *The Adventurers*. In those days I thought it would always be the same when he was working, that he would be nearby, available if I needed him, and that I would always do my best not to disturb him.

Through the years, however, it had become apparent that Harold needed or wanted *total* privacy when he was researching and writing a book. After the office at the 9000 Building on the Sunset Strip, he had taken other sundry places. In Cannes he had purchased a small apartment adjacent to the Croisette. I didn't mind; he hated to work and when he did, he drove himself to the limit. Furthermore, he had grown testy with age, and perhaps with success. "Privacy" meant he could concentrate on the task at hand with no outside interference; it meant he didn't want me, Adréana, or anyone else around who might bother him, if only for a moment.

At least that's what I thought privacy meant, until we had an unexpected tête-a-tête standing in the hallway of our home. Harold had been packing his bags for a trip to Detroit. When he saw me walk by, he came to the door of the master bedroom and said: "Tiger, we've gotta talk."

"Okay," I said, and started to walk away, assuming he meant we would talk about whatever he had on his mind later.

"I mean now," he said, although there was no urgency in his voice. "Okay," I said again. "What do you want to talk about?"

He came into the hallway and cleared his throat. "You know, I've got a lot of research to do on this next book and I get distracted easily when I'm working."

"Yes, I know, Harold," which was true. I remembered once when he was working in Beverly Hills and someone rang the front doorbell. He leaped up from his typewriter and rushed to answer it, although we had a houseful of servants to do exactly that.

"Well, from now on I've gotta get away when I'm working not only when I'm researching but actually writing. I'll be gone for as long as six to eight weeks at a time, depending on how things are going."

"I understand," I said, although I wasn't sure I did. In the present house he had an office fairly well isolated from other activities, but if he thought it necessary, then I wouldn't try to stop him from ensconcing himself in a cabin in the mountains, which is what I envisioned.

"I'm not sure you *do* understand," he said, and before I could concur again, he dropped a bombshell. "You've gotta realize that when I'm gone that long, I'll need a woman."

I was not only stunned, I felt as if I had been punched in the stomach. I was speechless.

"It won't be anything serious," he continued, "but I gotta have sexual gratification, especially when I'm away from you."

He looked at me then as though I was supposed to take this revelation in stride. Again, before I could say anything, not that I knew what to say, he said, "These will be brief meaningless affairs. You know, sort of research."

Research! Never in my life had I been at such a loss for words. I was devastated. Maybe he thought I was nodding my approval, but if my head was moving it was from a spastic, nervous reaction.

"Now, darling, I don't believe in double standards," he continued. "While I'm gone, if you want a man to replace me, that's okay. I just don't want any star fucking. Getting involved with a celebrity spells trouble." He paused, and then added, "And no long-term affairs."

By this time my head felt as though it were hanging down to my knees. I was more than devastated; I was in a torture pit. Yet, no words poured forth. I was not angry (I would be later); I was in shock. Then Harold did the most unexpected gesture of all: he took me in his arms and kissed me as though he were trying to expend his last ounce of passion. I don't know if I responded or not. I don't think so.

"One more thing," he said, after releasing me from his embrace. "I don't want any secrets in our relationship, Tiger. We have to tell each other everything, down to the last detail. If I were to find out from someone else rather than you, I'd feel betrayed, and it would be the end of us."

I already felt betrayed, so I didn't respond. Not that I could have anyway; I was still speechless. I needed to get away from him, to another room, anywhere, and think this through.

We were still in that hallway, which seemed suddenly confining. Harold said softly, "I'm glad you understand, Tiger."

And he left, almost humming under his breath. I ran to the bedroom, buried my head in the pillows, and cried my eyes out. It didn't help; I was so confused, even terrified. Here was a man who had responded to my passion and I to his for years. We were two people who had been totally committed to each other with hardly ever an argument between us.

Suddenly out of the blue he was dictating that henceforth we would have an "open marriage." I couldn't breathe. I felt claustrophobic.

That night in bed Harold again took me in his arms. "I love you more than anything, Tiger," he whispered.

"I love you too, Harold," I said meekly.

He made love to me with mad, rare passion, as though he never again wanted to let me go. All I could think after he was spent and sleeping was, *What is going to happen to us?* I was totally confused.

The next day he left for Detroit. He was gone for several weeks, although he called me daily. Occasionally he would reveal that he had met so-and-so (always a woman), but I did my best not to inquire what was really happening. I didn't want to know. In Beverly Hills, to keep my sanity on an even keel and not to think too much about Harold and his "research," I joined several new charity groups; but I was terribly unhappy and most eager to return to our villa in France.

True to his word, when Harold returned to Beverly Hills he told me several stories I didn't want to hear, very clinically, with all the sordid details, as if he were a doctor describing his latest surgeries. I had nothing to tell him because nothing had happened. In the beginning, I'm sure I was distant, but gradually our relationship took on the same verve and excitement it had enjoyed before he left; Harold was passionate, considerate, and totally devoted to me, as he had been in the past. And then he would take off again. I was not happy during his absences; I was still very much in love with him and somehow I rationalized his extramarital endeavors as some kind of necessity. Above all, I wanted to continue being his muse and in every way help and stimulate his creativity.

17

High Stakes Parties

*F*rance beckoned. To say I was happy when we returned that year would be a misrepresentation, but I felt better. After Harold's "open marriage" proclamation, Beverly Hills had turned sour for me, depressing and unsettling. The fresh air of Le Cannet seemed to clear my mind, and God knows I needed it—I had a lot of thinking to do.

The Villa Grazia was as though we had never left it (we kept our staff year round), and Smasher was delighted with our return. Harold went to work on *The Betsey* in his office in Cannes. He had a new electric typewriter and he pounded away a few hours each morning, but not with the energy I remembered when he wrote *The Adventurers* in the villa attic. I tried my best to act, even believe, as if nothing had happened to our relationship, but in my heart I knew our lives had been changed forever, no matter how much I loved him. Harold seemed unchanged: pompous and arrogant on the one hand, but passionate and charming on the other. As I reflect these many years later, I suppose he relished what was an obvious coup—he could do anything he wanted within the framework of the rules (which he had set) and I would still be there when he needed me. Nothing had changed, yet everything had changed, which added continual confusion to my mix of emotions.

We picked up our social life where we had left off, primarily with the Khashoggis, although our circle of friends began to expand. Soraya and Adnan had fantastic parties on the *Nabila* that took on the same luster and legend ours had attained in Beverly Hills. Their buffets were incredible, featuring gigantic bowls of beluga and sevruga caviar from Russia and Iran, smoked salmon from Scotland, and always rare delicacies from Adnan's native Saudi Arabia. From us they had picked up a taste for Dom Pérignon, and they stocked an inexhaustible supply of it in their galley.

They had homes all over the world, but when they were not on the Riviera they spent most of their time in London; as a consequence, they usually had a native Brit as their guest of honor. Among the celebrities I met on their yacht were actors Joan Collins, Cary Grant, and Michael Caine, Broadway lyricist Leslie Bricusse, singer Shirley Bassey, and they had so many princes and princesses that to keep up with who they were or where they were from was impossible. Their guest list was always long, and there would be dozens upon dozens of beautiful, nubile, young women dressed in the latest haute couture and dripping with diamonds. Adnan introduced them as starlets and models, but many of them were local prostitutes that he had personally dressed for the occasion as though he were the costumer in a movie company.

It was on the *Nabila* that I created a scene Harold later incorporated into his novel *The Pirate*. At Harold's request I had learned to belly dance, and when Soraya had a birthday party for Adnan, Harold encouraged me to perform. We were on the top deck and Adnan was seated on a huge pile of satin pillows like a Saudi prince. I began my dance, building slowly to the erotic and sensual climax my instructor had taught me. I had a captive audience that apparently included the captain of the yacht, for suddenly the craft made an unexpectedly sharp, right angle turn that sent the boat into a list and me into a lurch that ultimately dropped me hard to my knees. As the captain tried to right the yacht, its yawing tossed me from port side to starboard like a sack of potatoes. I hit the railing, but it saved me from going overboard. I was slapped to the deck with such tremendous force that I thought I was going to break through and fall to the hold below. At first I was more concerned about having damaged my elaborate costume (which Harold had bought from a professional belly dancer in Tehran) than I was of myself. Then I realized I was really injured. A great swelling began on the left side of my body, between the ribcage and the hip, which soon turned bluish black. Fortunately I had no broken bones, I just didn't wear a bikini for several months.

Harold's books were published in Great Britain like clockwork exactly one year after United States publication. For *The Inheritors* he promised New English Library, his London publisher, that he would do something special to promote the book. As the publication date drew near he was devoid of ideas. "I don't know what I'm going to do," he complained, "but I'm not gonna do it in England."

I shrugged. "You'll think of something."

He did. He decided to use Adréana's birthday party to fulfill his obligation. "We'll have it on the *Gracara*," he said.

I agreed wholeheartedly; we spent half of our time on the yacht anyway. I began to draw up a list of all the children we knew and, of course, their parents.

"I don't want any of the fathers invited," interjected Harold. "You don't *what?*"

"No fathers," he continued. "Make it explicit in the invitation that only mothers are invited. No men."

I shrugged, which was becoming my most common reaction to his whims. It took me a while to word an invitation, but I did as Harold requested and the party summons went out to several dozen high-society mothers and their children who were either living or vacationing in Cannes. At the same time, Harold contacted his London publisher and asked them to invite the British press. Meanwhile, he rented a baby grand piano and had it hoisted from the pier to the top deck of our yacht.

On the day of the party, Harold informed me that the press would not be allowed onboard until he gave the signal. Everyone responded to our invitation and we had present a horde of children and their glamorous mothers. Aside from the *Gracara* crew, Harold was the only man on the yacht. It was a warm, almost breezeless day, and the press, including the paparazzi, was forced to watch the festivity from the wharf.

To my surprise the party was quite successful. No one complained about the lack of fathers. The children, as well as their mothers, had a ball, but the impatient, standby journalists and photographers were unimpressed. They kept calling from the wharf, "Harold, let us come on board!" or "Harold Robbins, Harold Robbins, we need photographs!"

Harold paid them no heed, but I did. They were driving me crazy. I went to Harold. "You've got to let them come aboard. You invited them and they've been standing for hours in the hot sun. Let's at least give them something to drink."

"At the appropriate time we will," Harold said with that naughty grin of his, "but first of all this is Adréana's birthday party and I want her and her friends and their mothers to have fun."

They did, for several hours; finally Harold thought it was time to deal with the journalists and photographers. He asked all the exquisitely dressed mothers to join him at the piano, sorting them out equally on each side, placing himself in the middle, and then he told me to let the press come aboard.

Our crew threw down the gangplank and the press boarded in a steaming, sweating, thirsty rush. They found Harold and the beautiful mothers singing

"Happy Birthday!" Camera bulbs flashed a thousand times as Harold gathered the nearest women ever closer, kissing them on the cheek, switching from left to right and right to left, rotating the women, until at last, satisfied, he opened the bar to the journalist and photographers.

The next day pictures of Harold and all the beautiful women guests were splashed across the front page of virtually every newspaper in Europe. It was a publicity man's dream come true. Each headline was a variation on "Harold Robbins—What a life! Better than his books!"

"Hey, Tiger, said Harold, "why don't we take the *Gracara* down to Sicily and surprise your relatives."

We were breakfasting at Villa Grazia. I was elated at his suggestion. Six years had lapsed since I was last there, when I had promised my Uncle Andrea I would one day return with his favorite author. This time I would not only have Harold with me, but Adréana, too.

We left that afternoon, the American flag flying from our mast, and cruised quietly down the shin of the Italian boot. As the crow flies, it was hardly a two-day cruise, but we hugged the Italian coast before turning due south at Naples. It took us seven leisurely days.

I doubt if Garibaldi, when he sailed into Marsala harbor with two thousand soldiers to conquer Sicily during the Risorgimento, received more attention than we did. A yacht flying an American flag was more than a rarity in 1970s Sicily, and townspeople began to gather on the wharves to see who was aboard. By the time we pulled into port, a huge crowd had gathered; they were throwing flowers and offering gifts of fruit baskets and Marsala wine. It was exciting, but when I surveyed the crowd I saw none of my family.

People were quizzing us all at once, to the degree that I could not understand them. Then a dashing-looking gentleman edged close to the yacht and called out my name; he remembered me from my visit years before. He volunteered to take me to a telephone, where I could call my uncle.

"Go with him," said Harold. `Let's get this show on the road!"

I was helped off the yacht and onto the quay. The man had a tiny Vespa that was hardly large enough for him, much less for the two of us. Nevertheless, I hopped on behind him and we wound through the cobblestone streets to a pay telephone. I dialed and Uncle Andrea answered.

"Oh my god!" he said. "Grazia, I've been waiting here all this long while, waiting for this call! Is your husband with you?"

"Yes, and our daughter, too!"

"Oh, my god," he moaned. "At last! At long last!"

His sincerity was so touching that I almost cried. I felt terribly guilty I had made him wait six years. I hopped back on the Vespa behind my gallant knight and we took off, retracing our path back to the yacht.

Soon, Harold, Adréana, and I were gathered with the entire family at Uncle Andrea's home. The clan had grown since my last visit and not just through babies. I had more cousins than I had seen before, and then second cousins, and third cousins. The house could hardly hold us all. Finally, I realized it was Harold, the famous American writer, rather than Adréana or me, who was attracting them.

Time was not a problem for the Robbins family, but in two weeks we packed in more sightseeing, dining, and drinking than most people would do in two years. Every night we joined some branch of the family at a charming Marsala restaurant, where special arrangements had been made to serve the very best Sicilian food and always the famous Marsala wines.

Never one to penny pinch or avoid paying a bill, Harold still didn't spend a lira. My family members were too proud to let him. He always tried, but to no avail. He returned the favor by inviting everyone aboard the *Gracara* for a Robbins luncheon party and a cruise around the island.

All in all, it was a memorable return for me to my mother's home country. I hated to leave, but after a couple of weeks we again sailed away, heading back to France, but only for a brief stay. "I haven't done enough research to be able to finish *The Betsy*," Harold announced, and with that we were once again off to America.

After a brief reunion in New York with Paul and Zelda Gitlin, we returned to California, from where Harold immediately took off to continue his "research." That I knew he was philandering while he was away bothered me immensely, but once he returned it did not have a lasting effect on our relationship, at least not yet. I was in love with him, very forgiving, and never once did he act as though any of his extramarital affairs had been anything more than what he claimed they were, "just a piece of ass to satisfy my sexual needs when I'm away from you, darling."

Once again I threw myself into charity fund-raising, saw my friends, and answered the same questions with the same pat answers over and over again.

"Where's Harold?"

"Oh, he's off researching his next novel."

"What's it going to be about this time? Who is he going to base it on?"

"Oh, you'll see soon enough," I answered coyly.

Harold's comment to a newspaper columnist had made his roman á clef method of writing a titillating conversation piece: "I write under the guise of fiction to protect the guilty."

I took care of Adréana, attended charity functions, and planned parties around the days I knew with certainty Harold would be home, if only briefly: Halloween, Thanksgiving, Christmas, and of course New Year's. One season seemed to mesh into another, and our lives went on as if there were no extraneous interferences.

The guest list for our parties had grown into a Who's Who of Hollywood personalities, and our waiting list was a mile long. At one of our parties we had dressed the swimming pool to look like a tropical lagoon, and a canoe filled with exotic fruit floated on the water. For whatever reason, Shelley Winters decided to go boating. Before I knew it, she was paddling away, throwing fruit at bystanders, and singing a song in Italian. Fortunately, she didn't sink.

That was the party where Harold injected a bit of his own creativity. "Why don't we hire a bunch of beautiful masseuses and handsome masseurs," he said, "and let everyone who gets tired have a foot massage?"

I wasn't certain it was such a good idea, thinking perhaps feet weren't the only thing he had in mind to get massaged. But we did it and it worked beautifully. Soon, everyone seemed to be in bare feet, and the masseuses probably did more massages than they'd done during the entire past year. Apparently some guests got too tipsy to remember where they left their shoes, for the next morning several pairs were found in the aftermath debris of the party.

At the same party, while Shelley was paddling her canoe and the masseuses and masseurs were rehabilitating tired feet, British actor Laurence Harvey got married, precisely at midnight. A rabbi performed the service, and when it was completed Larry lifted his daughter Domino into the air and exclaimed, "My darling, you are no longer a bastard child!"

Larry's favorite wine was Pouilly-Fuissé, and he drank bottles of it. A couple of years later, when he was dying of stomach cancer, I visited him in his hospital room. He was very ill but undaunted.

"Is there anything I can do for you?" I asked.

"Yes," he said, watering at the mouth. "You can bring me a couple of bottles of Pouilly-Fuissé.

"But Larry," I protested, "are you sure the doctors will allow you to drink alcohol?"

"Of course the doctors won't allow me to drink alcohol!" he exclaimed. "But for God's sake I'm dying, so who cares?"

The next time I visited him I sneaked in a couple of bottles of his favorite beverage. He was delighted; he immediately uncorked one and shared a secret sip with me.

Unfortunately, Larry died at his home in Hampstead outside of London just a few weeks later. He was only forty-five.

When Adnan and Soraya Khashoggi visited us in Beverly Hills, Adnan asked Harold if we might have a party and invite some famous movie stars.

"Of course," said Harold, and he put in a call to the reliable Gene Schwam, his publicist.

We had a grand party in the Kashoggis honor, attended by a host of stars from motion pictures and television. Unfortunately, Adnan had grown up watching movies that had been made in the thirties, forties, and fifties. He didn't know Jack Nicholson from Warren Beatty or Jane Fonda from Faye Dunaway. He wanted stars! Throughout the evening he kept cornering Harold, "Is Clark coming?"

"Clark who?" asked Harold.

"Clark Gable."

"No, Adnan," said Harold. "Unfortunately Clark was unavailable for tonight's party. Very unavailable."

Adnan sighed, but he didn't give up. A little later he cornered Harold again. "Where is James?" he asked hopefully. "Will he be here?"

"James who?"

"Cagney."

"Oh, Jimmy's back East, Adnan, but he sent his regards to you. He told me to say hello on his behalf."

And later, "Is Humphrey Bogart coming, Harold?"

"He's already here, Adnan. I saw him cut by the pool with Errol Flynn just a moment ago. But you'd better catch them before they leave. I think they have a second engagement to attend."

Harold never told Adnan that the stars he wanted to meet were either dead or long since retired from the entertainment world. It made little difference, for the next morning Adnan was certain he had talked at length with Bogart, who had died in 1956.

Unlike Harold's ploy with the press at Adréana's birthday party on the *Gracara*, we always invited members of the Hollywood press to our California parties and treated them with respect and courtesy. Invariably they requested a guest list to run in their stories and columns the next day. One time Harold got tired of the requests and decided to make up a special guest list, one that was almost totally fictitious. He began jotting names in a registration book, the Duchess of so-and-so, Baron von whomever. It was great fun for him, and all day long before the party he kept coming up with new names, each more farfetched than the one before: His Honorable Milton Glubber, the Duke of Arlington; Count Egore Stoltz, fourth cousin of Czar Niklas Romanoff II. He would come up with a new idea and rush to write it down, laughing."Princess Carlotta von Havenhurst de Rothschild, grandniece of Queen Kathryn Anne Hiperia of Slovakia. That'll get them. It's a great name!"

By party time he had registered about thirty absurd names in the book, each time with a great horselaugh. I said, "I know you've been having lots of fun, Harold, but I don't think you can really give these names to the press."

His face fell. "Why not?"

"If they find out you've misled them, they'll be upset and won't come to any more of our parties."

"Bullshit!" said Harold "Ten to one they'll never know the difference. Not one of them."

I didn't take his bet. Needless to say, he left the book out for press perusal. Not one crazy name was questioned.

Harold was a compulsory gambler, which is not to say that he was a bad gambler. No, he was a good gambler, very good and very smart; one of the few I ever saw who won as often as he lost. I loved gambling, too, but I limited it to random casino visits in Monaco, and during infrequent trips to Las Vegas. Not so Harold. After we moved to 905 North Beverly Drive, he turned one of Gloria Swanson's former salon parlor's into a private gaming club replete with a slot machine, roulette wheel, craps and blackjack tables—the works.

Occasionally at a party some of the men (and often a woman or two) would resort to gambling at one game or another, small time stuff, betting a few dollars if not just the change in their pockets. One night some of the more serious fellows—a trio of heavyweight television stars—wanted to gamble higher stakes. Never one to pass up fortune's opportunity, Harold chose, naturally, to be the banker. After all, it was his casino. The gamblers were Ernest Borgnine, Vince Edwards, and Bob Newhart, a sailor, a doctor, and a funny man respectively in their big television hits. By midnight they'd lost collectively over $20,000 to Harold.

Our other guests had departed, and it was time for me to follow suit, if for no other reason than to call a halt to the illegal gambling. "Goodnight all," I told them. "I'm going to bed."

"Goodnight, Grace."

"Are you coming soon, Harold?" I asked.

He followed me out of his casino, whispering in my ear that he would be up to our bedroom very shortly.

I went to bed. I woke up a couple of times and could still hear the men downstairs in the casino, cursing, groaning, and laughing intermittently, but mostly cursing. I sighed and went back to sleep.

When Harold finally came to bed the first light of day was sifting through the curtains. He flopped down on the side of the bed, exhausted. I lifted my head and sleepily squinted my eyes.

"Don't tell me you gambled all night?" I said.

"Gambling? It wasn't gambling. I had to cheat them!"

I bolted to a sitting position, suddenly awake and wide-eyed. "Cheat them!" I cried. "Surely you didn't cheat you friends?"

"I swear to god, darling," said Harold. "Those guys are such lousy gamblers that I had to cheat in order for them to win their fucking money back!"

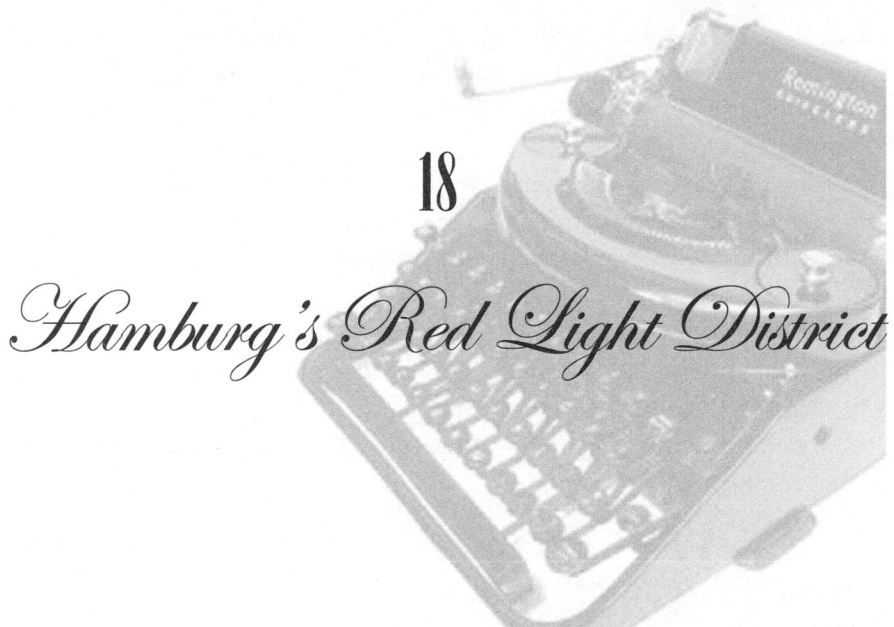

18

Hamburg's Red Light District

*P*aul Gitlin was calling. Leon Shimkin was calling. Harold's editor at Simon & Schuster was calling. As usual, Harold was behind on his book—months behind. He rented a small apartment in Westwood, moved in his electric typewriter, and hit the keyboard with a spurt of energy that reminded me of the old days. I checked on him periodically, usually by phone. I seldom went by to see him for fear of catching him in the "act of research." In truth it seemed to be actual work for a change, and one afternoon when I was resting in the master bedroom, the one Harold claimed was the trysting place of Gloria Swanson and Joseph Kennedy, Harold burst in and said, "Let's make love, Tiger!"

"What?"

"Let's make love and then go celebrate. I just posted the final manuscript of *The Betsy* to the Big Apple!"

"I'm sure Henry Ford will be pleased," I laughed. Little did I realize how terribly displeased he actually would be.

We made love, and then we wined and dined—not just that one evening but for several weeks of similar evenings—at all the hot celebrity spots Beverly Hills, Santa Monica, and Hollywood were famous for. Harold seemed to be Harold again. Then we boarded an airplane for a brief stay in New York, prior to making our annual pilgrimage to Europe.

The novel was due for publication in late spring, and one day Harold brought the galley proofs to our hotel. 'Take a look at this," he said, which was a first, since he was already thinking about his next book and had never once asked me to look at galleys. For that matter, Harold seldom looked at proofs himself; he left it in the hands of his editor. I usually saw the book in its first edition hardback.

I took the pages and began to read. I didn't have to read far to realize why Harold had given the proofs to me. The dedication read: "This book is dedicated with love to my wife, Grace, for whom the name—and the word were created."

Tears came to my eyes. I looked at Harold; he had that silly grin on his face, the one that always made me go aflutter inside. I threw my arms around him. "Oh thank you, darling!"

"Anything for my, Tiger," he whispered. "You're my muse, darling, and don't ever forget it."

"I won't."

"You sure?"

"I'm sure."

"Positive?"

"I'm positive," I whispered, but of course I wasn't.

The next day we were airborne for the Riviera.

Harold's next book would be *The Pirate*; his next "victim" would be Adnan Khashoggi. "Victim" is a misnomer; with the exceptions of Lana Turner and Henry Ford II, every so called victim I knew of, and many who imagined they were, was delighted to be named the archetype for one of Harold's fictional characters. Rumor had it that Howard Hughes had gloated for months after the success of *The Carpetbaggers*, although Harold later admitted that Jonas Cord was modeled more on William Lear of Learjet fame than on Hughes. Regardless, I was pleased Adnan had been targeted, as I knew Adnan would be pleased, too. I remembered that gold coin spinning on the marble floor of the *Nabila*. Besides, Harold's research might keep him closer to home. We had hardly entered our villa when Harold encouraged me to call Soraya.

The timing was perfect. Adnan was preparing to throw a yacht party in celebration of Soraya's birthday. If Harold spent buckets of money on our social life, Adnan spent barrels; but then for all of Harold's incoming millions, they were but a drop compared to Adnan's deluge. As Adnan's business empire expanded, so did the number of his homes—in Kenya, Paris, Cannes, the Canary Islands, Madrid, Marbella, Rome, Jeddah, Riyadh, Beirut, Monte Carlo, and Paris, but on the *Nabila* was where he felt most comfortable.

The Khashoggis were a fun but odd couple. Adnan usually displayed a calm, even stoic, demeanor, masking his feelings regardless of the circumstances; Soraya was his opposite, emotional, fiery, and quick to lose her temper. When we arrived at their party on a glorious starlit Mediterranean evening, we were unaware the host and hostess were in the midst of one of their frequent marital squabbles.

Hundreds of people were present. An orchestra provided music, the notes wafting in the cool night. At a signal from Adnan, the musicians began to play a special number dedicated to Soraya. Adnan approached her with a thin smile, gently took her hand, and led her to the dance floor. They began to dance, with the rest of us circled around. I thought it was so romantic, and when the music paused Adnan, presented her with an elegantly wrapped jewelry box.

All eyes were on them as Soraya opened her present. The box contained an absolutely gorgeous diamond necklace that must have cost Adnan a million dollars. He beamed; Soraya did not. She suddenly flung the priceless gift across the deck, no doubt aiming for the harbor waters. A collective gasp issued from the guests, but fortunately the necklace did not go overboard. Adnan simply shrugged and motioned for the musicians to begin anew.

During the course of the night the reason for Soraya's hostility was lost in the good spirits of the party, although not on Harold. Like my belly dancing episode of the year before, he used the necklace incident in *The Pirate*.

Soraya and Adnan stayed together many years, but it seemed inevitable their marriage would eventually fall apart. They argued constantly, although until the very end they always made up. Like Harold, Adnan had his rules of the sex game; unlike me, Soraya had hers too. Each had numerous affairs outside of their marriage, but unlike Harold with me, especially Harold, they didn't tell each other.

Some of their entanglements were utterly comic, at least in retrospect. Soraya's eyes roved as much as Adnan's, and while he was away on business, which was often, she likely had a gorgeous young man as her temporary companion on the *Nabila*. Soraya was a stunningly beautiful woman, and handsome young men, hungry for both sex and money, lusted after her.

Often, however, Adnan returned from his business ventures earlier than expected (probably by design), giving Soraya only a few minutes' notice to dispose of her present lover. For all of the Khashoggi wealth, she seldom had a franc or pound or dollar in cash aboard the *Nabila*. Frantic for emergency help, she would telephone me.

"Grace, Grace, I need some money, fast! Please, can you hurry, darling? Adnan will be here at any moment!"

I learned the routine quickly, but sometimes I was at our villa rather than our yacht, so it wasn't always easy to expedite the task. I would drive madly down the narrow road from Le Cannet to Cannes and then to the port, always wondering why Soraya couldn't just send her paramour on his way without payment, for surely he had received riches already beyond his wildest dreams. But that wasn't Soraya's modus operandi: she wanted the young lover out of her life, and thus provided him with enough money to leave town by train or plane, to what destination she did not care, as long as it was fast. I always made it just in the nick of time, and was often there to welcome the return of Adnan in the wake of Soraya's lover's hasty departure. Secretly Soraya would describe to me in detail how sexy her lover had been and how much she had enjoyed him. "This one went on and on and on; he just never seemed to come," she would say dreamily. "He never stopped making love to me, darling! Never! Oh, it was wonderful!"

Neither Adnan nor Soraya was stupid; they knew of each other's infidelities, although not to the degree that Harold felt "open marriage" couples should know. In other words, they didn't tell each other, but the knowledge was there, if only intuitively.

Not long after the Khashoggis broke up, Harold and I were having dinner at Moulin de Mougins, the famous restaurant that was patronized more than any other by celebrities during the Cannes Film Festival. Soraya tracked us down there. I had not seen her in a while and I was shocked. Compared to her former stylish self—always immaculately coiffed and richly dressed—she appeared disheveled and disoriented.

"Do you know any Muslims?" she asked.

Harold and I looked at each other. Off hand, the only Muslim we knew was Adnan.

"How about your husband?" said Harold.

"Oh god, Harold, I can't go to him!" She slapped some papers on our table. "Look at this!" she said. "He's getting rid of me!"

We looked; they were divorce papers.

"Oh, Soraya," I said sincerely. "I'm so sorry."

"I need three Muslims to sign this document," she continued.

Apparently Islamic law (Adnan had filed for divorce in Saudi Arabia) required each party to attach three authentic Muslim signatures to the divorce decree. Eventually she found her Muslims and the divorce was settled, temporarily. Soraya received only a modest sum. Then she counter sued in Britain, and won. The press said the settlement was the largest in history: one billion pounds or $1,874 million dollars. The true amount was considerably less.

That year we renewed our friendship with Frederick Loewe, whom Harold had known for years. I had not talked to him since after the performance in Rome of *My Fair Lady*.

Fritzi was a colorful eccentric. The composer (with his partner Alan J. Lerner) of other world-renowned classics, such as *Camelot*, *Gigi*, *Paint Your Wagon*, and *Brigadoon*, had retired to Cannes and Palm Springs and was splitting his time—as we were—between France and Beverly Hills.

A heart attack had prompted Fritzi's retirement, although it had not slowed him down. In his midseventies, he was still full of energy. He had never been married, but he had a timeless appreciation of beautiful women and was constantly on the lookout for one that would spend some time with him, if not the rest of his life, at least for one night. Fritzi was a strange-looking man for a wannabe Adonis: short, stocky, with a leonine mop of hair on an overly large head. He had apparently thrown away his suits because he invariably wore short-sleeve shirts with only one pocket and Bavarian-style short pants. He had a suite at the Carlton Hotel and a rented 100-foot yacht in the harbor named *The Seagull*.

A potential movie deal for one of Harold's books surfaced unexpectedly with Polygram, then headquartered in Germany. At lunch aboard the *Seagull*, we told Fritzi we were going away for a few days.

"Where are you going?" he asked.

"Hamburg, Germany," said Harold.

"I have to go with you," responded Fritzi excitedly, "because I was conceived in that gloomy city." And then he added, "And my birthday is coming up!"

"Pack your bags," said Harold.

When we arrived in Hamburg, we discovered that *My Fair Lady* was being performed in a local theater. My first reaction was fear that Fritzi would find the German translation as abominable as he had the Italian. I should not have been concerned. He was thrilled by it, perhaps more because his name was billed on the marquee in the city of his birth than he was impressed by the quality of the production.

We decided to honor Fritzi with a party at our hotel. We invited the entire cast and crew of the production without knowing a soul of them. I think Fritzi was nervous that no one would show up. Harold didn't give a damn if they did or not, telling him, "Don't worry, Fritzi, if they don't come, others will. Someone always shows up at a Harold Robbins party, even when they're not invited."

To Fritzi's relief and delight the entire cast and crew arrived after the performance to celebrate the man who had provided them with what one member called "such heavenly melodies." Fritzi beamed, and then he set his eyes on one of the young would-be stars of tomorrow, a young *Fraulein* he trailed after until the wee hours of the morning.

Although Fritzi grew up in Vienna, he knew his birth city intimately, especially the sex clubs on Reeperbahn Strasse, its infamous red light district.

When he suggested that we make the rounds with him, Harold did not take time to consult me. "Let's go!" he said, and we went.

The Reeperbahn was in St. Pauli, a city quarter near the harbor that seemed quite incompatibly named considering its reputation for wicked behavior. The erotic acts on stage were explicit, as I knew they would be, but I was surprised at the blatant activity and stark nudity of the waitresses, who bounded about, hopping in the laps of willing men. Fritzi was not only willing, but seemingly well known, as though he was a regular patron of the clubs.

At one point, while a hot and heavy sex act was being performed on the cabaret stage, Fritzi was trying to outdo it with a naked waitress who was squirming delightedly on his lap. When Fritzi whispered something in her ear, she looked surprised, and said, "Oh, but I can't, Leibling. My husband would kill me."

"And where's your husband?" asked Fritzi.

She pointed to the couple on the stage that was engaged in a very explicit sex act. "Why that's him, up there on the stage!" she cried.

Fritzi stared at the act for a moment, and then he said, "Your husband has great stage presence."

At that very moment the good-looking young man suddenly lost his "presence." Something went down on stage and boos went up in the audience.

The girl in Fritzi's lap said, "If you want him to really perform, stand and applaud him. The louder the applause, the better his performance."

Fritzi stood and began to applaud, gesturing for us to copy him. We followed suit, clapping our hands, and then others in the audience did the same thing. I felt a little ridiculous, but suddenly the young man's penis began to rise, and he regained his sexual momentum.

We laughed and sat down, but the instant the applause subsided, the man lost his erection again. We stood again and applauded, and that's the way it went until the man reached his climax, up and down, up and down, for both the audience and the performer.

After the show was finished Fritzi asked the girl in his lap, "What does he do at home when there's not an audience, when he's just with you?"

"It's embarrassing," said the girl.

Fritzi's face beamed with a sudden idea. "I know just the thing," he said without further explanation.

The next day he actually bought an "applause" record and a phonograph and had them delivered to the girl and her husband. We thought he was joking, but he wasn't.

Fritzi had a loyal and efficient German crew aboard the *Seagull* that catered to his every need. A couple of them would go out each morning to scour the beach for available girls to join Fritzi for lunch on the yacht. He never ate by himself.

Occasionally he had a formal lunch, inviting friends such as Harold and me to join him and his bevy of girls. He always had ten guests—not nine, not eleven, but ten, always—at a sit-down affair, and his chef served the best grilled fish in the harbor, with fresh vegetables and a crisp salad.

Fritzi considered himself a cheese gourmand, and at each function he took pride in presenting his cheese tray personally. It was one of the few really formal aspects of his gatherings, made dramatic by his recitation of each cheese as he laid the tray before his guests. It was actually a lecture, although quite educational for those not in the know, for he always instructed his audience on the quality of each cheese, its age, how and with what to eat it. He compared his cheese to women.

"We will start with this delight," he would say, gently taking a wedge from the tray. He would then sniff it and say, "It is like a sixteen-year-old girl."

Everyone then would follow his lead, taking a piece of cheese and sniffing it before eating it. Then Fritzi would proceed to a different variety.

"Now, this one"—sniff, sniff—"ah, she is a twenty-one-year-old."

Again, we smelled and ate, gradually working our way up to a mature, gorgeous, very ripe cheese.

Harold and I were invited often and therefore the cheese ritual became tedious for us, if not boring. One weekend at the Cannes marketplace, Harold found two cheese wedges made of rubber. "Look at these," he said. "Don't they look real?" I looked; the bogus cheeses looked absolutely authentic. Harold laughed mischievously under his breath and bought them, "The next time Fritzi invites us to his yacht, we're gonna have a little fun."

We didn't have to wait long. A few days later Fritzi called, and the following Sunday, a truly glorious day, we made our way to the *Seagull* with the rubber cheese wedges wrapped in market paper. Fritzi and his guests were in good spirits. After a few salutations Harold slipped away and took the cheese below deck to the galley. He explained his ploy and asked the kitchen crew to include the two fakes on the day's cheese tray. They were delighted to conspire with him.

When he returned to the top deck, I asked Harold what he had done with the cheeses. He grinned. "They're gonna be front and center on Frtizi's tray. I told the chef you brought them from Sicily."

I gulped. "You told him that *I* brought the cheese?"

"Sure," grinned Harold. "You're Sicilian. They're Sicilian cheese. It makes sense."

I was nervous to begin with, and now perturbed. The cheese ritual was so important to Fritzi that I was afraid he might really become upset, even humiliated. At an opportune moment I slipped back to the galley to cancel Harold's prank, but the cook and crew wouldn't hear of it. "No, no, we serve, we serve!" They too were bored with the usual routine and they begged me to let them go forth with the phony cheese.

I sighed. *Well,* I thought, *c'est la vie.*

A few minutes later the tray was delivered. I held my breath as the servant whispered in Fritzi's ear. His face beamed and he immediately stood up. I was seated directly opposite him at the other end of the table. He looked at me with his bright, blue eyes and smiled with pleasure.

"I take pride in my cheese tray," said Fritzi, "but today I have extra pride because Grace has added two rare and special cheeses from her native Sicily to our menu." He was very serious, using the soft *a* of the French pronunciation of my name, saying "Grahss." I began to squirm because I knew I was doomed.

With that, he picked up a knife and began to slice the Sicilian cheese, or rather *try* to slice it. As he carved here, and then there, punched and poked, perspiration began to bead on his forehead. Simultaneously I slipped a little deeper into my chair.

"Good Sicilian cheese is harder than Italian parmesan," said Harold, biting his lip.

"Yes, I can see," said Fritzi.

He tried again, stabbing, punching, poking, and finally swinging the cheese knife like a hatchet. *Why isn't it squeaking?* I asked myself. Nothing happened as Fritzi poked and sawed, and then the rubber did let out a shrill, piercing squeak. Fritzi froze.

"Grahss!" he suddenly sneered, and my name sounded like a four-letter word. He then grabbed the bogus cheese and actually flung it at me. It bounced off my shoulder like a tennis ball hitting a brick wall and rebounded back to Fritzi, almost hitting him in the face.

Harold and eight guests laughed uproariously; Fritzi and I did not. The party went on, but Fritzi continued glum. When Harold and I left, I knew I had been banned from the *Seagull,* probably forever. Harold was more optimistic: "Don't worry about it, Tiger. He'll cool his heels for a couple of weeks, and then he'll call. Count on it."

Two weeks later Fritzi telephoned. "I need ten people for lunch," he said, "but so far I only have eight people. Would you and Harold please join me?"

When Harold finished *The Pirate,* and we returned to California, via New York City. The book came out in the spring; it was his twelfth consecutive best seller. He dedicated it to Adréana, who was approaching her tenth birthday, and to

Caryn, who was quickly becoming a young, albeit troubled, woman. Time was flying by.

Warner Bros. bought the film rights to *The Pirate*, and when they finally went into production in France on a four-hour television movie, they requested Harold's presence during the Christmas holidays in case the screenwriters ran into problems. Harold had begun to look forward to our New Year's Eve parties with such excitement that the idea of not having one was a downer for him.

I looked at Harold's downcast face. "Why don't we have the party in September, before we leave for Europe?" I suggested.

His eyes flashed with excitement. "That's a terrific idea," he said, "And you know what? I can promote *The Pirate* at the same time."

What he meant by that remark I didn't understand until later. It was one of the few parties I did not plan. It was held on Warner Brothers' huge Sound Stage One at the Burbank Studios. It was a bash, and true to his word, Harold certainly promoted *The Pirate*. Huge klieg lights were set outside the sound stage, which gave the effect of a world premiere. A camel stood languidly chewing its cud on the fringe of the red carpet that led to the entrance. The animal was appropriately named Clyde, and it took the festivity in stride.

Inside the decorations scavenged from the Warner Bros. property department displayed a lavish make-believe Arabian Nights world, hinting at the background of Harold's protagonist in the novel. The sound-stage floor was covered with Persian rugs and piles of Persian pillows. An oil derrick rose from the middle of the gigantic cocktail bar. Belly dancers danced, fortunetellers told lies, and harem girls sashayed erotically among the guests. Bedouin desert tents were stationed throughout the stage, resting places and rendezvous points for the thousand guests. At precisely midnight, as if to remind the guests that we were symbolically celebrating the arrival of a new year, a giant mock-up of the book cover descended from the ceiling.

When we returned from Europe, we decided to buy our own home in Beverly Hills. Harold began scouting, much as he had done on the French Riviera years before when we purchased Villa Grazia. He found a spectacular mansion in the hills on ritzy Beverly Estates Drive. Ironically, the owner was Stephen Crane, a successful restaurateur who had not only been one of Lana Turner's husbands but was also the father of Lana's daughter Cheryl, around whom the Stompanato scandal had swirled.

Harold bought the house for around a million dollars, and I set about having it renovated and refurbished. We probably bought the house too quickly, for after the deal was done, there were several things neither of us liked. In particular, Harold hated the reflecting swimming pool. "I like blue," he complained, "not black." In fact, it was a bad luck house, although our misfortunes while we lived there did not start immediately.

The changes we made in the house were much more of a reconstruction than a renovation, and it took months to complete. Life did not slow down, however, nor did our imaginations. For Harold's sixtieth birthday celebration I came up with the idea of having a "hard hat" party at our future home, which still had bare walls and floors. Each guest was given a hard hat as he or she entered the house, including our guest of honor, Mayor Tom Bradley. I decorated the interior with construction equipment and materials—hammers, screwdrivers, saws, electrical cords, and the like, and wheelbarrows filled with crudités. Sawdust was strewn on the floors. I hired four Chippendales dancers to entertain the ladies. They followed them from empty room to empty room. Who doesn't love a half-naked man in a hard hat!

That year when we were in France, Harold began to complain about a swelling in his groin area. By the time we returned to the States, it had grown more intense. It was September, the time of year I usually began planning our annual New Year's Eve party. Our mindset had always been to outdo the party of the previous year, but this time my imagination was exhausted. After the fabulous Thousand and One Arabian Nights at Warner's the year before, which had been our eleventh straight party, I thought, *Well, maybe we should forget it this year and attend other people's parties*. I mentioned dropping the party to Harold.

His face screwed up. "Oh, nooooo!" he exclaimed. "We've got to have the party. It's become a tradition! Now, do me a favor and call my fucking doctor."

After an examination, Harold's doctor diagnosed a hernia and recommended an immediate operation. Harold grunted with displeasure at the idea, but reluctantly shrugged his approval, knowing he had to do it. He was a man of unlimited energy and he hated to be confined anywhere for any length of time. Following the surgery, he had to spend several miserable days recuperating. I virtually lived in the hospital suite with him, going home only to check on Adréana or to sleep at night. One morning when I arrived at his room, his mood was in a high spirit. He had a big grin on his face. "Grace, I've got it," he said.

"Got what?"

"The idea for our party!"

I had been more concerned with his health than I had been with the party, so my mind was still blank of ideas. "Well, what is it?" I asked.

"We'll get twelve beautiful girls, one for each month of the year," he said enthusiastically, "and we'll have them pose for calendar photographs, you know, real sexy, and then we'll give the calendars to our guests as New Year's gifts, and we'll have all of the girls present at the party."

It wasn't a bad idea, although I had reservations. "Where do you plan on getting the girls?" I asked.

"Don't worry about it, darling," he said. I could see ideas dancing in his mind. "We'll get Pasqual to cast the calendar girls and we'll get Joe Cassini to choreograph the thing."

They were friends of ours. Pasqual had a photography school and Cassini was a dance choreographer. The idea of Pasqual having a casting session with his innumerable models made sense, but what Joe would choreograph, I had no idea. I looked at Harold. He was ecstatic, thinking no doubt about the casting sessions.

"Okay," I said, and since I had once been a casting director at Grey Advertising, I added, "I'll help you with the casting."

Harold frowned, as if it would be an imposition—whether on him or on me, I wasn't sure. "That won't be necessary, darling." He may have discerned my own frown, because he quickly added, "But of course you can sit in on the sessions if you want to."

We discussed the idea for a minute more, and then I left to check on Adréana. As I was exiting the suite, Harold called out, "But remember, Grace, I am going to choose the girls!"

"Right," I said.

When he was out of the hospital and ambulatory, Harold began to spend a considerable amount of time at Pasqual's studio, so much time that one would have thought he was casting all three volumes of Gibbons's *The History of the Decline and Fall of the Roman Empire.*

One morning when he was leaving the house, I said, "Wait up, Harold. I think I'll go over to the studio with you and see how the casting for the party is coming along."

I expected him to find a reason why I shouldn't go, but he didn't. "Okay," he said. "Come on, let's go!"

To my surprise the audition was professionally organized, which I assumed was Pasqual's contribution rather than Harold's. God only knows how many young women had paraded before them in previous days, but the day I was there they saw at least forty girls. Harold sensed that I thought the time he was consuming in the sessions was ridiculous, considering that I happened to know something about the casting game. On the drive home, he said, "You know, it's just too much. It's too hard to choose from all of them."

"Are you giving up on the idea?"

"No," he said, "but I think we need some outside help. I think I'll have a calendar girl contest."

"How will that work?"

"Easy. I'll personally appoint a panel of judges and we'll stage a beauty pageant at a club somewhere. It will be fun that way, and it'll give this year's party some extra publicity. What do you think?"

I shrugged. It was November. He had been casting for weeks and it was another month-and-half before the end of the year. Before it was over with I suspected he would have spent almost four months on the calendar idea. "Whatever, Harold," I said, "But do you think you'll ever write another book?"

"Baby, baby, I'm working on it," he said. "You know that I've always got an idea churning in my head."

He narrowed the girls that he and Pasqual had interviewed down to seventy. He then booked an audition date at the Roxy on Sunset Strip, a fairly new club and theater that Lou Rawls and a couple of friends had started as a showcase for rock bands. He did not "personally appoint" a panel of judges; rather, he had Gene Schwam send invitations to Alan Alda, Sonny Bono, Edward Asner, James Brolin, William Shatner, Lloyd Bridges, Bob Crane, Dick Martin, Marty Allen, and Vince Edwards.

"What if none of them come?" I complained.

"Who gives a shit?" Harold responded. "We'll still get maximum publicity."

Only Marty and Vince showed up to be judges, but Harold didn't consider the absence of the others as a rebuff. After all, he was going to be the final judge, whether he admitted it or not. To make the panel a quintet he appointed my friend Linda Christian, Tyron Power's ex-wife, and me as judges.

On the given day the seventy girls showed up, plus a few dozen more, all would-be actresses. Most of them were gorgeous, some were intelligent, and a handful were stupid. Harold had put together a conglomerate of prizes for the winners that included free composites, modeling fees, beauty products, and a day at a fancy Beverly Hills spa. Thus the show went on, with Robert Q. Lewis as the master of ceremonies. It lasted four long hours, with the girls parading back and forth on the Roxy stage, posturing, posing, and answering questions asked by Lewis.

When one girl was asked what interests she had outside of show business, she answered, "Astronomy."

"Oh," said Lewis, "what sign are you?"

"I said astronomy, not astrology," responded the girl testily. She didn't become one of the calendar girls.

Lewis asked another girl if she wanted to be an actress. "Is a bear Catholic?"

Everyone looked at each other; even Lewis's usual witty retorts were stopped cold. She wasn't selected.

A third girl, when asked why she had entered the contest, said, "Because I would just love to work with Harold Robbins!" She was one of the winners.

Among the sparse audience was a reporter from the *Los Angeles Times*. After the dozen winners were announced, he approached Harold. "Why did you stage this event?" he asked.

"Because it's fun," said Harold. "Everywhere I go it's business and gloom, business and gloom. I like to inject a little fun into life. And how better to do it than expose twelve beautiful girls as calendar girls for my New Year's Eve party?"

Our twelfth holiday party was another smashing success, and for the first time it was due almost entirely to Harold's imagination. Again, we held it in the Crystal Ballroom at the Beverly Hills Hotel. From the photo sessions at Pasqual's, Harold had enormous blow-ups printed of the calendar girls, splashed against the walls of the party room. The girls, attractively clad (actually close to being unclad), did a terrific dance routine staged by Joe Cassini. Our friend, Tony Martin, entertained with a song—what else? Neil Sedaka's "Calendar Girl."

19

Partying on My Own

*I*n the years following Harold's "open marriage" proclamation, his need to "research" his books independent of my presence and his desire to be "isolated" when he wrote a novel became ever greater. In many ways we entered into a life of subtle estrangement. During the first couple of years he would be gone for a few weeks, return for a few days, and then be off again. Gradually, his time away from home grew longer and longer, and then he returned to me in Beverly Hills, only to stay a few days and then he would leave for France. No matter where he was or how long he was gone, we talked by telephone every day; when he did return, it was as though there was absolutely nothing awry in our lives. We made passionate love constantly and he treated me as if I were the end all in his life. No wonder then that I continued to think I was. I was still crazy about him. When he related his experiences with other women, I simply paid no attention, although it was never easy.

I never felt independent of him, but circumstances required that I fashion a life for myself, and I gradually did so. I enjoyed a liberty in Cannes that I did not seem to have in Beverly Hills; the South of France was filled with people from all walks of life and all strata. Through the course of time, I made innumerable friends and none were more colorful or eccentric than Gustav Levin and Tommy Kyle. They were a gay couple who lived in a beautiful villa atop the highest point of Cannes.

Gustav—Gussie to his friends—was a reticent man, stiffly handsome, very formal, and the heir to the Perrier water fortune. Tommy was his young

American lover, tall, slender, blond, and drop-dead gorgeous; he was the mirror image of a slightly effeminate Marlboro Man. Gussie was austere, but Tommy had a wild sense of humor and he loved to entertain up at Gussie's villa. The villa service staff reflected Gussie's staid formality. From butler to waiter they were always dressed in immaculate white uniforms and donned white gloves as if they were attendants to members of an old aristocratic family. There was nothing aristocratic about Tommy, except his lavish style. He loved parties, and he used the liveried staff to the hilt.

I recall a dinner party he held in the villa conservatory, where all the guests sat on low-slung, down-filled couches in the midst of a jungle of exotic flora, all kinds of plant and flower species that ranged from the simple rose to the more exotic belladonna. Tommy himself sat on a throne on a slightly raised platform, from where he could lord over us.

"Tonight, we are having a special dessert," he announced flamboyantly from above us after we had finished dinner. There was a chatter of curiosity among the guests, then Tommy continued, "Cecil is going to drive me down to the Croisette in the Corniche." He made a gesture to the English butler, who took his cue and promptly exited toward the garage. Tommy laughed hilariously and called after him, "And have the top down, Cecil!"

We stirred, some of us standing, and all of us thinking we were going to pile into the Rolls Royce and tour the boardwalk. Tommy gestured for us to remain seated, and the servants began to pass out pens and pads of paper. Tommy was in his element.

"Each of you jot down exactly what you would like for dessert—man, woman, boy, or girl; height and weight; blonde, brunette, or redhead!" He giggled. It was like ordering from a takeout restaurant. We quickly wrote something down and soon Tommy was off into the starlit night with Cecil at the wheel of Gussie's convertible.

By day the Croisette was famous for its gardens and palms and casual social milieu, but once night fell, it was infamous for its young women and men who promenaded along the boardwalk showing their physical endowments, each in hope of being picked up for the evening. Tommy returned in less than an hour with the "desserts," each matching a specific order. Although the dinner guests were primarily heterosexual, I noticed that not a single one of the "orders" Tommy brought back from the street was a girl.

What followed was not what I would consider an orgy, although most everyone paired off with whoever matched their criteria and made off to the privacy of one of the innumerable bedrooms in Gussie's magnificent villa. I stood in the shadows watching the dispensation, quite gladly alone until a voice behind me said, "You must be Grace."

I turned. He was a tall, gorgeous young man in his midtwenties, a bona fide Adonis with a thick French accent. My heart thumped. Was I ready for this? "Yes, I'm Grace," I said softly.

"I am Jacques," he smiled, "your dessert." He took my hand and kissed it, very tenderly, very formally, as if we had just been introduced at a formal banquet.

I looked at him and thought fleetingly of Harold. Where was he? Who was the subject of his research tonight? The young man continued to smile at me, not lecherously but seductively, and the anger that had been building within me for years suddenly reached its critical mass and exploded like a bomb. Yes, I was ready.

It was said the next day that Tommy's dinner guests ate sumptuously. Tommy, as per usual, paid for everything, including all the desserts with Gussie's money.

The atmosphere at Tommy and Gussie's parties was so far removed from what most people would call reality that almost everyone ultimately joined in the dream, knowing that it would seem to be just that, a hallucination, when they went home. Yet it was real while it was happening, and many a personal hang-up was temporarily suspended.

I took Soraya Khashoggi to one of the dinner parties. We were seated next to a young, Italian couple that had recently married. They were very sophisticated and the young man was a titled member of an ancient family of Roman nobility. During dinner the young bride began to tell us what a superb lover her husband was. "He didn't propose until he took me from the rear," she said candidly. "Now I prefer it that way because I can't get pregnant."

Soraya and I glanced at each other, not that we were really surprised, for parties at Gussie's villa seemed to unleash innumerable repressions and people talked of things they wouldn't dream of bringing up at other venues.

"I don't want to have children," the Italian woman continued, "because when my husband dies, I don't want to have to share the inheritance." She laughed as though she wanted us to think she was joking, but we both thought, *Oh no, she's not!* Her openness, however, was relaxing, and the table conversations around us picked up where she left off.

Across from us was an older, British couple. The man had a stiff upper lip and a vivid imagination.

"A friend of mine who was my age," he told us, "married a much younger woman. When he discerned that he wasn't satisfying his wife, he purchased an ape that he kept in a cage in the master bedroom. Every night he watched as his wife entered the cage and engaged in intercourse with the giant primate." He shrugged as if his ridiculous story were a commonplace event. Again Soraya and I glanced askance at one another.

"Finally his wife became pregnant," the British gentleman continued. "After she had a miscarriage, her husband felt he should get rid of the ape, and so he did. He gave it to the London Zoo. You can observe the poor lonely beast to this very day."

We waited for him to laugh at his own story, but he didn't. Soraya then took over the conversation.

"I've always wanted to be the madam at a whorehouse," she fantasized aloud, "but the prostitutes would be all boys, each one handpicked and personally trained by me!"

I heard a chuckle or two, but not nearly the laughter one would expect under other circumstances. Soraya's tale of desire, perhaps a fantasy that she had really dreamed of before, opened the floodgate for a whole series of tall tales, all sexual in nature. Some of them were so fascinating that hardly anyone touched their food, even though we were being served a seven-course dinner by Gussie's army of uniformed servants.

One of the most dramatic dinner parties I ever attended was at an alfresco restaurant in St. Tropez. Harold and I were yachting along the coast and decided to drop anchor in St. Tropez harbor and go to one of the popular restaurants ashore.

One of our dinner companions was the Prince of Baroda, hailing from a southeastern state in the Republic of India. I'd heard stories of rich rajahs, but this prince didn't seem to have a rupee, much less a franc. Despite his titles, he never stayed at a hotel; rather, he depended on the kindness of strangers, always helping himself to the generosity of one of our group (this time me) who put him up at their villa or on their yacht. On this particular evening, others joined us at the table, including several handsome visiting doctors who were friends of Tommy Kyle.

At some moment Prince Baroda, or Princey as we called him, suddenly left the restaurant without explanation. After a while I noticed he had not come back.

"What happened to Princey?" I asked Tommy.

"How should I know?" Tommy responded with an unconcerned shrug.

I began to worry. Time passed and still there was no Prince of Baroda. I decided to check our yacht. I had a weird premonition that something might be wrong. I ran across the cobblestone streets in my high heels to the dock where we were moored. I boarded and went immediately below deck.

When I entered the first stateroom, I stopped short at the threshold and gasped. There was Princey, lying on a couch, completely nude, sort of semiconscious. His face and penis were of the same shade of purple. I rushed to him, not knowing what to do. When he saw me, he tried to speak, but he couldn't. He choked and pointed to his throat. I was beside myself.

Unexpectedly, Tommy arrived just a minute behind me. Despite his earlier indifference, when he saw Princey's condition he started screaming like a mad person. Realizing that Tommy was not going to be of help and that Princey was on the verge of dying, I suddenly went into crisis mode. It was an era, however, before anyone had heard of the Heimlich maneuver and I didn't have a clue as to what to do.

Princey continued to gasp and choke; he began turning an even deeper shade of purple. Tommy was still screaming. Something had to be done and fast, or the man was going to die. I dashed down to the galley. I searched the cupboards, not really knowing what I was seeking, but when I saw a jar of honey, I grabbed it. I have no idea why I thought it would work, but I rushed headlong back to Princey. He was virtually unconscious by now, and without prelude I grabbed his hair, pulled his head back, wedged his mouth open, and poured the entire jar of honey down his throat.

After a moment he began to cough. I grabbed a wastebasket and stuck it under his chin. Suddenly, he coughed violently and whatever was lodged in his throat popped out fully honey-coated.

"I couldn't breathe," he said, gasping for air. "That's why I left the dinner table."

By this time Tommy had regained his composure. "Princey," he said angrily, "with all those doctors at our table, why didn't you let us know you had a problem? Why didn't you ask one to go with you and assist you?"

At that Princey laughed, and I knew he was going to be all right. "Why, I didn't think of it," he said.

He was still naked, of course, and I noticed that as his face regained its natural color, his penis remained purple as a plum. I assumed that's the way it had always been. After the incident, I secretly thought of him as the "Purple Prince."

Another incident began one evening when we were dining aboard the yacht in the St. Tropez harbor. Yolanda Kluge, the wife of the American billionaire, was one of our guests. We had been cruising most of the day along the coast, and as we were finishing dinner, she suddenly said, "Let's go cruising on land."

Her suggestion hit the spot with a few of us, and we took off. St. Tropez was a small town with a lively nightlife, and I think we hit every club and bar on its map before the night was over, at least Tommy Kyle and I did. At one stop Yolanda began flirting with a cute gigolo; before I knew it, she and the young man were off into the night, without us. Tommy and I shrugged it off and continued to barhop.

At last, having coursed through the night on more drinks than I care to remember (since I was never a big drinker), we decided to return to the yacht.

As soon as we got onboard, we heard the sounds of passionate lovemaking echoing from below deck. Well, we didn't want to interrupt anyone, so we stayed topside.

A few minutes later silence fell. A few seconds after that Yolanda emerged.

"Did you have a good time?" I asked cheerfully.

"Yes," she whispered frantically, 'but I don't have any francs to pay him with!"

I bit my tongue, opened my purse, and ended up footing the bill for what had started out as Yolanda's land cruise. Oh, the things that happened in St. Tropez!

On another occasion in St. Tropez an entrepreneurial woman named Marie invited me to a party at her deck side restaurant. "Bring all your friends," she said, "especially the young men, because I'm going to have a cock contest."

"A what?" I asked curiously.

"A cock contest," she repeated. "You'll see. Just bring all the handsome young men who are friends of yours."

I was young myself and in those days I seldom passed up an opportunity to partake of a party. I had no idea what Marie was talking about, but I remained curious. I rounded up as many of our gang as I could.

It turned out to be a dinner party, and rather tame by St. Tropez and *Gracara* standards. Finally, however, Marie took the floor and announced that it was time for the contest.

"All of you men stand up," she demanded.

The men stood up, nonplussed.

"Now, I want you to pull down your pants and measure your penis," said Marie, "either in inches or centimeters. The girls present can help you. The winner will receive a prize."

Marie didn't say what the prize was, but I suppose it made no difference. Most of the men sat down. Some of those present were her own friends and she tried to encourage them to participate, but again she had no takers. Finally all of them were seated again. Marie became annoyed and began to curse.

"*Sacre bleu!* Are there no real men here? Is there not one of you with a *zizi*?"

Finally, one of my friends, Gary Pudney, a famous television producer, stood up. He unzipped and then quickly zipped up his pants. He looked around rather sheepishly, and then said with a shrug, "It looks like I'm the only competitor, so I guess I'm the winner!"

Everyone but Marie applauded.

In Cannes, Florence Gould was the grande dame of our social set. She was old, a scion by marriage to the infamous Frank Jay Gould, the legendary manipulator of stocks and a pioneer in railroads and communications.

Florence did with her share of Jay's fortune what he had failed to do himself—
she became a respected member of the world's rich and glamorous society. She
knew everyone, and she was gracious enough to introduce me to the créme de
la créme in the South of France. Her friendships ran the gamut from aristocrats
to artists. She invited me to many of her parties, and each one was something
to look forward to.

Florence was approximately eighty when I met her. One couldn't tell her
age because she had not a single wrinkle in her moon-shaped face. Certain
minutely swollen aspects of her face, however, indicated that she might have
had silicone injections, which had become the rage in those days before the
dangers of the procedure had become known. I remember vividly her voice,
for she spoke distinctly but strangely. It was obvious she had false teeth, but
they were only noticeable when she finished speaking a sentence, always with
a sharp click as though the sound were a punctuation mark.

It was difficult to classify Florence. As a young woman, she had been a
Ziegfeld Follies showgirl. Her beauty had attracted young Frank Jay Gould,
who had inherited much of the family fortune. They married, and thus she
began her own Cinderella story.

When I met her, Florence alternated between her villa in Cannes and a
summer home on a private beach at Juan-les-Pins. Florence's private art
gallery included works by Gaugin, Toulouse-Lautrec, and other major artists,
primarily of the postimpressionist group. As a collector, however, she was both
eccentric and eclectic. In her villa basement she had an incredible array of
stained-glass windows, some as large as doors, even walls, running from floor
to ceiling, all created by Bernard Buffet, the French existentialist painter whose
favored tragic subject was usually taken from the passion story. The religious
theme was also reflected in the panels in Florence's basement, where there
were portraits of Christ, the Virgin Mary holding the baby Jesus, Joseph, and
various saints.

Florence wanted to leave her collection to the French government. Her
plan called for her villa to be turned into a museum upon her death, with all
of her art and jewelry on display. When the French government heard of her
munificent offer, they decided to take inventory of her treasures. The result
was not in Florence's favor. The auditors decided her possessions were greatly
undervalued and they raised her taxes. Florence was so outraged that she
changed her will. Today, her paintings hang in the Brooklyn Museum of Art.
What happened to the stained-glass panels, I don't know.

Of all my wonderful friends, however, the dearest and closest was Princess Marusia Toumanoff. She and her husband Nicholas became an integral
part of the fairy-tale life I lived during those year. Marusia had a network

of friends that extended around the world. She introduced me to fascinating people, from the South of France to Beverly Hills (where the Toumanoffs also had a home), and from Marbella on Spain's Costa del Sol to Acapulco on the Mexican Riviera.

The Toumanoffs were childless and Marusia took me under her wing. She acted like a proud mother and loved to show me off in the best of society. Although she was not a great beauty, Marusia was striking for her age. She wore her light blonde hair down; her eyeliner was always too dark and the line extended too far from her eyes; yet, she remained a commanding personality. She had a stunning figure and she loved to flaunt it by wearing sexy blouses and tight slacks. She was nimble and could kick her gorgeous legs up to her chin, even at an advanced age.

Marusia was a night person and she loved to make the rounds to the myriad discothéques. A native of Poland, she spoke in an affected Russian accent that had been inherited gradually through time from Prince Nikki. Her words were a fractured combination of French and English, and her expressions were priceless. She used slang terms that one would deem vulgar coming from most people, but from Marusia's lips they were adorable.

"Dollink, qui cares?" she would say. "I never look at or want to remember any ugly faces. I must have only the beautiful and the young preeks around me."

She loved young men and she didn't hesitate to use her acquired expertise to round one up for a one-night stand. If a healthy young stud was to her liking, she would say, "You little preek, if you are alone, then come with us and you'll have a good time." I don't recall anyone ever turning her down, and the rest of our group always welcomed the new addition.

Marusia was not in the least discriminatory; she loved the gay discos and clubs as well as the straight ones. She demanded front and center seats, close enough to the stage to stuff dollar bills in a stripper's G-string. One night when we were in a male dancer's club I followed Marusia's suit and stuffed a dollar bill in the dancer's crotch. Marusia gasped, gave me a strange look, and said, "Dollink, what are you doing?" She then stuck her hand into the surprised dancer's jockey-strap and plucked the dollar back. "Here, dollink? Don't spoil them!" She handed the bill back to me; I had inadvertently stuffed a one hundred dollar bill instead of a single. Then she saw the dancer's fallen, disappointed face. "Later, dollink, we'll make up for it," she said to him, but there was not going to be a "later," as he probably knew.

A certain type of personality loves life with extra enthusiasm, and Marusia had that personality. She enjoyed every moment of her life and didn't care who saw her getting what she wanted out of it. One night when I was leaving a party, I went to the bedroom to retrieve my coat. I found Marusia lying naked on top of a huge pile of fur coats. One of her little "preeks" was right there between her open legs. I was shocked, although I later wondered why, since Marusia was outlandish in practically everything she did.

She drank only vodka and had the habit of tossing her empty glass into a fireplace. When a fireplace wasn't available, she used corner walls, "So, dollink, no one steps on the cheeps." Luis Palacio was a leading Spanish couturier. At a party in his home in Marbella, Marusia persuaded all of the guests to hurl their empty glasses in the fireplace. When it filled up, she used the floor. Everyone did the same. Soon, glass was everywhere and we were walking about like people on hot coals.

Like so many couples in the fast lane, Marusia and Nikki decided to get a divorce. The aftermath of their marriage was as strange as their lives together had been. Marusia married a young Frenchman many years her junior, Etienne, but Nikki continued to travel with her, not just her—them! The trio even took holidays together. Meanwhile, Nikki dated other women, which enraged Marusia. Whenever possible, she always sought revenge.

One of Nikki's girlfriends had the audacity to ask Marusia what his favorite food was. "I want to make him a home-cooked dinner," she cooed.

"Why, it's cheese, dollink," said Marusia sweetly. "Cheese from the beginning, cheese to the end."

Nikki hated cheese. The instant he got a whiff of the smell of his girlfriend's treat, he retreated back into the street. The girl was dumbfounded. She called Marusia to find out what she thought might have gone wrong.

"Why, dollink, you probably did not have enough cheese!"

I introduced Nikki to his next princess. She was a wonderful woman and an excellent wife, but the truth is that Nikki remained in love with Marusia. It was mutual, and today they lie side by side at Forest Lawn Cemetery in Los Angeles. Harold, in his generosity, paid for Marusia's funeral and burial. Her death left a void in my life that was never filled.

Another colorful couple we befriended in the South of France was the Baron and Baroness di Portanova, known as Ricky and Sandra. Marusia introduced them to us in the bar of the Hotel du Paris in Monte Carlo. They were a good-looking couple; Ricky was handsome in a swashbuckling, devil-may-care fashion, and Sandra reminded me of Vivien Leigh in the role of Scarlett O'Hara. They were immensely wealthy by virtue of Texas oil wells, with a huge home in Houston and one of the largest villas in Acapulco.

The di Portanovas spent the summers on the Riviera, taking a suite at the Hotel du Paris and alternating between the hotel and their yacht, as Harold and I did in Cannes. After dinner they always repaired to the bar of the hotel where they treated guests to pink Dom Pérignon and bowls of caviar. They were even more extravagant with their caviar than Harold had been at the Four Seasons Restaurant when I first met him. I remember being at one of their parties when the waiters were actually ladling caviar onto plates in huge scoops. The di Portanovas had a huge circle of friends and therefore always many guests in the evening. Harold once speculated quite seriously, "Their hotel bill each summer must be at least a million dollars."

If it was, it meant that money wasn't everything to the hotel management. In an absolutely screwball display Ricky got himself barred from the hotel premises, at least for a time. He got so drunk one night that he mistook a lobby flowerpot for the men's room urinal in full view of a dozen horrified guests. The hotel management's decision was embarrassing enough, but higher authorities made it known to the couple that they were no longer welcome in the principality itself. Fortunately, their banishment was short lived. They soon returned and nothing more was said about Ricky's misbehavior. They spent their summers at the hotel in Monaco and their winters in their villa in Acapulco. Both are now deceased, but I think of them from time to time with the fondest of memories.

20

Lovers and Calendar Girls

espite the many wonderful friends we made and the social set Harold and I belonged to on the Côte d'Azur, other people entered our lives who brought with them a great deal of anguish and despair, at least to me. Harold's philandering, which had been invisible in the beginning, became more obvious as time went on. I was with him because I loved him, and after that day of revelation standing in the hallway in our Beverly Hills home, I had learned to take his brief flings in stride. "She meant nothing," he would reassure me, "just a woman's body to satisfy my urges when you were not there." I believed him, or tried to. Open marriages were not uncommon; in fact, the very term had come to symbolize a new and healthy liberalism in American relationships, somewhat of a carryover from European customs that had been around forever. Harold had become famous, and women, especially young women, followed him in packs. He loved the attention, but never did he pursue one of them, or them him, in my presence. My imagination, however, was vivid and therefore tortuous. It was not easy to handle Harold's flings when he was away from me, but at least I did not know the women, which helped overcome my disquiet; that is, until Gabriella entered our lives.

She was a baroness from St. Tropez, where she lived in a beautiful apartment overlooking the harbor. She had a Russian lover named Wally, who was a retired field operative for Interpol. I liked Wally; he was courteous and congenial. His huge handlebar mustache gave him the appearance of a walrus, which is what I called him: Wally the Walrus. He seemed to like the nickname.

Gabriella was an attractive woman with a mysterious air about her. One had to take in the sum total of her looks to recognize her beauty. Her hair was midnight black, usually pulled back in a peasant bun; but her skin seemed flawed as if she didn't use quality creams. Her bone structure, however, was superb, and the fact that she rarely spoke intensified her mystery. She was a big woman, resembling my idea of a dominatrix, and since she wasn't remotely the type of woman Harold liked, I hardly gave her a second thought.

She and Wally were not members of our social set, although Harold and I dined out with them occasionally and a couple of times we invited them to join us on the yacht. When it was time for Adréana to begin school again (we had decided she should go to an American school), I returned with her to Beverly Hills, leaving Harold behind in Cannes to work on his next book, *The Lonely Lady*. It never entered my mind that he would philander with Gabriella, an oversized baroness, far removed from his usual taste.

When I returned from the States in the fall, Harold said nothing about her. The crew of the *Gracara*, being loyal to their master, also remained mum, although they treated me with their usual courtesy and fondness. A friend of mine, however, was more revealing of the facts.

"Grace," she said confidentially, "I think you should know that when Gabriella was in Paris recently she told many people that she was going to become the next Mrs. Harold Robbins."

Other friends followed suit, and I began to realize that in my absence Gabriella had become a regular visitor on the *Gracara*. There was a constant repetition of Gabriella's statement: "I'm going to be the next Mrs. Harold Robbins." For one of the few times in my life, I confronted Harold.

"Oh, Tiger," he said nonchalantly. "She was just research, that's all. You were gone and I had to fulfill my needs. She does some pretty weird things, but it was just research."

Research? It was probably Harold's most creative effort at justifying an affair. But he didn't stop there; he proceeded to give me every detail of their sexual fling down to the minutest detail. "She didn't mean anything, Tiger," he reassured me. "I love you, darling, and don't ever forget it."

"Well, I think you should know that your baroness is telling people that I'm out and that she's in. She's even describing your forthcoming nuptials. So tell me, is she going to be the next Mrs. Harold Robbins as she says?"

For once, Harold was stumped for words. He seemed both embarrassed at Gabriella's behavior and concerned for my feelings. In a way it was amusing. He was suddenly a little puppy dog, following me around, which told me that in his heart Harold only wanted me, or at least that's what I wanted to believe. He dropped Gabriella immediately and I don't think he ever saw her again.

Her memory wasn't forgotten, however, and after a lapse of time, Harold mentioned her penchant for lovemaking. She had a foot fetish, he said, and would begin their rounds by sucking his toes. If he thought I would repeat her performance, he was wrong. I was disgusted, and I told him so.

Another time he mentioned the Chinese sash maneuver or "ribbon trick" as he called it.

"What's that?" I asked.

"She stuffed a silk sash or handkerchief up my ass," he said. "While we're fucking, just before I reached a climax, she pulled it out. It intensified my orgasm."

Once the baroness was out of our lives, I tried to forget her, and finally Harold did also. She was just another passing fling, although one with a vivid imagination in reference to Harold's feelings for her. At last, her name or his experiences with her were never mentioned again.

Judy Starger was of a different ilk than Gabriella, and Harold's dalliance with her took a new turn. It happened virtually before my eyes, rather than when Harold and I were separated by time and distance.

When we met Judy, she was married to movie producer Marty Starger, who at varying times was president of ABC Television and of Marble Arch Productions. They seemed a lovely, happy couple, and they joined us on the *Gracara* for a cruise to Marbella. As usual, I tried to be the perfect hostess, and we all had a great, fun time. A few months later Judy showed up at our villa in Le Cannet, alone. She had gained weight and had a tarnished appearance. She and Marty had split up, she revealed.

"I just had to get away," she said rather pitifully. "Can you put me up for a few days?"

I felt sorry for her, and Harold and I agreed to let her stay on the *Gracara* until she could put her life together, while we remained at the villa. It was perfect for Judy; she had a ball, exercising, swimming, jogging along the Croisette, and partaking of all the luxurious amenities our yacht and crew could afford her, which was a lot. She lost weight, toned her body, and slowly reverted back to her former, attractive self.

In those days Harold had an office on avenue de Madrid in Cannes. He would drive down every morning and begin his work anew. What I didn't know was that he began to make a pit stop every day at the *Gracara*, and Judy apparently did the same thing at his office when she was out jogging.

One day I needed to ask Harold something and I popped in unexpectedly at his office. Judy was there, just emerging from the shower. I didn't say anything, but they both knew I wasn't pleased. Finally Harold began to sputter an explanation. "That damned shower on the yacht," he said, "it's plugged up again and Judy had to come here to bathe."

He wasn't very convincing. We had a full crew to maintain the yacht and keep it in tip-top shape. Thereafter her presence created constant tension, and I was relieved when she returned to the States to finalize her divorce from Marty. When she left, she did not show me the courtesy of a thank you, even though I personally drove her to the airport. Frankly, I didn't care.

When we returned to Los Angeles that year, Harold said he had to contact Judy regarding a real estate transaction. Today, I realize it was a bogus excuse to see her. Although I didn't know it until years later, he bought a house for her in Malibu that she was supposed to resell and then share the profits with him. None of this came out until our own divorce proceedings in the early nineties. Harold was beginning to stretch the concept of open marriage further and further, changing his original edict at random to fit his needs.

Leslie was a homeless Australian waif who lived on the beach at St. Tropez. She always had sand in her hair. With Gabriella and Judy, Harold maintained a pretense of keeping his girlfriends under another roof, but he actually invited Leslie to move in with us—and she did. I was beside myself. What attraction he found in her was beyond the pale. She was a filthy little vagabond that resembled a drowned rat. She even had fleas! For the most part I had kept my mouth shut concerning the baroness and Judy, but Leslie was too much. I confronted Harold.

"This unattractive little creature," I began. "What on earth can you possibly find alluring about her?"

"The poor girl was a heroin addict, Tiger, but she kicked the habit. Now, that's a hard thing to do, and I admire her for it."

Puh-leeze! He admired a homeless junkie to the degree he felt she should move into our villa? It was strictly sex, and I knew it—but what to do? I still loved Harold; all I could do was suck in my gut until he grew tired of Leslie, which didn't happen overnight.

They grew inseparable, a condition most women in my position would not have tolerated; somehow I did, but it was insufferable. This little nothing not only lived in my home, but Harold launched her into a variety of ill-fated business ventures, simple things like a beach rental agency that had surfboards with sails on them. It was ludicrous; Leslie had no more business sense than a monkey, and every enterprise failed after a brief period of time. Harold finally realized there was a limit even to my patient tolerance and at last he moved Leslie into an apartment in Cannes. It didn't change his relationship with her, but at least he wasn't cavorting with his mistress under our roof.

Leslie kept hanging around, and her presence caused a massive rift in our marriage that was probably irreversible, although I didn't realize it at the time. The truth is that I had always missed Harold's presence when he was off writing, researching, or doing whatever. I found solace in the knowledge that when he returned home our relationship would continue as though nothing had or possibly could thwart it. But now for the first time, when we were actually in the same place together, Le Cannet, he was in fact with Leslie more than he was with me. When I expressed my jealousy and anger, indeed, my outrage, Harold tried to whitewash it.

"You can't be angry over Leslie," he would say, "she's just a meaningless kid. But she has spunk. After all, anyone who can beat heroin has got something!"

"Harold, you're making a fool of yourself first and of me second," I retorted.

"Tiger, darling, you're my woman. Don't forget that. Leslie won't be around forever. She has her own life to live."

His words did little to soothe my anguish, but I learned restraint and gradually coped with Leslie's presence, trying to avoid her whenever possible. I sought help in marijuana, which I had never used before. It often helped to ease the pain, but also it sometimes made things worse. Once I baked a batch of brownies that were loaded with weed. I was standing in the kitchen stuffing my face with them when Harold and Leslie entered. I realized suddenly that I was nude; I was mortified. Harold thought it was hysterical, however, and he roared with laughter.

I grabbed a brownie and then gave Leslie a hard glare before I retreated to my bedroom, the one sanctuary where I knew I wouldn't bump into her.

In hindsight I've often wondered why I didn't sit down with Harold and explain how much this affair hurt me. Harold could be very understanding, yet we never had that discussion. For some reason, I just couldn't force myself to confront him. I kept thinking of that day when he first proposed the idea of an open marriage in the hallway in Beverly Hills. I had been so stunned and emotionally injured that I simply had not argued with him or told him what I thought. Thus, it began a situation that was never to end, except in divorce. We had become real-life prototypes of the fictitious characters in his novels.

One of the happiest days in my life was when Leslie finally returned to Australia. Harold, at long last, had grown tired of her as well as her many failed business enterprises. God only knows how much money she went through in Harold's puny effort to help her become a business woman. The minute she left, Harold and I became lovers again, as if there had never been an interruption.

I found more satisfaction in my charity work than ever I did in marijuana. It kept my mind occupied while Harold was working or cavorting. I started a project in France in the seventies that I supported and supervised for seven years. It was a fundraiser for La Famille du St. Vincent, the only orphanage in the South of France. The event itself was called A Tout Coeur (With All My Heart) and was held annually at the Palm Beach Casino in Cannes.

The French government was noticeably absent when it came to financial support for the orphanage, and I wanted to do something to correct that. Before the charity came to its infamous end, I raised many millions through my galas, with multi-million dollar contributions from people such as Adnan Khashoggi. But there were many others who gave of their time as well as money, and my friends, like Florence Gould, served on the fundraising committee.

The main event was always held on the last Tuesday of July. Princess Grace's more famous Red Cross Ball was held a week to two weeks later, on the first Friday of August. Of course, the Red Cross event was held in Monaco, a skip and a jump from Cannes.

Harold and I always attended Princess Grace's ball, although she couldn't come to mine, which I understood, always sending in a sizable monetary contribution. I was surprised then, although I wouldn't be today, when the British tabloid press fabricated a feud between us, with headlines proclaiming the "War of the Two Graces." I was outraged but Harold thought it was great, being savvy about publicity of virtually any kind.

I will not compare my galas with Princess Grace's, but they were top of the chart nevertheless. Friends from Hollywood always volunteered to enter-tain; for example Cyd Charisse and Tony Martin once flew in direct from an engagement in Las Vegas. The most fabulous participant was the legendary chanteuse Josephine Baker, whom I secured through the efforts of my friend Florence Gould. Although Miss Baker had been invited as a guest only, she volunteered to perform, and she made that year's gala a memorable event.

A Tout Coeur became a major social event as well as a distinguished fundraiser; unfortunately, an unsavory incident marred the seventh year event. Jerry Lewis was supposed to perform, but he stayed in his dressing room so long that the guests became restless. By the time he managed to get onstage, most of the audience was intoxicated, particularly the titled members of the global aristocracy who were sitting at Florence Gould's table.

The French people loved Jerry and thought him a comedy genius, but not so the international set seated with Florence. They pelted Lewis with dinner rolls until he fled the stage, humiliated. Harold and I ran after him in an effort to save the moment, but there was no comforting Jerry. He locked himself in his dressing room. We could hear him sobbing. "I will never, never, never return to France!" he screamed. That was the end of Jerry Lewis at my fundraiser; it was also the end of the fundraisers themselves.

To stage such a gala was a fulltime, year-round job, and I was always exhausted by the time the event actually started. Harold would practically pick me up and carry me in his arms to the yacht in the harbor when it ended, from where we always departed the next morning for a recuperating cruise. After seven years, I felt I had raised enough money and had done my share for the orphanage. Because of the cautious frugality of the Mother Superior and the contributions garnered from A Tout Coeur, the orphanage had become self-sustaining.

In September, we returned to California; I was happy to be home in the United States, where I planned to relax for a few months. I had decided that our calendar girl New Year's Eve party had been our last; and once we were settled again in Beverly Hills, I refrained from even mentioning a renewal. Then one day Harold said, "Hey, Tiger, what are we gonna do this year for our New Year's Eve party?"

"Harold, I haven't the slightest idea," I told him. "Perhaps it's time to stop having them. After all, it's going to be awfully difficult to top last year."

"Maybe not as hard as you think," he said, and I knew he had an idea. He grabbed a paper and pencil and began sketching, talking all the while. "We'll hire two beautiful twins, and we'll dress them like this. They'll be nude except for the seven. Together, they'll be the New Year's Girls." He handed me the drawing: "Here, what do you think?"

He was not a sketch artist, but his picture was decipherable. It was of the costume he had in mind, worn on the chest of a girl, curving down to her crotch. The horizontal top of the "seven" would cover her breasts and the bottom of the slightly vertical curve would cover her genital area, barely. Side by side, the twins, if he could find them, and I had no doubt that he could, would represent the number 77 for the year 1977.

"I think it's a superb idea, Harold," I said, quickly acquiescing, "but this year I think we should have a smaller, more intimate affair, just with our close friends."

He agreed, and we decided to have the party at Gatsby's, a restaurant in Brentwood that was owned by our friends Helen and Bill Rosen. It was a medium-sized, adorable, very cozy, and a perfect place to host our last New Year's affair, for I was sure this really would mark the end of them. For the thirteenth time in the same number of years (that first party suddenly seemed so long ago) I sent out invitations, although this time to a much shorter guest list.

Alas, Gatsby's turned out to be far too small for the number of people who came to the party, which was three times as many as we had actually invited. I wore a dramatic chiffon gown with a ribbon trim and a shoulder cape; Harold tried to upstage me with a bright pink ruffled shirt under his tuxedo jacket. By midnight the restaurant was so packed that the twins hardly had room to make their entrance. Some of the waiters cleared a table and the twins climbed aboard in their sheer-beyond-sheer costumes just in time for the countdown to the New Year.

It was another memorable party, attended by over 300 people, many of whom had to celebrate it on the sidewalk outside the restaurant's entrance because there wasn't enough room inside. Among those who did manage to get in were two Bradleys, our friend the Mayor Tom and the five-star General Omar, Eisenhower's protégé in World War II and the former chairman of the joint-chiefs-of-staff, who came with Paul Gitlin.

21

Ménage a Quatre

The fact that Leslie had left our lives during the previous year did not change Harold's philandering. He simply sought new mistresses, and the more he did, the more our marriage deteriorated. In retrospect I can see that it was a no win situation. I desperately wanted to hold our marriage together. There were so many wonderful memories; and when we were together, Harold still treated me as his "number one woman." I had not been a saint, but I had refrained from doing anything monstrously awful and I had done absolutely nothing to injure our public and social reputation.

Without question drugs played a role in Harold's next game plan, and that's precisely what it was, a grandiose plan that consummated in a game. When Harold was working, he always refrained from alcohol; but as time went on, as he pushed his deadlines to the ultimate, he used drugs to keep himself going, stretching his usual twelve-hour days into sixteen, sometimes even more. At some point I began to realize he wasn't stopping his use of drugs when he completed a book. When I questioned him about it, he fended me off, saying, "Oh, I just use them occasionally at parties, darling, like everybody else."

The next time we had a party, he took himself at his own word. He brought in enough drugs for every invitee—cocaine, uppers, downers, you name it. But the drugs were only props for Harold's real plan; they were substances made available to those who needed to lose their inhibitions. His real plan was a grand orgy, I was aghast. "Ah, come one, Tiger," said Harold, "we know what the rules are. We're in love with each other. If I go with this woman or you go with that man, what difference will it make? After it's over and done with, we'll never see them again. We only live once and we should experience everything we possibly can."

The gross details aside, Harold had his way. More often than not I did not know any of the people who suddenly showed up on our doorstep to participate in a party, although many of them were celebrities that I could identify from their movies or publicity. Harold had an acute eye for "swingers" and he wasn't shy when it came to inviting them. With lines of free, high-grade coke in parallel lines on our bathroom counters and with booze flowing like water, it took little persuasion for our "guests" to lose themselves in what Harold called "my dolce vita."

I was always personally hurt by Harold's adultery, but I wasn't vindictive. I never planned to do injury to our marriage by my own actions, but when it happened, by rote as it were, the old cliché of "turnabout is fair play" was suddenly a misnomer in Harold's addiction to open marriage. He didn't chastise me, however; he used my actions as an instrument of liberation for even greater scandalous actions.

It began one year when we returned to Beverly Hills from the South of France. We went to a surprise birthday party for Sammy Davis, Jr., given by his hospitable and beautiful wife Altovise. It was a costume party and the guests were asked to dress like children or babies. Perhaps it is because of the motion picture industry and the many costume houses in Los Angeles, but there is no place that I know of where guests take to costumes more seriously than in Beverly Hills. Hugh York, the famous hairdresser, for example, wore a christening gown with a beautiful ruffled bonnet and baptismal dress that fit him perfectly. He had it made especially for the party, but he would have looked even more baby chic had he cut his full beard and shaved his mustache.

I dressed as a cute little brat. I wore a pinafore, Mary Jane shoes with straps, and a necklace that had the word "Brat" spelled out in gold. I rented the outfit from Western Costume. Harold went as a swashbuckler, which fit more perfectly the image he had of himself than it did his true physical image. He was over sixty now, and his muscle was going to fat.

In typical star fashion Sammy was the last person to arrive at his own party. He took one glance at the outrageous attire of his guests and ran out of the house. Altovise chased after him with his costume in hand. He soon came back, this time wearing the Dr. Denton pajamas that his wife had ordered for him to wear. His costume was actually the real thing, complete with a buttoned flap in the rear and a zipper in the front. He even wore slippers that were sewn to the bottom of the legs.

Ronald McDonald showed up in his red wig and baggy clown outfit, representing Altovise's caterer, McDonald's. He wheeled in a huge cart overflowing with hamburgers and French fries, giving everyone an excuse to go off their diets. It was great fun, stuffing our faces with junk food.

Costumes often inspire brief personality changes, and the theme that day seemed to make us feel naughty and frivolous, like the children we once were. I knew Altovise much better than I knew Sammy, but when I was dancing with Harold, I noticed Sammy was following my every move. Every time I glanced his way, I found him again staring at me. When the party was finally wearing down and Harold was off talking or flirting or doing whatever he was doing, Sammy cornered me. He took me by the hand and sort of tugged me. "Little girl," he said, "you come with me."

I took on the posture of a timid little girl and followed him. Actually it was fun and titillating, the little girl-little boy game.

"Where are we going, Sammy?" I asked in a little girl's voice.

"Just come with me," he said, also affecting his voice. "Have you seen what I've got downstairs?"

"No, Sammy," I said like a little brat. "What do you have to show me downstairs?"

He took me into a small trophy room that contained his memorabilia: gold records, statuettes, and dozens of plaques. It was impressive and fascinating, although I knew he had not tugged me in there to impress me with all his awards. There was a small wet bar in the corner.

"Let's have a little drink," said Sammy. He started for the bar, but suddenly turned back to me. "No," he continued, "I have a better idea." Slowly, he began to unzip his Dr. Denton's.

I was fascinated, sort of frozen in place, almost breathless.

"I'll show you mine if you'll show me yours," said Sammy, again affecting a childlike voice.

I did not have time to answer, for suddenly he whipped it out and was indeed showing it to me. There was hardly anything else that I could see. Sammy was a diminutive person, but his penis seemed larger than his body. I was breathless.

Finally I gained my senses. "You know, Sammy," I think *yours* is gorgeous, but this just isn't the time or the place."

We could hear the remaining revelers upstairs, not to mention the near presence of Altovise and Harold. Although I was tempted in a moment of childish haste, I refrained. I didn't want to do to Harold what he had done to me so many times with the likes of Gabriella, Judy, and Leslie, and who knows who else.

Sammy did not argue with me. "Okay," he said with a smile, "when is a good time?"

"Tomorrow," I told him.

"Meet me at the Beverly Hilton," he said.

I nodded and we went back upstairs. We met as planned the next day at the Beverly Hilton, and we met a few times after that. Sammy was very busy with his career in those days and finding free time was difficult for him, yet he always made time for me. I enjoyed it, every minute of it.

When we were leaving the Hilton one day, I mentioned to Sammy off the cuff, "Harold throws orgies up at our place."

"Hey, why don't you include me next time," said Sammy enthusiastically.

Harold was unaware that I was seeing Sammy, but now I knew I had to tell him. I arrived home before Harold, and I was nervous waiting for him. I had no idea how he would react, but I remembered that day so long ago when he had forewarned me not to be a "star-fucker." I was nervous, but I wanted the truth out. The minute he came home, I said, "Harold, I've been having an affair with Sammy Davis, Jr."

He gave me a look, but he did not appear to be upset.

"Sammy, huh?"

"Yes, and he wants to come to the next orgy," I continued.

Harold's eyes lit up. "Hey, that's a great idea," he said. "Why don't you invite Altovise, too?"

That was it—no argument, no angry scene. Perhaps by that time Harold had violated his own rules so many times that he knew it would be ludicrous to reprimand me.

When Sammy and I next met, I told him that I had mentioned him to Harold.

"Yeah, and what did he say?"

"He wants you to come to the next orgy."

Sammy leaned back and smiled.

"He also wants you to bring Altovise," I added hesitantly.

To my surprise, they both came, although only once. It was a small gathering, with only three other people, none of whom I knew. It did not matter, because I gave Sammy all of my attention. I did notice, however, that Altovise was having a great time with none other than Harold. Wife swapping was popular at the time, although it wasn't something Harold and I liked to do. Switching partners with the Davises was unusual and I don't think we ever did it again. On top of that I rationalized it as not being technically a wife-swap, since others were involved also.

I realized that night, that orgies only work if you don't know the other guests very well. It has something to do with fear on the one hand and intimacy on the other. We never had another orgy after that. Casual group sex had lost its allure and excitement. Perhaps, too, we were getting jaded, although Harold had one more idea for a sexual experience we had never engaged in.

"I want us to go to bed with another man," he said.

"What?" I was startled. For all of our sexual experimentation, never had he mentioned a ménage a trois.

"It's for your pleasure, Tiger," he began to explain. "When one man is fucking your pussy and the other is fucking your ass, and the two cocks touch, wham, it's supposed to bring you your greatest orgasm."

Great or not, it never happened.

Harold, however, quickly replaced it with a new idea: a ménage a quatre—three women, including me, and of course him.

He was lunching at The Bistro when he spotted an attractive woman seated at another table. That she was a total stranger did not faze Harold in the least. He moved in on her. "I'm Harold Robbins."

"I'm Gina." And before he was finished, she returned home with him for dinner.

"I'm a witch," Gina told me, "and I have supernatural powers."

She did not demonstrate her "powers" before dinner, but she did mention that she had a girlfriend named Wendy.

"Why don't you invite her over?" said Harold enthusiastically. "She can join us for dinner."

"When?"

"Now!"

We had a great chef and to add an extra person to a guest list at a late hour was no problem. Wendy arrived and the four of us enjoyed dinner. The women were obviously impressed, but what happened next was risk-taking at its highest level.

"Let's have some dessert," said Harold.

He excused himself for a moment, and then returned with his stash of drugs and paraphernalia. He got pharmaceutical grade cocaine from his chiropractor; it came in huge spheres the size of golf balls. Now, he shaved some off and chopped it up. I glanced at Gina and Wendy; they were excited.

Like everything else he did, Harold made "doing drugs" into a production. He had a collection of brass coke spoons and straws, including one that was a miniature Hoover vacuum cleaner. He was always experimenting; he had learned to roll out the tobacco from a filter-tip cigarette with his fingers and then replace it with marijuana. The filter eliminated the harsh, burning sensation that raw weed usually gave.

The sight of drug paraphernalia was mood setting in itself. As Harold proceeded through the ritual of shaving and rolling, then added some amyl nitrate poppers to the cocaine, all of us were already rising to a new emotional level. I knew the drugs were simply a prelude to Harold's desire for all of us to have some kind of scene together and I was a bit hesitant, inhibited. I had never been with a woman before and I needed a massive hit to go through with it.

I don't remember exactly how Harold orchestrated it, but soon we four were in the same bed. We were coupled off at first, Harold and I making love, and Gina and Wendy making love. Suddenly Harold passed me to Gina and he took up with Wendy. *No*, I thought, *I don't want to do this. Harold has to stop these fantasy experiments with me.* I sprang out of bed and excused myself ever so politely.

It was almost impossible to second-guess Harold, but I was truly surprised he had not reprimanded me for having an affair with Sammy Davis, Jr. For that matter the flame Sammy and I had shared faltered quickly to a flicker and finally went out altogether. We remained friends, but I became much closer to Altovise, who was caught up in the same crazy quilt of adulterous marriage that I was in. She and I often comforted each other about the wayward ways of our husbands and the paths that our own lives had taken.

No, Harold said nothing about my affair with Sammy, but I've often wondered if next he did not purposely pursue a well-known French actress in an effort to wreak unspoken revenge upon my violation of his rule against our having affairs with celebrities. Angelique was a beautiful young woman who had starred in a series of epic costume movies that had been box office hits around the world, elevating her into the limelight of movie stardom.

Angelique was married to a successful French movie producer. Harold and I had been introduced to them one time at the Cannes Film Festival, Harold had not expressed any interest in her in France, nor she in him, but not long after my affair with Sammy, Harold ran into her one day at The Bistro where he was spraying willing noses from a special coke pen. He apparently took a closer look at Angelique, and this time he liked what he saw.

Harold had long since stopped working at home. He needed "quiet and peace of mind, total concentration." He was working hard on *Dreams Die First*, and as a result he had taken an apartment in suburban Brentwood Village and converted part of it into an office. It was not unusual for him to sometimes stay overnight at the office. He always called if he was not coming home, so I did not doubt his sincerity and honesty. After all, he had no qualms about telling me of his extramarital activities, even when I really didn't want to hear about them.

One night when he was home, he made a half-hearted attempt at making love to me. His caresses and kisses seemed minus his usual efforts and his thoughts seemed to be elsewhere. He tried, but when at last he could not get an erection, I was concerned. This sexual dysfunction was a first in our long relationship. I knew that some men, when under pressure, had a problem, and often Harold complained that he didn't want work to interfere with fucking. I did not want him to be upset with his momentary impotence, so I decided to soothe what I assumed was a bruised ego with understanding.

"I'm sure it's because you've been working so hard at the office."

His face screwed up, but he didn't say anything.

"Is there something wrong that I am unaware of?" I continued.

"I'll tell you later," he said. "Let's try again."

We finally made love, due to considerable effort on my part. When we were finished, however, I thought Harold had a bored expression on his face, as if to say that my exertion had made lovemaking rather humdrum.

"Now what's wrong?" I asked.

He leaned back on a pillow and lit a cigarette. "Well," he said with a shrug. He took a quick drag and exhaled. "You see, I was with Angelique this afternoon. Two times so quickly in a row is almost too much for me to handle anymore."

I didn't say anything. I went into the bathroom to collect my thoughts. I was angry and hurt, but when I returned to the bedroom, I couldn't think of anything to say except, "So, how was she?"

To my undying chagrin, Harold perked up at the question without realiz‐ ing it was angry rhetoric. I could have killed him, yet I did not interrupt him as he vividly described his encounter with Angelique earlier in the afternoon. Again, I tried to let his words go in one ear and out the other, and to a degree I did, but some of them registered.

"She's a beautiful woman," he said with enthusiasm, "and she has the most incredible cunt."

I gasped silently. Later, I actually rationalized his behavior away by comparing his description of Angelique's genitals to his description of mine. He had called hers a "cunt," whereas he always referred to mine as a "pussy." Every other woman had a cunt, but I had a pussy. Harold made that differentiation, and I decided I could live with that—in fact had to if I wanted to keep our relationship intact.

Angelique apparently used a lubricant before intercourse and Harold reveled in telling me about it. "It made her cunt so goddamned slippery and soft and silky," he said with glee. "I mean, Tiger—it felt great!"

"Find out what it is and I'll use it too," I answered gamely.

Harold never found out because his afternoon's fling with Angelique turned out to be a one-time stand. She, too, revealed what had happened with Harold to her spouse, and her husband wasn't as understanding about it as I had been with Harold. The only positive outcome was that I didn't have to use a lubricant to compete with Harold's latest experience.

The incidents with Sammy and Angelique represented a major turning point in our relationship. Things had been out of hand for a long while, but I had not been willing to face up to them, usually losing myself and hiding my feelings in marijuana. I seldom argued with Harold. I began to realize that I had not argued with my father either, who had been the dominating force in my family's domestic life when I was a child.

Was I still in love with Harold? Yes, there was no question about it. For me, he was still the most exciting person in the world, and for the most part, when we were together, he treated me like a goddess. Even when he revealed his sordid affairs, he always spoke of them to me in a clinical fashion, as if they had been nothing more than laboratory experiments, just "research" that he could use in his novels, which he often did.

Perhaps I thought he would slow down with age, but he didn't. His sexual appetite seemed to increase in direct proportion to his sense of midlife crisis. He often complained of his early years, when he was absent of money; one statement became a litany; "I wish to god I had made money when I was young, so that I would have enjoyed it more." As far as I was concerned, he seemed to be doing his utmost to make up for those lost years of his youth. He became a machine, both in writing and sex.

However, there was a price to pay. I cannot say that Harold was a "dope fiend," but as the years ensued he became more dependent upon a variety of drugs to help him keep up the pace. When he wrote, he still did not drink alcohol, but he used drugs more and more to stay the long creative surge. The books tumbled forth as they always had, one every two years or so, written in a great spurt of continuous pounding at the typewriter keys, but after *The Pirate* was published in 1974, there was a definite slowdown, except for the spending.

Every million dollars he made, he spent a million plus, although I was unaware of our finances. Harold was old fashioned in that way; he thought of himself as the leader of the clan, the wage earner, the masculine source of income. And, of course, because the money did keep rolling in, much of it in advance of his actually writing the book for which he had been paid, he waited until the last minute, even second, to begin it.

Paul Gitlin, whom I came to believe manipulated Harold as much as Harold manipulated others, told many stories that weren't far from the truth. Paul's favorite was when he locked Harold in a bungalow at the Beverly Hills

Hotel, not allowing him to have as much as a sandwich until he passed a given number of pages over the transom. The story was not true, as Paul well knew, because no one, not even Paul Gitlin, could tell Harold Robbins when he could eat, drink, or fuck. Yet, there was an element of truth in it.

Stories fermented in Harold's imagination, sometimes for years, before they blossomed into a cohesive idea. "That's the creative part," he said, "developing the idea into a book." In later years, with the "good life" taking its toll of creative time and a deadline always imminent, I think he often began a book before the story had totally jelled in his mind.

He had always researched the background of his stories in depth, and by the late seventies he used that as an excuse to go his way alone, always. Gone were the days when we went to the studios together, where he sought out the source of his inspiration in the mountain guerrillas and discussed his every move with me. Now he said he needed to be isolated more than ever during the research phase, although I knew it was an excuse to continue his life of promiscuity as much as anything else.

Yet, Harold always did something to rekindle our love, or so it seemed. *When Dreams Die First* was published in 1977, I was as thrilled with its dedication as I had been with the one in *The Adventurers* eleven years before. It read: This book is for Grace because Grace is for me." Two years later when our lives seemed to be totally falling apart, he did the same with *Memories of Another Day*, "For Grazia Maria con amore." Sucker I may have been, but his sentimentality always affected me.

Nevertheless, Adréana was still the primary reason for my life, and after she started going to school I tried to be near her. Harold would go off to Europe, to do "research" or write, and I would stay in Beverly Hills with Adréana, or when she went to school in France, Harold would "work" in the States and I would accompany Adréana. Our relationship began to be one of distance; we talked far more on the telephone (usually daily) than we saw each other. Not one time, however, did Harold ever indicate to me that I wasn't the woman whom he truly loved, and I had no reason to think otherwise, even with the course our lives had taken. He was still my man, my love, and lover, although for the first time I suppose I was consciously looking upon him as my father, too.

I was not blameless, although after Harold had dictated our "open marriage" the affairs I had were fleeting and usually quite impromptu, certainly born of a certain loneliness and innocence, if not innocent in themselves. I was not interested in other men, but after the Sammy Davis affair and Harold's tryst with Angelique, my mindset changed. It did not happen overnight; it was a gradual downslide, but the gulf between Harold and me began to grow wide and then wider.

The words that best describe my mental state are "lonely and bored." To escape them I began to socialize compulsively, perhaps in an effort to escape my imagination concerning what Harold was doing. I had always been involved in selective charities, but now I joined every charity group that would have me or that I could help, and I accepted every invitation that was extended to me.

In the process, I became Harold's preeminent publicist. I used events to promote his career. I gave hints of the subject matter and storyline of what he was currently working on. Since Harold was a supreme storyteller, everyone wanted to know what famous personage or celebrity he was dissecting next, so I started rumors. Actually it was fun; Harold got a kick out of my efforts, always wanting to know every little detail of the latest function I had attended. I told him most of the facts, but not exactly everything.

While attending a society dinner, I met an actor who had gained fame as one of the James Bond leading men. We were introduced at the reception, but during the dinner itself we were separated by several tables. Richard Gulley, the transplanted British noble and longtime aid to Jack Warner, was the emcee; when it came time for the dessert to be served, he suggested that we take a "seventh-inning break," stand, and wander about until we found new seats, surrounded by new people.

Need I say who sat by me? It was James Bond, and it was his doing, not mine. He had stared at me during the first four courses of dinner, forcing me to coquettishly avert my eyes so many times I couldn't count them, and now he slipped in beside me at a new table, incredibly handsome and seemingly as debonair and seductive in real life as he was on the screen. It was non-other than Roger Moore. He made some small talk and then got to the real gist of his interest.

"Is it true that your husband has actually experienced everything he writes about?" he asked.

For whatever reason Gina and Wendy popped into my mind and I thought to myself, *If he only knew!* Not only had Harold experienced most of what he had written, but there were experiences we had both engaged in that could not be placed on paper even with the liberated standards of the present time.

"Some of it," I said rather coyly, quite ready to pursue my usual bent of publicizing what Harold was presently working on in our villa in France. But 007 stopped me cold with his next question.

"Is it true you've shared his experiences?"

I gave him a curious look. He was staring at me with great anticipation. After a moment I gave a subtle nod and said quietly, "Of course it's true."

"How marvelous!" he exclaimed. He lowered his eyes to my décolletage and then lifted them back to my face. "All the sex and drugs?" he continued. We were on the verge of finishing the final item of a heavy, five-course dinner, but his eyes were sparkling with hunger.

"All of it," I said.

"How marvelous!" he repeated, and then he leaned ever closer to me. "Do you happen to have anything with you?"

"No," I told him, "but I know where there's some wonderful grass." He smiled with pleasure.

"And maybe some other things too," I added.

With my addendum, he almost fell out of his chair with excitement, rather unlike James Bond. The cool "stirred, not shaken" cliché was lost in his excitement. The dessert was served and he gobbled his down as though his action might speed up the end of the dinner.

At last I was exiting the premises with James Bond hot on my trail. We talked briefly, and then he followed me home, which was just a few blocks from the Beverly Hills restaurant. It was a tailgate job from beginning to end, although I was not driving slowly at all. Ian Fleming would have been proud. James Bond was not going to let me out of his sight.

After I parked, he was at my car door before I could turn the ignition key off. He swung it open and I got out.

"You're one of the most gorgeous women I've ever seen," he said flatteringly. "Has anyone ever told you that Elizabeth Taylor looks like you?"

He did know how to ooze the charm. It was not unusual for people to say that I looked like Miss Taylor, but that *she* looked like *me* was a new twist on flirtation. Unfortunately, it pretty much ended there in the driveway.

Once we entered the house, Roger's interest riveted almost exclusively to Harold's stash. He rolled a joint almost faster than one could snap his fingers, lit it, and began a series of heavy, deep drags. We were in half-light, but the pupils of his eyes changed with each puff. He grew giddy and then he entered into a sloppily amorous effort to seduce me. It was halfhearted and I fended him off. It was obvious he was more interested in the grass than he was with sex. I decided ditto for me. I rolled a joint and joined him in his reverie of relaxation.

The next day I thought, "So much for James Bond!" without realizing there would be another James Bond.

I was at a party at Zsa Zsa Gabor's home. She greeted us and showed us the bruises from the policeman, handcuffs (She had slapped him refusing his citation). The guests of honor were the Prince of Thurn and Taxis and his new wife Gloria. It was a typical Zsa Zsa party, with an eclectic mix of people, many beautiful women and an abundance of handsome men. I had spotted the other James Bond early on, but without any interest whatsoever, perhaps associating him with my first Bond experience. However, after the wine and champagne had cascaded for a while, I lost my inhibitions and grew suddenly interested in meeting him, perhaps to make a comparison.

I observed him standing quite alone in a corner, just watching, and not conversing with anyone. I made my introduction, full of curiosity.

Hello," I said, "I'm Grace Robbins. I think you know my husband Harold."

"Yes, I know who you are," he said, and he introduced himself out of courtesy, as if I didn't know who he was.

After a moment of chitchat he said, "It's a rather boring affair, don't you think?"

I agreed (not really), and before I knew it, he was driving me home. I had not yet mentioned Harold's coke and marijuana, nor did I ever. This James Bond was the bedroom type, and it didn't take much to seduce me. In fact, he overwhelmed me, sort of guiding me to my own bedroom as if he knew the way better than I did.

"Be still," he whispered quietly, holding me in his arms. "Don't say anything."

I tried not to do either, but I was certainly trembling uncontrollably, which seemed to titillate him. We made love, or to put it in more accurate light, he made love to me. I got stirred and shaken. This guy was the real James Bond, Sean Connery.

That my relationship with Harold was changing was emphasized the next day when he called me from France. "What did you do last night?" he asked.

"Nothing," I said. "I went to a boring party at Zsa Zsa's."

"Oh, who was there?"

"Nobody," I told him. "The same old crowd."

"Did anyone hit on you?"

"God no," I said.

"No one at all?" he repeated.

"No one."

He then proceeded to tell me about his latest laboratory experiment. I yawned.

When Harold returned to Beverly Hills, it was the same as it always had been during the first days of his arrival. He treated me as though we had just met and that he was pursuing me. It was wonderful, and yet I knew that a wrench had been thrown into the machinery.

For my birthday he suggested a small, intimate party of friends at the fashionable Chez Moi disco in Beverly Hills. Small and intimate was fine with me, except when we arrived, it seemed that Harold had invited the entire city. It was fun and unexpected, very typical of Harold. Everyone was wearing a bright yellow T-shirt with my face silk-screened on the front. It was very flattering, the image having been taken from an oil painting of me done by an artist who claimed to be the nephew of the famous Russian dancer Nijinsky. What with a few hits of grass, the party image became psychedelic, with everyone wearing two faces, theirs and mine.

As usual, Harold spared no money or energy. The party was a production. After a sumptuous dinner, the tables were cleared and the guests danced to the music of a live band. I loved parties and I was in my element, ready to dance with whomever asked me. Harold, however, had other plans.

"Come on!" he said, tugging me out of the crowd and toward the kitchen. I thought for a moment we were leaving, which would not have been unusual at all. Many had been the time Harold had left a $50,000 party we had thrown on the *Gracara* in Cannes because he had become suddenly bored. I followed him like a puppet on strings. As he tugged me into the kitchen, however, I stopped short at the threshold.

Four incredibly handsome bodybuilders were waiting. They were nude, except for their flimsy G-strings. Each of them supported a pole attached to a divan in the style of the conveyance of an Indian Rajah.

"Climb aboard!" ordered Harold.

I climbed in and the male models transported me back to the dining room proper. Harold had pre-orchestrated my return entrance and our guests were now seated at the tables that had been placed against the walls surrounding the dance floor. The divan stopped at the first table and the hunks lowered it, but not enough for me to get out. Someone handed me a glass of champagne.

"Take a sip, Tiger!" cried Harold.

I did, to great applause. But then there was the next table, where Harold urged me to repeat the gesture. I made the rounds in the divan, from table to table, taking a sip of champagne at each stop, and by the time I had been served at the last table, I was truly sloshed. At that point I could have easily gone home or passed out, but I was carried again back to the kitchen with Harold gaily at the side of my handheld carriage. At last they sat me down.

"Now for your birthday present!" cried Harold.

I looked around and saw nothing except the four bodybuilders through a haze of alcohol fog.

"Where is it?" I asked.

"It's them!" said Harold excitedly. "We're taking them home with us. You can have one or all of them!"

He had once suggested the idea of me making love with him and another man simultaneously, but this was too much.

"Oh no," I said. "Oh no!"

Harold's face fell.

"What do you mean?" he said.

I climbed off the divan, wobbly but determined. "Oh no. That's what I mean," I told him. "Ohhhh no!"

"But Grace!"

"No, not me, Harold. That's your fantasy, not mine!"

The next day the party was forgotten. Harold never mentioned my indignity at his preposterous birthday present. On the surface life went on as usual, but there was an unmentioned twist in our relationship: I had finally defied Harold! What would come of it? Nothing seemed to change. I did, but not Harold. Life continued on from one party to the next.

One memorable party, not ours, was Wes Farrell's Halloween bash. He was a former Beverly Hills playboy who had married Tina Sinatra, although they were separated at the time.

Unlike the birthday party Harold threw for me earlier in the year, this party apparently bored him. He touched my arm and whispered, "Think you can get a ride home? I'm tired of this place."

I nodded yes, kissed him on the cheek, and he was gone, where to I had no idea.

Soon after, a couple I knew approached me. They were dressed as a bride and groom, although they were not married. The woman was the estranged wife of a famous member of Frank Sinatra's Rat Pack, but they were nevertheless a handsome couple, one of the most popular pair of our set. I liked them both.

As the party was wrapping down, they approached me. "Grace," said the man, "some of us are going over to my place and continue the party. Why don't you come with us?"

I begged off.

"Oh, come on!" said the make-believe bride. "You only live once, Grace. We'll have fun."

Well, I needed a ride and the groom promised to take me home when things broke up at his house. We said our good-byes to Wes Farrell and took off. When we got to the house in the flats of Beverly Hills, no one else was there. I didn't say anything at first, but after we were in the house for a while and no one had arrived from the other party, it dawned on me that we were the party.

"I don't think anyone else is coming," I said.

"Oh well," said the groom, "that's the way it goes."

The house was a large, rambling, ranch-style structure expensively but informally decorated and appointed with rustic, country furniture. It was charming and different. The host put on some slow, seductive music and dimmed the lights; the atmosphere was mood setting. He then brought out some marijuana, rolled a joint, lit it, and passed it around. It was excellent stuff and I felt its effects immediately. It didn't hurt that I had consumed a great deal of champagne at the party.

Suddenly, the bride took me by the hand and led me down a hallway. I followed her dreamily into a bedroom, admiring her beauty. In my state, time meant nothing, but in retrospect I think things happened very quickly. She began to undress me in a gentle, caressing way. I don't know why, but I felt very special. I was now nude and she was still wearing her bridal gown. It wasn't a fantasy, but it certainly seemed to be. Here was a bride on her wedding night, but she was making love to me, not to her new husband. Later I thought that perhaps I had dreamed the scene, but believe me, I hadn't. What I did do, however, was get completely caught up in the fantasy, enjoying every touch, kiss, and caress of my partner.

And then something happened that almost spoiled the moment. My eyes adjusted and I saw the groom watching us from the shadows of the room. Even in the moonlight, for that's what it was, I could discern his immense pleasure at being a voyeur. I must have started briefly, for suddenly he moved closer to the bed and began to praise the bride's efforts and to encourage us to continue. The last clear thought I remember was, "If only Harold could see us. He'd love it!" How could I be thinking of Harold? It was always Harold. He had me so mixed up.

22

Sizzling Acapulco

On December 31, 1978, after we decided not to have any more lavish New Year's Eve parties, Harold and I settled on having a quiet dinner at Verita Thompson's La Cantina Restaurant. Caryn was visiting, and we took her and Adréana with us. Caryn was now an attractive young woman in her twenties, and Adréana had entered her teenage years. Walter Thompson had died a couple of years before and Verita had become a successful restaurateur. Although the evening was uneventful, I nevertheless enjoyed seeing Verita, who had become a lasting friend.

The next day Harold and I went to the Polo Lounge at the Beverly Hills Hotel. By chance we met a man who would come to have a great influence on our lives and relationship. He was Oscar Obregon, a wealthy, Mexican playboy whose great grandfather had been President of Mexico. He was with his girlfriend (one of many), and once he discovered who we were, he descended on us and virtually demanded that he buy us a drink.

"Harold Robbins, the famous writer who throws the famous parties!" he cried out with glee. "We've been looking for you for days!"

Harold and I glanced askance at each other. Who was this guy?

Oscar explained that he had cancelled his own famous New Year's Eve party at his mansion in Acapulco at the insistence of Marianna, his present girlfriend, who thought if they spent the holidays in Beverly Hills, then perhaps they would somehow finagle an invitation to our party, such was the legendary status the festivity had gained. They had been hanging around the Polo Lounge for a week.

"You've been waiting around here for a week?" Harold repeated, incredulous.

"Yes," said Oscar enthusiastically, "and at The Bistro and La Scala and Scandia and Chasen's. But you were never there!"

Harold laughed and asked them to join us.

I explained that they would surely have been welcomed to our party, but that we had given it up this year for the first time in over a decade. Oscar's face fell, and then lighted up again. "Then I'll have a party for you in Acapulco!"

We ordered drinks, and Harold and Oscar began to swap stories. Oscar told us about some of the parties he had thrown through the years at Nirvana, his Mexican villa. They sounded lavish, very upscale, sophisticated, and a bit on the wild side.

"My next party is this month," said Oscar. "*Town and Country* magazine will be there to do a piece on the beautiful people of Acapulco! And we want you to come!"

It was a pleasant meeting, fun. Oscar was engaging and full of energy, and Marianne was a beautiful but quiet young woman with the physical attributes of a model. Finally it was time to leave.

"Please, please come to my party. I want you to be there," pleaded Oscar. "I want to be able to tell my guests that Harold Robbins, the famous American writer, and his lovely wife, Grace, are my dear friends."

It was to be a photo shoot, and Harold, ever willing to take the opportunity to promote his next book, agreed we would go, even though we knew nothing about this man. Little did we realize how much Oscar Obregon would change our lives.

Two weeks later we were on our way to Acapulco, not having the least idea of what to expect; but when we saw Nirvana, it certainly lived up to its heavenly name. It sat high on a hill overlooking the city and the Pacific Ocean. It was more than a mansion; it was a palace, and each room seemed to be more lavishly decorated than the preceding one. It had an Olympic-size swimming pool surrounded by Ionic Greek columns, each with a flaming torch atop, and at night from virtually anywhere in Acapulco one could see the blazing flames and pinpoint the location as Obregon's Nirvana.

Oscar had a magnificent staff headed up by a world-class chef. Acapulco catered to an international clientele that rented villas during the season, and its chefs had to learn the cuisine of many nations. At Nirvana, you could order any dish you wanted, regardless of whether it was American, Italian, German, French, Swedish, or Mexican; when it was served, it was easy to believe you were actually in the native country to which the food was indigenous. Our French chef in Le Cannet had spoiled me, so I wasn't easy to please, but Oscar Obregon's cook was a genius. The servants, who indulged us like royalty, seemed to exist just to please us, not in a wholly subservient way but more out of pride in demonstrating their incredible skills. They were highly accomplished at everything they did and were unabashedly grateful at the least amount of praise. We had very courteous and responsive help in France, but the attitude in Mexico bordered on adulation.

We had hardly arrived when Oscar gave us a brunch "in order to introduce us to the beautiful people of Acapulco." It was sumptuous and well attended. Among the guests were our old friends Sandra and Ricky di Portanova and Princess Marusia Toumanoff.

I fell in love with Acapulco. The people were wonderful, the climate was perfect, and the beach, aptly called the Mexican Riviera, reminded me of Cannes. Better yet, Acapulco was only a two-and-a-half hour flight from Los Angeles International Airport.

"I love this place," I told Harold one day. "Why don't we buy a home here?"

He was hesitant at first, but after mulling it over he agreed with me. "Yeah, it's a hell of a lot closer than France," he said. "Let's look around for something."

Thus we began our search for a new "casa" in Mexico, much like we had done in Cannes years before. We found a four-level house owned by an American named Bernie Gimble. It needed a lot of work, but as Harold said, "It has a good floor plan, and if you put a little effort into it, you can probably turn it into a showcase, Tiger."

I agreed. It was beautifully laid out, although not on the magnificent scale of Nirvana, which was the ultimate in luxury, but it was larger than our villa in France, with the components to make a great home. It had a lovely swimming pool with a lanai. On the first floor were two master bedrooms adjacent to each other and two smaller bedrooms that could serve as guestrooms. On the second level was an exterior terrace dining room with a view that was perfect for the Mexican climate. The third level had three more bedrooms and the fourth floor consisted of two elegant but simple drawing rooms. The more we looked at it, the more Harold liked it.

"I can work here in any one of a dozen rooms," he said excitedly, rushing up and down the stairs with the abandonment of a child in a toy store.

He talked to Bernie Gimble and cut a deal. We now had homes in France, California, and Mexico, three of the world's greatest locations.

The renovation was a mammoth task and a slow process. When I realized it would be finished in April, I vainly decided our first big bash would be my own birthday celebration. "That's a great idea, Tiger!" Harold agreed exuberantly, and we set about planning our premier party. As it unfolded, our first social function in Acapulco was almost our last.

"Let's recreate the fireworks scene from *The Adventurers*," said Harold. We owned some unused land on a sloping hill in front of the house and he wanted to set off the pyrotechnics from there. It seemed like a colorful idea to me, so I offered no argument. Fireworks were a given at fiestas in Mexico and planning the display gave Harold something to do in the absence of writing.

On the day of the party, Harold stationed an army of men and materiel on the sloping hill, where they would be out of sight of our guests. Later, the party began as scheduled and it was terrific. At a given time the fireworks were set off, a thousand Roman candles flaring skyward in the night and a host of other explosives that lit the sky with the words "Happy Birthday, Grazia!" I was thrilled.

The fireworks continued deep into the night, as did the music of the strolling mariachis and the continuous consumption of margaritas, which we served by the pitcher. We did not realize until the next day that Harold's fireworks display had almost burned down the neighborhood. His army had taken no precautions as to where the fireworks were rocketed and almost every vacant lot on our side of town was burned black as coal, including our hillside that served as the launching pad. We were relieved that none of our neighbors complained.

We picked up our friendship with Sandra and Ricky di Portanova where we had left off in Monte Carlo. They had just built a new home in Acapulco that they named Arabesque; it was an extravagant compound so huge it required forty servants. The most striking thing about it was a watchtower that rose thirty feet high, its guardhouse complete with a small, machine gun–armed security force.

"What are they all about?" I asked Harold one day, pointing to the armed guards in the tower.

"Damned if I know," said Harold. Maybe Ricky has his money stashed in a private vault in his house."

We laughed it off, but we should have taken Ricky's security precautions more seriously.

The rest of the di Portanova home and compound was done with exquisite taste. It was absolutely enchanting. Waterfalls came cascading from the roofs, beautifully backlit at night, adding a touch of class to their alfresco dinner parties given on the terrace. The interior of the main house was decorated in an Arabian theme that would have made Adnan Khashoggi groan with envy. It included an array of life-size camels sculpted by the famous Mexican sculptor Victor Salmones. Victor was a stickler for details and he made certain his animals were anatomically correct. A rumor circulated that Sandra, deciding the male camels were too well endowed, castrated the dromedary statues with a sledgehammer.

Several guesthouses dotted the compound and each was as magnificent in its own way as the main house. The furniture had been designed by another famous artist who had whimsically crafted the ends of the armrests of the chairs with humanlike hands and the legs of the chairs with humanlike feet.

My favorite part of the di Portanova home was the disco, where they held many private parties and charity events. It was a vast room with an underwater theme, Every time I walked into the disco, I felt like a mermaid.

One night I met a Scandinavian woman at one of the di Portanova's disco parties. Her name was Inga. She was accompanied by an older gentleman who turned out to be not only her lover but also a former president of Mexico; although in his eighties at least, he was still a handsome man. Inga, who was decades younger, was blonde and beautiful in a vivacious way that seems exclusively indigenous to Scandinavian women.

"She's a ten," said Harold, "very definitely a ten."

She was also promiscuous, and her lover was possibly the only person present who did not have knowledge of her legion of infidelities. Many of them were revealed to me in a spate of time shorter than it took to sip a margarita. Frankly, I didn't have to believe the rumors; before the evening was over Inga took me into her confidence and between dances she freely described her assorted affairs.

"I conquer whomever I desire," she said. Although I believed her, she offered not a hint that she had placed Harold and me on her list of new challenges.

A few nights after the di Portanova party, Harold ran into Inga at a popular public disco. Undoubtedly heated up anew, he invited her to drop by our house. She came, full of her sexuality, and she spent a considerable amount of time flaunting it, unbuttoning her blouse as if absentmindedly, then buttoning it again, raising her skirt to her thighs when she was sitting down, and making other, more subtle, gestures. Harold was so enticed he didn't realize Inga was putting on her act for me, rather than him.

At the door when she was leaving, she whispered to me, referring to the di Portanova party, "Next time we meet, let's skip the dancing. Shall we?"

The "next time" did not include Harold. A few days after Inga visited our house, he flew to Beverly Hills to renew work on *Dreams Die First*, his next novel. Although he had a spring deadline, I think the purchase of the Acapulco property was the real motivating factor in his getting back to work. A couple of days after he left, I had a telephone call from Inga.

"Grace, why don't you join me for lunch tomorrow?" she said.

"I'd love to," I responded. "Where?"

The next day I went to Inga's luxurious home on the beach. Frankly, I don't remember what the main course was, but it quickly became apparent that I was on the menu as the dessert. She started making advances.

"I prefer men," I said, very sweetly. Inga and I never reconnected sexually, even though we still saw each other socially, and today I think of her with fond memories.

Sexual activity and particularly promiscuous sex was more commonplace in those days than some people want to believe. Both the South of France and Southern California were world-renowned playgrounds, but Acapulco put both of them in the shade. I called it the "beach-boy/beach-girl syndrome" because I suspected the inclination was due to all those bronzed gods and goddesses walking half-naked up and down the beach all day long. I never met anyone who became jaded to them; rather, their continuous presence served to set a mood for the others.

Acapulco was not only a romantic city, it was the sexiest city I had ever been to. There's no question that the climate, too, helped set the stage for lovemaking, and the social conventions we all adhered to was a factor also. Following a relaxing siesta, we'd get dressed for dinner, which usually didn't begin until 11 p.m. Following dinner, the party would continue at one of the city's many discotheques, perhaps at several of them before the night was over. After dancing for several hours the cool, humid air and clear sparkling sky put one in the mood for romance. It was almost inescapable. One night seemed to blend into the next, but each one seemed more incredible than the night before.

Oscar Obregon was a delightful man, and as time passed, our friendship with him grew stronger. He seemed always in good spirits and game to try anything new, which was right up Harold's alley. Oscar claimed to have a successful law office in Mexico City, but he spent so much time with us and at his Acapulco mansion that I didn't know how he found time to practice law. I began to realize his wealth came from old money and that he was essentially a spoiled, rich playboy, although chock-full of fun.

When Harold returned from Beverly Hills, he and Oscar took up where they had left off, like two teenage boys on a lark. Oscar loved Harold's lifestyle and he would latch onto every goofy idea that Harold came up with. Most disconcerting, they wasted enormous energy and time in their efforts to turn the ideas into realities.

Harold claimed he used drugs responsibly, for sexual reasons, and to keep himself going when he was working, but in retrospect I realize he had begun to mix them with all aspects of his life, equal with his consumption of alcohol, which had begun to increase. He was now in his sixties, but his antics were frequently more akin to those of a teenage boy running rampant with wild imagination.

The craziest idea he came up with was the establishment of a Mexican beauty parlor designed to "style" the pubic hairs of its clientele. Oscar was enthusiastic for the project, and they set about designing the coifs with glee. In a playful moment Harold had once shaved a heart on my vagina and now he wanted to take that idea to a commercial level. He suggested to Oscar that they open a shop called "Cunt Coiffures." It was absurd, yet Harold was serious, which gives one a vivid indication of how drugs and booze had come to affect him.

"Acapulco is the perfect place for such a business," said Harold with the seriousness of a corporate executive. "What do you think?"

"I think it's crazy," I responded.

He turned to Oscar, whose eyes were as hazy and dilated as Harold's.

"Magnifico!" cried Oscar. "No one has ever thought of this before. What a business we will have! But how do we go about it?"

"First we have to practice," said Harold. "We have to come up with some designs. Hearts, diamonds, stars. We need some hands-on experience."

I thought they were joking until Oscar brought a new girlfriend over one night to practice on. She was quite attractive and very willing. After a few drinks, Oscar said, "Come on, baby. Take your clothes off. I want Harold to show me how to become a pussy stylist."

When Harold went to the kitchen to find some scissors, I followed him. "Surely Oscar is not serious," I said.

"I don't know if he is or not," Harold answered, "but I am."

He found the scissors and then we found Oscar and the girl, now in one of the bedrooms. The girl was sitting on the edge of a bed, naked. Harold placed a towel on the floor to catch the pubic hairs, and then he said, "Okay, lean back and spread your legs a little."

I left the room, but I could hear them tittering through the course of time. After a while I heard Oscar say, "That's great, Harold! Let me try it!"

Later, when Oscar and the girl were leaving, I heard Harold say with a laugh, "Okay, Oscar, tomorrow we hang our shingle!"

Of course, they never did.

Poor Oscar. He loved life, but he didn't have the same freewheeling backbone that Harold possessed. He committed suicide, allegedly by jumping out the window of his high-rise office in Mexico City. It seemed inexplicable to me, because he always seemed so happy. Later I heard rumors he had been pushed.

Oscar was only one of the many high-living international set who welcomed us to Acapulco. It seemed everyone wanted to meet the famous novelist who had just bought a home on the Mexican Riviera. Shortly after we moved in, we were invited to brunch at a restaurant. Harold declined because he was immersed in his writing, but he urged me to go. I'm sure the other guests were disappointed when I showed up alone, but soon they made me feel welcome. Despite their disappointment at Harold's absence, they treated me nevertheless as the guest of honor. They were a much younger crowd than we usually associated with, but I detected from their questions that they were swingers.

As the brunch progressed, I wondered if Harold's reputation and therefore mine had preceded us. Again, the questions seemed to presuppose that we were actually characters in Harold's novels. Harold would have loved it, but I felt uncomfortable.

Following the brunch, one of the young men asked me if I would "please" look at his apartment, which was located just above the restaurant. He was a handsome young man, truly a Mexican Adonis, all bronzed from the sun and lean as tenderloin. His manners were impeccable and I felt obligated to join him, if for only a moment.

It was a modest apartment, rather sparse of furniture, nothing really to brag about. The second he closed the door behind me, I knew I had to get out of there quickly. His expression changed like the skin of a chameleon, and I saw nothing but sexual hunger, as if he thought I would hop into bed with him like one of Harold's fictional characters. I did not want my name bandied about the rumor mill any more than it probably already was and I rapidly fended the boy off.

That was really my introduction to Acapulco society and it wasn't exactly what I had in mind. I wanted to be a prominent hostess and to continue my efforts toward charity by sponsoring various functions. I excused myself as courteously as possible and got the hell out of there with the realization that I was being tested. Isn't Grace Robbins a swinger? The answer, at least for the moment, was no.

It was not easy, however, to establish and maintain the reputation I wanted in Acapulco. Harold was getting worse, rather than better. If there were any rules at all, he prided himself on breaking them. I had become numb to his one-night stands and casual sex, but he never entered into a longtime relationship, except for the little Australian waif Leslie, who was no threat to my marriage. That circumstance was about to change; in fact, it had begun to change the very moment we arrived in Mexico for Oscar's *Town and Country* photo shoot.

The magazine was represented by two people, Linda Ashland, a writer, and her live-in lover, the photographer Slim Aarons. Linda was a cute girl and a competent journalist who interviewed everyone at the party, which was a good cross-section of Acapulco society. I noticed she gave Harold particular attention, although it didn't surprise me. As the party progressed and the interviews were finished, Linda became very coquettish and continued to go back to Harold. As usual, Harold responded to her flirtations in kind. I was not happy, but there was nothing I could do about it, except hope for a short dalliance. It wasn't to be, that is, short; eventually Linda dumped Slim and became Harold's mistress, although it took me a while to discover the truth.

We spent November through April in the balmy clime of Acapulco, with many commutes to Beverly Hills for business and social reasons. It was not unexpected that Harold would stay alone in Beverly Hills for a few weeks to write; his need to be alone had become a given. But suddenly he found reason to be in New York periodically for an unseemly amount of time. He blamed it on business, "A new deal that Paul Gitlin is cooking up. And believe me, Tiger, it's all above board. No hanky-panky. I've got too much work to do."

The trips gradually became extended. Three days became four, four five, and so forth. Zelda Gitlin had passed away and Harold now stayed at Paul's home rather than in a hotel. When I made my usual daily telephone call to Harold, Paul often answered with a banal excuse for Harold's absence. "He stepped out for a minute, Grace," or "Oh, Grace, he's in the shower. I'll have him call you when he gets out." True to Paul's promise, Harold would return my call in just a few minutes.

Intuitively I knew Harold was having a serious affair with Linda Ashton. First of all, when he came home, he didn't take the time to tell me about his sordid one-night stands that he usually relished in describing. Finally, I didn't need intuition. Unlike his previous liaisons, Harold began to flaunt Linda openly. I didn't have spies per se, but I didn't need them. Word simply flowed back to me unsolicited.

When I joined Harold at various places where he was researching, it was always apparent Linda had just been there, for she would purposely leave Chanel toiletries and other clues behind for me to find. She pretended to be an artist and she once left a sketch of a nude woman prominently displaying her ass with the words "Do you want some?" scribbled underneath the picture in her own handwriting. When I went to Cannes alone, the villa and yacht staffs spared no details in giving me a full report of Linda's affair with Harold, information that frankly I could have lived more peacefully without hearing. It was significant, too, that the fellows on the yacht did not keep the secret to themselves; that's how open the affair had become. Even Harold's secretary took me aside and showed me bills for a variety of expensive clothes Harold had purchased, which certainly weren't for me. When I saw bills from Paris, I was heartbroken. I remembered that wonderful time when Harold had taken me to the couture houses, when any- and everything was mine for the having.

I decided to confront Harold. If he had set some rules that day so long ago in Beverly Hills, he had now broken them all. I waved a bill in his face. "You didn't tell me you went to France," I said.

"I . . . I . . . it was just a quick trip."

"Oh, and what's this?" It was a Parisian clothing bill.

"That's . . . that's . . . it was for research on the book." He was then working on *Goodbye, Janette*, a story set in the world of high fashion. "I needed to go backstage at the fashion houses," he tried to explain.

"With Linda Ashton?" I cried, waving another bill.

"She met me there," he continued. "I needed her to introduce me to the couturiers and other figures in the industry."

"You certainly didn't need any help when you took me there the first time we were in France!" I screamed.

It was insulting, as if Harold Robbins needed an introduction. Nevertheless, the confrontation had a beneficial result. Harold eventually broke it off with Linda, who I understand finally lost her job as a journalist. The benefit, however, did not outweigh the injury done to our relationship; I knew at last that a breakup with Harold was somewhere in the future.

Meanwhile, I met a very young man named Skip at the annual SHARE charity fundraiser in Los Angeles. I loved the SHARE galas because they weren't stuffy and pretentious like many of the gown and black-tie affairs. In fact, the dress code for the SHARE functions, as always, was country and western, and Skip seemed to be a perfect urban cowboy. Harold was in New York on "business," not that his absence cramped my social life, for he had stopped attending charity events long before. I had since become a loner in the charity world because he always had "work" to do.

Skip was in his twenties, tall and slim—a sort of male version of Harold's Leslie, now that I think back on it.

"Hi," he said with a sort of woebegone James Dean look, "I'm Skip."

"I'm Grace," I told him.

"Yeah," he continued with a shrug. "Somebody told me you were married to Harold Robbins, the writer. You know, *The Carpetbaggers* and all that other stuff."

I laughed. "Yes, all kinds of other stuff."

He smiled, rather sheepishly, and seemed to make a transformation from Jimmy Dean to a young Gary Cooper— a rugged, all-American cowboy come to save the damsel in distress. I liked him, although I didn't take the bait.

Skip was a friend of a friend of mine; it unfolded in the days and weeks to come that he was a drifter who moved from one friend's apartment to another, with no place of his own to call home. He had a bad boy attitude, little formal education, but a heavy dose of street smarts. Under normal circumstances, I wouldn't have given him the time of day, much less help him, but things were no longer normal.

When Harold returned, he tried to be all honey and dew, without mentioning anything about Linda, now stashed away in New York. Skip was in need of a place to stay and I felt sorry for him, not having yet become au courant about his real character. What to do? Well, I came up with a solution, which was one of the worst ideas I ever conceived.

After Harold bought the house in Acapulco, we knew our time in Cannes would be limited. We still had the *Gracara*, but we decided to get a smaller yacht to use on the Pacific. One day when we were at the Los Angeles Boat Show, we bought a forty-footer named *The Spellbinder* and anchored it in Marina del Rey, south of Santa Monica. Actually we had purchased the boat on a whim after *Dreams Die First* was published in 1977; as a result, we had rarely used it.

Since Skip was currently without a place to stay, I decided to let him stay on *The Spellbinder*, without mentioning it to Harold, who never went to the Marina. My rationale was simple: if Harold could keep his new mistress on the *Gracara* in Cannes, then I could let a potential "boy toy" use our yacht in Marina del Rey. Is this what was happening now, "tit for tat?"

Not long after Skip moved onto the *Spellbinder*, Harold and I took off for Cannes, although we knew in advance the trip's regular lengthy duration would be purposely cut short. After all, Harold still had his on-going "business" in New York, and I was anxious to return to Los Angeles.

Leaving Skip behind in Marina del Rey was a disaster. He was not only a loner and a drifter, but he was a thief, too. Not long after we arrived in the South of France, he sailed to Mexico with an accomplice, not on a pleasure cruise but for the purpose of selling the *Spellbinder* on the black market. Fortunately, or unfortunately, depending on the way one looks at it, the manager of the Marina del Rey marina noticed the boat was missing and called the police.

Almost immediately we received a telephone call in Cannes. Harold answered it. The *Spellbinder* had been intercepted as it sailed south, hugging the Pacific coastline. Did we know anything about it?

"No," Harold told them.

"One of the crew claims he's a close friend of Mrs. Robbins and that she gave him permission to use the yacht."

We got the *Spellbinder* back, Skip went on to his next victim, and I explained the circumstances in a roundabout way to Harold.

"He was just a young man I met at a SHARE charity event and he needed a place to stay for a while," I told him lamely. "How was I to know he was a pirate?"

Harold did not press me for more details, but I knew his indifference to what he considered my infidelity was another sign of the continuing deterioration of our marriage. In a way I felt self-satisfied, however perversely, for I thought I had achieved some sort of moral victory. Linda leaving her toiletries and sketches of her ass around for me to find were nothing in comparison to Skip's yacht-jacking.

Part Three

The End

"He was a genius, so you had to take his idiosyncrasies as a given. It was okay when he was with Grace; she was great for him. But all geniuses seem to have their downfall. Before he fell through, Harold had a great run."

—Gene Schwam

23

Stroke and Coke

When Harold and I returned to the United States, we stuck around only long enough for Harold to diddle around with Linda for a few days; then we were off to Acapulco. If I had lost the bad taste in my mouth in France, it returned in New York. I was angry again, seething silently, but when I had the opportunity to get back at Harold, I let it pass.

Acapulco is in the State of Guerrero, and its governor at the time was a big fan of Harold and his books. When he invited us to attend his birthday party, we were delighted and honored.

We were not surprised to be picked up in a limousine and have a police escort to the governor's mansion. Many times before, when Harold was in a rush, the state had provided the same service. In fact, from servants to politicians, the people of Acapulco always treated us with enormous—and what we considered very special—respect.

The birthday party was like no other birthday party we had ever attended or given. It was held in a huge, beautiful plaza enclosed by a forest of trees. Almost every important Mexican politician was in attendance. The governor welcomed us personally, played the perfect host, and then had us seated at a table on a very high dais overlooking the grounds. He then took his place upon a large throne-like chair. Important government officials were seated on his left and Harold and I were on his right. A sumptuous meal was served that can only be called a feast.

During this lunch an interesting ritual unfolded before us. Peasants and blue-collar workers formed a long queue, each bearing a gift for the chief executive. They were all dressed in white and their gifts were mainly food, produce or meat, except the meat was live chickens, turkeys, pigs, calves, lambs, and a ram goat. I was particularly interested in the ram because I had never seen one close up.

"What are you staring at?" whispered Harold.

"The ram," I told him.

"Why?"

"Because I'm an Aries. Remember? It's my astrological sign." He laughed.

The governor received each gift personally, handed it over to a lieutenant, and shook the well-wisher's hand, a ceremony that seemed to go on forever. I found the scene fascinating. Although Harold grew restless, he included a similar episode in a later novel.

Despite the interminable hubbub with the gifts and animals, I had undoubtedly caught the governor's eye. He kept glancing at me with unquestionable flirtation. He would receive a pig or chicken, hand it away, and then glance at me with a twinkle in his eyes. I was delighted, and when we returned home, I received an especially flowery thank you note from him for my having attended his birthday party; he didn't mention Harold.

A few days later, Harold returned to Beverly Hills to work on his latest book. The next day I received another letter from the governor, again thanking me for attending his party and telling me how delighted he was to have met me. In Harold's absence I decided to return the governor's favor. I invited him to a party at our villa.

It was a large party, and as far as I could determine everyone on the guest list showed up, except the governor. Deep into the party I expressed my disappointment.

"Oh, don't worry," I was told. "In Mexico it is traditional for the most important guest to arrive last and to leave first."

I held my breath at this news, but not for long. Sure enough, well into the party, the governor arrived with his entourage. The first problem was that it was so late many of the guests were already preparing to leave. They didn't, however, honoring the age-old tradition. The second problem was that the governor stayed and stayed and stayed. People were yawning, awaiting his departure. Finally, he slipped me a note, thanking me for the party and promising to return sometime. He left first, as was the custom; the minute his limousine drove away there was a rush to the door by the other exhausted guests as though a fire alarm had sounded. By this time it was in the wee hours of the morning.

The servants quickly cleaned up the place, the dozens of empty glasses and half-filled plates, and then I sent them to bed. Suddenly I found myself alone in the midst of memory. I was pleased, though, for it had been a wonderful party despite the governor's long stay. Finally, I decided to retire.

As I started toward the bedroom, there was a heavy knock at the front door. I listened and the knock was repeated. I went to the door and opened it.

The governor was standing on the threshold, seemingly as fresh as a daisy, and alone. The moment was awkward because I really didn't know what to say or do with him.

"Oh," I said, "won't you please come in?"

"Thank you."

He came in.

The party had taken place primarily on the terrace, so I asked, "Would you like to see our villa?"

"Of course."

I gave him a tour, making sure that I avoided the master bedroom. When we arrived at the top level, I said, "Would you like a cocktail?"

"Of course."

I mixed a couple of drinks at the bar, and then we sat down on barstools.

"It's a lovely home," he said, "very charming."

"Thank you."

"When will Harold return?"

"I don't know," I told him. "He's working on a book in the States."

With that bit of knowledge, the governor suddenly grabbed my breasts with both hands. I was so taken aback that I shoved him and leaped up from my chair. I was speechless and didn't know what to say. He stood in turn, obviously nervous at his overreaction to being alone with me.

"Respecto!" he muttered. "Respecto!" He said it over and over again, until I realized that it was his way of saying he didn't mean any disrespect.

I nodded my acceptance of his apology and escorted him down the stairs and to the front door. He sort of clicked his heels and I threw the door open. Outside was a huge cavalcade of cars, his entire entourage of officials, lieutenants, and bodyguards armed with automatic weapons. I could have died. I had just rejected their leader! I stared at this small army and thought, *My god, Grace, what have you done now? Are you in trouble or what?*

The governor went down the steps. At the bottom landing he turned back to me with a wistful but apologetic expression. "Respecto," he said for the hundredth time.

"Gracias," I said, "respecto tambien." And I quickly closed the door as I eyed several of the waiting cars.

When Harold returned, I did not tell him what had happened. Since his affair with Linda, our lines of communication seemed severed. Nothing had happened anyway, except for the brief and futile groping of a horny politician.

I had been a little afraid after the governor had left that night, knowing that some Mexican politicos were of ruthless character and had virtually unlimited authority to create problems for anyone who happened to get on their shit list, regardless of the reason. I need not have worried. The governor took my rejection in stride and became a good friend who never hesitated to help us when we were in need, no matter how menial the problem—that is, for the time being.

The incident with the governor occurred during the beginning of the eighties, the Decade of Greed. I did not know it at the time, but it foreshadowed a period of total and unmitigated despair, for Harold as much as for me. On the surface, however, it seemed we had all that a couple could want. For *Memories of Another Day*, Harold's last book of the previous decade, published in 1979, Paul Gitlin had engineered his largest advance yet: $2,500,000. "I've made him so much money this time that he can't possibly spend it all before his next book comes out," said Paul,

Actually, that figure was only the core of Harold's wealth. All of his books were still in print and selling well, although the critics were saying more and more that he was now rehashing previously told stories, changing the names of the characters, and giving each old story a new title. Harold pushed himself more than ever, but it wasn't because he anticipated writing a great book; it was because our financial obligations (regardless of what Paul Gitlin thought) were growing larger by the year. Although we had given up the New Year's Eve parties, we still had parties, plenty of them, some for Harold and some for me, usually in two different places. We had an 11,000-square-foot mansion in Beverly Hills, a villa in France, another in Acapulco, with fulltime staffs to go with them. We had a ninety-foot yacht and its paid crew in Cannes and a forty-foot yacht in Marina del Rey, not to mention a dozen luxury cars. We still used them all, but it was blatantly and terribly irresponsible—yet we were so caught up in our lifestyle that we couldn't see the foolishness of it. When someone compared our lives to the tragedy of Zelda and Scott Fitzgerald, I pooh-poohed it as nonsense. One evening at a party in Beverly Hills, when Joan Collins, who was starring in the television hit *Dynasty*, remarked, "My life as Alexis on television is fantastic, yet fictional. But for your fantastic life, Grace, it's for real and I want those twenty-four karat gold nails you wear for Alexis." I thought silently, *Yes, Joan, but if you only knew what took place behind the scenes.*

I had never been superstitious, but I began to think our mansion in Beverly Hills was cursed. So many needless calamities occurred there. We had not built it from scratch, but had spent a fortune in time and money to renovate and customize it to fit our needs and personalities. Not long after we had begun the project, I was told that a ghost lived in the attic, the ghost of a former owner. Allegedly the mistress of the house had discovered her husband making love to another man in the master bedroom. She had collapsed on the spot and subsequently died of heart failure, such was her shock. How her ghost ended up living in the attic, I don't know, but I began to believe there might be something to the legend.

Our first tragedy occurred in 1980. It happened in the bathroom, which came perhaps with a curse of its own. The portrait Tom Horky had painted of me half-nude, holding an apple like Eve in the Garden of Eden, was hanging there. It had always been Harold's favorite painting, and when we first got together, it was one of the few things I took out of the apartment Tom and I had shared.

Late one night when we were sleeping, the fire alarms went off. We awoke groggily, but quickly realized the seriousness of the situation. A thin veil of smoke permeated the room. We set out in search of the source of the fire. Harold went into the bathroom. A wastebasket was on fire with flames licking the air. One of us had dumped an ashtray without realizing a cigarette had not been extinguished. Harold threw some water on the fire, which was a mistake. The flames were replaced by heavy, dark billowing smoke.

Harold had always had lung problems, but two years previously his condition had been exacerbated when he ventured down into some West Virginia coalmines while researching *Memories of Another Day*. He had contracted coal miner's lung from the sifting coal dust. After inhaling so much smoke in the bathroom, he developed what was called fireman's lung. He never recovered and for the rest of his life he needed a canister of oxygen nearby in the event his ability to breath was diminished, which was often. It didn't help that he continued to smoke cigarettes, even when he was using an oxygen mask. He would lift the mask up, take a puff, and then lower the mask back to his face.

After other, even more tragic, events happened in the house, I began to wonder if Tom, through his painting, had somehow hexed our lives, taking revenge on us because Harold had taken me away from him.

Caryn had grown up now, and when we learned she had become engaged, Harold wanted to have a lavish wedding in our home. We planned a grand event, and on the wedding day the house looked gorgeous. A couple of hours before the ceremony, I began to get ready. Naturally, it was a formal affair, and when I finished dressing Harold suggested that I go downstairs while he jumped into the shower before putting on his tuxedo.

Something happened while he was showering, but none of us realized what, not even Harold. He dressed alone, but when he came downstairs he wasn't himself. The ceremony went off beautifully, but during the reception one of the guests of Caryn's new husband's family asked Harold who the subject was of another painting, one that hung in our living room. It was a portrait of me with the yellow sunflowers that Harold had commissioned a few years before by a Russian artist. Harold studied the painting for a long moment and then said, "I don't remember." He studied it again, just as fitfully as before, and then turned to someone and asked, "Who is that woman in the painting?" He wasn't joking, and I knew it. It was the painting he had used to silkscreen my face on the T-shirts at my birthday party five years before. I rushed over to him.

'Harold," I said, "why don't you sit down for a moment? I think something has happened to you."

He didn't argue with me. I sat him down and he seemed to stare blankly into space. After a moment, he said, "Why are all these people here?" That was it; I called 911. Harold had suffered a stroke while taking a shower.

For the next few days I was on pins and needles. Fortunately, the stroke was not paralyzing, but it created a condition called aphasia, which affects the victim's natural ability to juxtapose words and articulate ideas properly. In Harold's case the condition caused him to forget words and to write sentences backwards. For the average victim, it was a tragedy; for a writer, it was a catastrophe. Harold never fully recovered, but in a classic case of making lemonade out of lemons, he later fictionalized his stroke in *The Storyteller*.

Two years later the culminating factor that destroyed our relationship began. I represented Harold at the Cannes Film Festival because he wasn't well enough to attend. Meshulam Riklis, Pia Zadora's husband, had purchased the movie rights to *The Lonely Lady* as a film vehicle for his wife. He had planned several cocktail parties and luncheons surrounding the announcement of the forthcoming movie and a recognition dinner in Harold's honor. It was the type of media event Harold always tried to take advantage of.

"I know I can't go, Tiger, but you can. You'll have to represent me."

"But Harold—"

"Don't argue with me. You're the only person in the world who can stand in my shoes. You've been involved in everything that ever happened to me that was important. I'm counting on you, darling, like I always have. And you can also scout around for a buyer of the villa. I won't be able to ever return to France."

Of course, I went, and dutifully made my way from party to party, as well as speaking at the dinner honoring him. Had it not been for Harold's condition I would have had a ball, but frankly, it was no longer the same without him, regardless of the gulf that was widening between us.

When I returned to Beverly Hills from Cannes, he had a surprise for me. He had thoughtfully hired a personal assistant "to help you keep things organized." I had previously had a secretary, but she had left for a position in the motion picture industry.

The new woman was Jann Stapp who said that she was a former partner in an advertising agency in Oklahoma that had apparently gone bankrupt. I was surprised, not at Harold's generosity, which had not changed, but at Jann's appearance. Harold liked to be surrounded by beautiful girls, whether they were employees or not, and Jann was not remotely the type of girl Harold had always appreciated in the past. She was plain and rather frumpy, a bit overweight, and her hair was a fright. Harold liked attractive young women who took care of themselves and flaunted their beauty. She was obviously one of those women who didn't pay much attention to her physical appearance. Jann reminded me of a stereotypical schoolmarm with a certain librarian aura. Linda Ashland she was not, and therefore I felt absolutely no threat from her whatsoever. I didn't even remotely consider it.

Besides, I liked Jann. She had a nice smile and she was friendly, although in a sort of distant way. She proved herself valuable, too, not only for me with my hectic charity work while serving on dozens of fund-raising committees here and abroad, but also for Harold. He had ever increasing medical needs and she attended to them diligently.

One day I remarked to Harold, "I don't know what I would ever do without Jann." He did not say a thing.

"You know what?" I added. "She's so good to you that you should remember her in your will."

He shrugged lightly, again without comment.

"You might at least consider it, Harold," I continued.

"Do you think I'm gonna suddenly fucking die or something?" he asked caustically.

"No, and I didn't mean it like that," I said, and let the moment pass.

As Jann continued to work for me, I noticed that her physical appearance improved considerably. I had always prided myself on looking as attractive as I possibly could, and I thought maybe the fact I took a little extra time in preparing myself, whether for work or for a social function, was having a beneficial effect on Jann, that setting an example had motivated her.

I went on my merry way, innocently watching Jann's improvements, even though some of them didn't make sense to me. One day she asked, "Would you mind if I got my breasts enlarged?"

Since she didn't need my permission for such an operation, I was taken aback that she posed it as a question for my approval. I didn't know what to say. Suddenly I became suspicious.

"I've always wanted to do it, but I couldn't afford to," she said. "But now that I have some extra money . . ."

She explained that her grandmother had recently passed away and left her a small inheritance, which she could use for a boob job. That Harold might be her "grandmother" began flashing in my mind. The big bad wolf after Little Red Riding Hood, maybe, but then I thought Jann was a far cry from the image of a cute little nursery rhyme girl. So I dismissed it.

"I'll be very honest with you," I told Jann in a motherly fashion. "I wouldn't advise you to spend your money that way. After all, you don't go out very often and outside of me the only ones who see you are Harold, Adréana, the servants, and the dogs." It had become apparent she had no friends, but I let that pass. She looked at me with a sad pouty expression. So I reconsidered, "If it will make you feel better about yourself, then go ahead and do it."

She went ahead and did it. After the surgery she flaunted her new breasts around the house. It was almost ridiculous, until I realized one day she was trying to act like me with her every gesture. My breasts were real and what flaunting I did came naturally, but I knew, too, that it was much more than the breast thing. She asked me if she could have some of my old dresses.

"Where would you wear them?" I asked, trying to mask my growing suspicion.

"Well, when you have parties," she said. "I'd like to dress up and look nice."

Her answer seemed honest and logical, so I gladly gave her some of my wardrobe. My clothes, however, weren't enough. Next she went to a beauty salon and had her hair coiffed almost identical to mine. No, not almost—exactly like mine. When she showed up at the house wearing one of my dresses and coifed with my hairstyle, I thought, *My god, the woman is trying to become me!*

Next she excitedly showed me a new, outrageously expensive BMW. For a bankrupt advertising agent now on a slightly more than modest salary, she was doing quite well for herself. Her grandmother must have died wallowing in hoarded money.

For all of my wondering about Jann's behavior, I was still terribly naive. I said to Harold, "Don't you find her actions peculiar? She's wearing my old dresses, has new artificial breasts, has taken up my hairdo, and now she's gone out and spent a fortune on a fancy new car."

Harold shrugged nonchalantly and said dismissively, "Who cares? Let the girl have some fun with her imagination. She certainly doesn't have anything else going on in her life."

For Christmas, Harold gave me a karaoke machine with his own personal instruction: "Have a ball, Tiger!" He knew how much I liked to sing, although I'd never had any professional training. I loved the songs of Frank Sinatra and Cole Porter is my favorite composer—I knew all of their songs by heart. 'You're really great, Grazia. You could have been a professional singer," Harold often said. He thought the karaoke would help me improve what talent I had, and I took it as the most thoughtful gift he had given me in a long time.

"Don't you want to go to Acapulco?" he asked later in the day.

"Of course I do!" I exclaimed with excitement. "When do we leave?"

"Hell, I can't go. I've got to work on this goddamned book and besides I can't walk" he said, "but I know how much you like it down there this time of year."

"Oh, Harold, I wouldn't leave you here alone during the holidays," I protested.

"Are you kidding?" he responded. "I don't have time for a holiday. I'm gonna be pounding the fucking typewriter keys. Besides, if I need anything, Jann will be here. What the hell do you think I'm paying her for?"

I went to Acapulco. Whether Harold had anything to do with it or not, I don't know, but almost immediately the entertainment director of the new Acapulco Plaza Hotel asked me to perform at its opening night charity gala. I was thrilled and began to rehearse for my world premiere as a café society chanteuse.

Meanwhile, Harold was struck by a new tragedy. As usual, he had been putting in his grueling twelve-hour days at the typewriter, although his aphasia made his work more difficult and frustrating. On the night of February 23, 1984, he and Jann joined some friends of ours, restaurateur Bif Caruso and his wife Patty, for dinner at a local restaurant in Los Angeles. I discovered later that Harold and the Carusos had snorted an enormous amount of cocaine while they were out on the town.

When they returned home, Harold went upstairs to take a shower in the bad-luck bathroom. Jann was in the kitchen on the ground floor. At some point she noticed water seeping from the kitchen ceiling. She rang the phone in the bathroom, but there was no answer. She rang again: still no answer. In a sudden panic she rushed upstairs.

Harold was sprawled unconscious on the bathroom floor. Later, press accounts reported he had tripped on the tub and hit his head on a marble counter. In an interview with *People* magazine, Harold gave his personal recollection of the accident, which was accurate but incomplete. "After hitting my head I slid unconscious across the bathroom floor with such force that I hit the toilet bowl, knocking it off its pipes. The water began pouring out. My legs wound up on either side of the bowl." His left hip had been badly shattered and his pubic bone broken.

He didn't mention to *People* that he had suffered a cocaine-induced seizure, which caused him to lose consciousness and fall. We managed to keep the truth out of the scandal sheets and mainstream media, even though the doctors who ministered to Harold at UCLA Medical Center confirmed the truth, which included a devastating prognosis concerning Harold's recovery. It was going to be a long, long while before he was himself again, if ever.

When Jann found him that night, she first placed a call to 911 and then called me. I was on the next flight to Los Angeles.

During the next eight months, Harold underwent three complicated operations. His bones, however, never mended. He was in constant pain and confined to a wheelchair; gradually he managed to ambulate slowly for a short distance on crutches, but it was never easy. There was one brief period when he managed to use a walking cane, but it didn't last.

The medical bills were horrendous. Although we had insurance, Harold claimed he ended up paying over one million dollars out of pocket. I believed him at the time, but much later I came to the conclusion he was trying to hide money from me.

A couple of weeks after the accident Harold said to me, 'Why don't you go back to Acapulco. I don't want you to miss your singing debut."

"Oh, Harold, don't be silly. There's no way I'm going back while you're in this condition."

"There's nothing you can do for me, Tiger. Only time can take care of my problems. You've put in too much rehearsing to miss your big moment down there."

"No, I don't care about it that much," I told him adamantly and sincerely. "It's just a hotel in Acapulco, Harold. It's not like it's a command performance for the Queen."

"Goddammit, the show must go on. You're scheduled to perform and that's what you're going to do! Now go pack your fucking bags! If for no one else, I want you to do it for me."

It seemed for a moment that the accident had somehow propelled Harold back into the person he had been in the early years of our marriage, always the considerate husband, so eager to please me.

"Okay, Harold," I said tenderly and honestly, "I'll do it for you."

"That's my girl," he said. As I was leaving the room, he added, "Besides, if I need anything, Jann will take care of it."

Reluctantly, I returned to Acapulco. I performed at the charity event, and although it was a certified smash, it was bittersweet even with Tony Bennett there. I had too many other things on my mind, considering what had happened back in Beverly Hills. I returned to California as quickly as possible.

Things were not better. Harold was not recuperating from his surgery as well as his doctors had hoped he would. Besides the debilitating effects of not being able to walk or write easily, he required more than thirty medications a day. Even with Jann helping me, I realized we needed professional assistance. I contacted an agency and signed on for a private registered nurse.

She was disastrous. She looked like a *Playboy* centerfold in costume for a photo shoot. Her bust line was forty-plus and her body seemed poured into a uniform two sizes too small. She spent most of her time staring at her image in the mirrors on the walls and ceiling of our master bedroom. Harold, of course, thought she was great, but she wasn't worth the enormous cost of her "services." Jann hated her, which didn't strike me as odd at the time, and she was delighted when I finally dismissed the woman. Jann assured me she could do everything the nurse did, and more. Little did I know . . .

Although Harold and I had been drifting apart long before the accident, we still slept together. But now, because of his extraordinary sensitivity to touch, I moved into a separate bedroom. He yelped like an injured dog at the slightest physical contact, so it became a hands-off relationship. I was afraid of doing irreparable damage to him. It was a lonely period and I cried a lot. Even after Harold began to mend somewhat, the medications served to kill his sex drive. Although he finally adjusted to the wheelchair and became mobile, he didn't want to go out anymore. Our once magnificent jet-set lifestyle suddenly came to a screeching halt.

Our problems were compounded by secrecy. Few people knew of the seriousness of Harold's infirmity. He was adamant that we maintain his image of the dashing globetrotting novelist. Our friend Couri Hay, of the *National Enquirer*, helped considerably in keeping his true condition out of the press, just as we had managed to do with the real cause of the original accident. I couldn't even confide in friends. Adréana was in Paris going to school and thankfully didn't have to deal with the problem, but her absence increased my own sense of isolation.

Harold's loss of sex drive was not the only side effect he suffered. The painkillers deadened his nerve cells that were critical to motor coordination; now he had difficulty writing. I talked to our long-time friend Larry Flynt of *Hustler* magazine fame who had been paralyzed in an assassination attempt some years before. Larry loved Harold and would have done everything to help us. But, alas, Harold went back to the hospital for more surgery. An electrical device was implanted in his spine that allowed him to mask his pain via electrical shocks from a remote control box. It wasn't 100 percent effective, but it eliminated enough pain to let him keep his mind clear for writing. Later, he sold an interviewer: "If you pour on too much juice, it can knock you on your ass. Drugs are either a high or you go to sleep, neither of which I wanted. I just wanted to stop the pain period, and get back to work."

After many months word of Harold's physical predicament finally leaked out. One day Beverly Hills philanthropist Arthur Spitzer called. He wanted Harold to talk with Norman Cousins, the dynamic editor of the *Saturday Review* who had written a best seller describing his own debilitating illness and how he had coped with his pain. At that point Harold was willing to talk with almost anyone. He asked me to invite Arthur and Norman over.

They came, toting along with them Cousins's biofeedback machine. After a brief explanation of how the machine worked, Harold sent them away, rather rudely. "That goddamned contraption would never work for me!" he complained angrily.

Although Jann had been hired as my assistant, gradually she became Harold's full-time nurse. A full year after Harold's accident, it seemed at last that things were getting better. He was at least mobile, although he was in a wheelchair but unable to travel. We spent an uneventful Christmas and New Year's together, and bided our time. I had told friends that I would return to Acapulco after the first of the year, but I caught a mild case of the flu and canceled my trip.

Luckily, Ricky di Portanova had persuaded us to have our home guarded, and we finally stationed a guard with a rifle on the roof of our house. Because of the threat of kidnapping, almost everyone in upper-class society had precautionary security. Although we followed suit, I never gave it much thought.

Apparently, the word did not get out to everyone that I had canceled my trip to Acapulco. January 6 was a national Mexican holiday, Three Kings Night. That evening a young and inexperienced maid was the only person at the villa; the others were attending a church service.

Someone knocked on the door. The maid looked through the peephole, but no one seemed to be there. When she returned to her room, the knocking resumed, louder. Again she went to the door. This time, however, she made the mistake of opening it. Three men wearing ski masks pushed her aside and rushed into the house.

"Donde esta la señora?" they demanded. "Where is the mistress of the house?"

"She isn't here," the frightened maid told them, but they refused to believe her.

"Take us to her bedroom!" they said.

Under the threat of violence she led them to my bedroom. The door was locked.

"Open the door!" they told her.

"I don't have a key," she said, which was true. When we were out of town, we left the key with our attorney Señor Ayela, who also managed our property.

At that moment the rest of the staff and their families returned from the church services. They were lined up and interrogated as to my whereabouts. Everyone said the same thing, "La señora is not here." The three men became so enraged that they battered down the door to my room. Realizing my absence, they then proceeded to beat the male servants and to rape the women. I was obviously an intended kidnap victim, since they did not loot the house. In fact, they took nothing, except the dignity of my staff. It was a terribly violent assault.

Suzi, the *New York Post* gossip columnist, broke the story in the United States and it was soon in all the major newspapers. How she found out, I never knew. In Acapulco the story was a public relations disaster. The tourist industry began to suffer; the rich Americans who normally left the frigid north after the holidays failed to arrive. As a result there were many empty villas and unoccupied hotel rooms. For some reason the local press vilified me as the cause of the problem, as if I, rather than the armed intruders, had committed a crime.

We then received a call from the governor of Guerrero. "Do not worry," he told Harold and me. "I will find the culprits and they will be punished."

Sure enough, he called again two days later and said the men had been captured and were being dealt with. In fact, the men had been killed by state policemen. All I knew was that we would never be able to enjoy Acapulco again without fear of something bad happening. It was a sad revelation.

I returned to Acapulco alone to sell the house with my dear friend Fernando Allende. Fernando was both a great actor and a singer, renowned and loved throughout Latin America, especially in his native Mexico. He helped me immensely during the period when I had to let the staff go. It was unsettling because most of them were related and I saw a family disintegrating, something I could certainly empathize with. I loved them all, but the property had to be liquidated.

When I left to return to Beverly Hills, I had misgivings. Our time in Acapulco had begun with a serendipitous experience, coming about because of a chance meeting with Oscar Obregon in the Polo Lounge at the Beverly Hills Hotel. Our time in Mexico had been wonderful, but as I was beginning to realize, all good things really do come to an end.

24

Things Fall Apart

*I*n June, I went to Paris to attend Adréana's graduation from the American School. She was no longer my baby girl. I wondered where all the time had gone? It seemed like yesterday that I had given birth to her in the clinic in Cannes, but here she was now a beautiful young woman.

The weather was still chilly in Paris at night, and I noticed that one of the windowpanes in Adréana's apartment had been broken out.

"What happened to the window?" I asked.

"Oh, it was like that when I moved in and the landlord refused to fix it," she said.

I was shocked. She had endured the frigid Parisian winter with what amounted to an open window. My maternal instinct kicked in immediately. "Pack your bags," I said. "We're going to Cannes."

We went to the villa in Le Cannet, but a terrible transformation had taken place since I had last been there. A crime wave had swept across France and the Riviera was infested almost as badly as Acapulco. Many of our old friends had moved. Wealthy Arabs had begun to buy up the villas in Cannes, Le Cannet, and in the area north of our property, ironically named Californie. Foolishly they flaunted their wealth and the criminal element came pouring in, the way tourists had done years before. I heard all kinds of rumors about criminal activity; whether they were true or not did not matter. I was frightened. Everything had changed. The once sleepy village of Le Cannet was now dangerous terrain laden with strangers; I wanted nothing to do with them.

I wondered if I was overreacting, but my staff was just as apprehensive as I was. They were inordinately cautious and the butler had taken to walking the grounds at night with a police dog and a shotgun.

I knew that Harold in his debilitated condition would never be able to jet back and forth as we had done during the old days, which seemed suddenly so long ago. Even now, after an absence of only a year or so, he would not have recognized Cannes, the colorful beachfront town that he had once loved as much as I had. It was dull now, lacking color, and the spontaneous fun we had enjoyed seemed no longer. I called him and suggested that we sell the Villa Grazia. He didn't even question me.

"Sell it by all means," he said instantly.

Within two months I managed to divest ourselves of everything we had accumulated in France during two decades. I put an ad in the *International Herald Tribune* announcing the sale of the villa and the smaller house, where the servants lived. I sold them almost immediately to a building contractor who asked if he could keep the name Villa Grazia. Another ad served to dispose of our fleet of cars, including Harold's prototype red Jensen and my white Cadillac convertible. I gave his moped that he used to scoot around town on to one of the crewmembers of the yacht. I wanted to keep the gold Mercedes, but when I mentioned it to Harold, he was obstinate: "No, get rid of it! Sell everything, including the *Gracara*!"

His office on avenue Madrid went over night to an elderly French couple who loved it. I thought it would take more time to find a buyer for the *Gracara*, but I was lucky again. While I was in St. Tropez, I bumped into a friend of Adnan Khashoggi who had heard the yacht was up for sale. He bought it and changed the name. The last I heard it was still docked in St. Tropez. I wanted to ship our lovely and elegant furniture to Beverly Hills, but again Harold wouldn't hear of it. All of the proceeds from the sales were going to Harold's attorney in Paris; when I asked for an accounting, he wouldn't give me one, saying that most of the money was going to the French government for payment of back taxes. Upset, I called Harold.

"Don't worry about it," he said.

Meanwhile, in the States, Harold was liquidating our other holdings. He sold our Beverly Hills mansion. He then rented a four-house compound in Palm Springs. For the first time in over twenty years we owned no property.

When I left France for the United States, the contractor who bought our property had already begun to demolish our villa and the two-story servant's house. He started construction of an apartment building, which he called Villa Grazia. The name was the only remaining vestige of the wonderfully extravagant life we had lived in Cannes and Le Cannet.

I did not stay long in Los Angeles. Harold wanted me in Palm Springs to decorate our new compound. His breathing had become difficult and cumbersome, and when the remodeling began he couldn't take the dust the contractors kicked up. He and Jann checked into a suite at the Maxim Hotel, while I oversaw the renovations during the hot month of August.

For two months I lived amidst the dust and hammering and sawing. At night, Harold and I would meet for dinner at one of the local restaurants. Jann always came along, and after we finished dining she would take Harold back to his luxury suite at the hotel and I would retire to the hot compound. Harold was obviously ill, so my suspicions were not aroused. Someone had to make sure he took his daily dose of medicine, which still included thirty odd pills.

The main house at the compound had two bedrooms and a maid's room. I designed a room for Harold, which was across the hall from the room I chose for myself, after his doctor told me that it was still preferable for Harold to sleep alone. He was fragile and sensitive, and if I rolled over him during sleep I might injure him.

The property had three guesthouses. I decorated one for Jann, another for Adréana when she visited, and the third I turned into an office for Harold. It was finished in October 1985. Harold and Jann moved from the hotel and everything seemed to work out fine. Somehow, I had managed to fit all the furniture from the Beverly Hills mansion without cluttering up the place; in fact, it was quite comfortable.

We lived in the Las Palmas area; our immediate neighbors were the Kirk Douglas's and the Sidney Sheldon's. They welcomed us wholeheartedly and invited us to join their social set, although Harold reneged. I enjoyed the change; life in Palm Springs was very different than what it had been in Acapulco and Beverly Hills. The pace was slower, and most of our friends were older (although younger than Harold, who was now seventy), more established, and certainly more mature than our acquaintances had been in other places. It reminded me of our first, early years in Le Cannet. Our new friends loved parties and we received invitations constantly. I usually accepted, but Harold seldom went. "I don't want to participate in Palm Springs society," he often said with a hint of bitterness, and I wondered silently, *Then why did we move here?*

His health continued to deteriorate and he was again in constant pain. He was bound to his wheelchair, leaving it only for his daily therapy (for his damaged hips and withering lungs) and to sleep at night. Jann was quite strong, and she took over the chore of wheeling him into a restaurant when we went out for an occasional dinner.

Soon, however, Jann suffered from her own problems. Not long after we moved to Palm Springs, she developed diabetes and had to inject insulin into her navel before every meal. Harold became very solicitous of her. Before going to dinner, he would ask, "How do you feel? Did you remember to take your insulin?"

Even with her own ailments, I think Jann really loved taking care of Harold. It put her in her element. She had no other life and she became devoted to him. She was so attentive that sometimes it felt as though I wasn't even there. After years of organizing charity galas in California and France, I was restless. Thus I was pleased when Verita Thompson called, asking for my help. She had closed her restaurant La Cantina on Santa Monica Boulevard and was opening a new place on the Sunset Strip.

"Come over here and help me get this place off the ground," she said.

I was thrilled. I told Harold that she had asked me to help her with the new restaurant. Did he mind?

"Of course not," he said. "By all means, help her. One time when I was broke, she saved my ass with a personal loan."

I planned to spend the weekdays with Verita at her penthouse apartment in Los Angeles, and I would go back to Palm Springs to be with Harold on the weekends. The truth is that I felt far more needed by Verita than I did by Harold.

Her new establishment had a piano, which she didn't quite know what to do with. I knew a lot of singers, so I suggested that we bring one in with an accompanist and turn the room into a piano bar or small cabaret. Verita thought it was a good idea, but after a few weeks and several different performers, it just wasn't working.

"I have an idea," I said one night.

"What's that?" asked Verita.

"Would you mind if I tried performing?" I asked timidly.

"Grazia," she said (she always called me Grazia), "let's give it a try. Nothing else is working."

I managed to obtain the singers' standby manual, the so-called "fake book" that contained the lyrics and music of almost every old standard. Surprisingly, I already knew most of the songs and even the keys. I found a good accompanist and I began performing Thursday through Saturday evenings at Verita's—just like that!

My act received a lot of press attention because of a unique technique I used. When you sing at a piano bar, there are always customers talking, drinking, and smoking, so sometimes it's difficult to get their attention. I figured out an ingenious way to solve the problem. If I was singing a slow romantic song and noticed that no one was listening or that I was losing my audience, I'd simply stop and say, "Oh, I'll do that one later." Then I'd begin a number that was more upbeat. I noticed that I usually regained the audience. I remembered what Tony Bennett once told me, "If you can sing in a saloon, you can sing anywhere!"

After *Los Angeles* magazine did a piece on my cabaret act, I got a call from a producer of the television show *Lifestyles of the Rich and Famous*. He wanted to feature me in one of their segments. I was excited.

"Can I bring Harold?"

"Of course," he laughed.

I rushed back to Palm Springs the following Sunday to tell Harold. He was not in the least receptive.

"No, I don't want to be involved in that," he said, "but you do it. It's your thing. I don't want any part of it."

I believe it was the first time Harold had ever rejected helping me. Later, I realized he didn't want to be part of the show because he no longer wanted to be part of my life.

Lifestyle shot the first part of the segment at Verita's restaurant and then the crew moved to Palm Springs, where we did the final shots. True to his word and to the dismay of the producers, Harold was adamant about not appearing in the television program.

After the segment was completed the company sent me a copy of the edited master version, which was scheduled to air on television a few weeks later. I was pleased and anxious to show it to Harold. While we were viewing it on our VHS, he remained silent. When it was finished, he looked at me with a hostile expression and said furiously, "It looks like I'm dead and gone!"

Although I did not argue with him, I was terribly disappointed. I had wanted him to be on the program with me, and in his physical absence I had mentioned him at every opportunity, just as I did every evening when I performed at Verita's. It was apparent also that Jann disliked the *Lifestyle* piece.

From that point forward Harold gradually but dramatically began to cut me out of his life. Of course, it was Jann who filled the vacuum. I don't think I was ever alone with Harold for longer than a few seconds after we screened the television segment. When I entered his room, he immediately summoned Jann, and she would be there.

"Jann, come in here," Harold would tell her to stay when she entered, as though I were totally invisible. I began to feel like a visiting and unwanted guest in my own home when I returned to Palm Springs for the weekend after performing at Verita's during the week. I was even ignored at the breakfast table, where Harold and Jann would engage in animated conversation, including cute asides that at long last I realized were those of a couple who were in the first throes of a romantic adventure.

The most telltale sign was when Harold sat down one Sunday to watch a football game on television. He had always disdained sports, but since Jann was an avid fan, overnight he became an aficionado. Under other circumstances it would have been ludicrous, the two of them sitting in front of the television set cheering and booing in unison. I marveled at Harold's sudden fascination with something he had avoided and criticized all of his life. Yet, I tried to rationalize it; Harold had become, after all, an invalid, and I told myself that this new pastime was a therapeutic method of forgetting his pain.

It was bad enough that Jann had come to insinuate herself into every facet of Harold's life, but then she began to invade mine as well. The staff, my staff, was given explicit orders not to do anything without her permission. I realized that loyalty, ultimately, is tied to money, and since Harold paid the bills, well . . .

Once I asked our butler to take a pair of my shoes to be re-heeled. He looked at me rather embarrassedly and made no comment.

"What is it?" I asked. "Do you have a problem with that?"

"No, but I've been instructed to get Miss Stapp's permission for any extraneous expenses," he said sheepishly.

I confronted Jann.

"What did the butler mean when he said he had to have your approval for me to get a pair of shoes repaired?" I asked.

She hemmed and hawed for a moment, not wanting to respond without Harold being present.

"Explain it to me," I repeated.

"Because of his huge medical bills, Harold asked me to keep track of the money. He said there should be no unneeded expenses."

I was furious, but to no avail. The rejections continued. Jann countermanded everything, from one of my prescription pharmaceutical orders to my dry-cleaning. Once when I needed to send a fax, Jann told Harold, and he summoned me to his office.

"Tell her, Jann," said Harold. By now it was clearn that Jann had control of our household, and, our money.

"Your faxes are an unnecessary expense," she said, "and besides, the machine is too complicated for you to operate."

If I had been naive before, I wasn't any longer. The writing was on the wall. Harold resented my presence. When someone called me to invite us, or me, to a social function in Palm Springs, he blamed me for creating a commotion. "I need peace and quiet," he said accusingly. "I can't take the stress of your telephone calls and social life."

Singing at Verita's became my therapy; unwelcomed in my own home, I began to stay in Los Angeles through the entire week, returning only randomly to Palm Springs. Yet, one could never underestimate Harold, nor second-guess him. I was stunned one night when he and Jann showed up on the Sunset Strip to see me perform. I was further shocked when Harold called me the next morning.

"You're a star, Tiger," he exclaimed ecstatically, "a star!" It would have been easy to think he was mocking me, but after almost thirty years together, I knew Harold well enough to know when he was sincere. For a brief moment his comments lighted a spark; for the first time in months his once-loving self seemed to have been reborn. He asked me to come home for the weekend. I did, of course. When he suggested that we have a few people over for cocktails, he said, "And hire a piano player." I was thrilled, until he added, "But no songs, Tiger. I don't want any singing."

We had a small party, but it was Harold, like so many times before, who hogged the spotlight. Harold had become old; with age, infirmity, and his inability to write as he had through all the past years, was grasping for something that was impossible. At long last his enormous ego had replaced his talent and his drive. It was not a fun party.

A year or so before, I had introduced Prince Nikki Toumanoff to my friend Ada, and when they decided to get married in Monte Carlo, I jumped at the chance to go. It was Harold who encouraged me to accept the invitation. "You should be there," he said. "They're old friends of ours and we should be represented at their wedding."

I went to Monte Carlo, but upon my arrival I learned that Nikki and Ada had changed their plans in midstream and had already gotten married. They held a reception, however, at the Hotel du Paris, but for me the entire trip was a sad reminiscence. I went to Cannes and stayed at a hotel on the Croisette, but I missed our villa and yacht. I missed Adréana enormously, and the truth is, I missed Harold also. Life was no longer the same. I was sailing about without a place to drop anchor. My daughter had grown up and Harold was rapidly becoming a hermit holed up in Palm Springs, watching sports events with Jann.

The old ties to the South of France had been broken. I no longer belonged in Cannes. I preferred to return to Palm Springs with my memories. Upon my arrival back home, Harold immediately complained about my expenses, even though it was he who had encouraged me to go to France in the first place.

I sought refuge at Verita's, but my moment in the sun at that little haven was doomed to be short-lived. Although on the surface her restaurant appeared to be a great success—there was always a line of people waiting to get in, but it was deceptive. Verita was having financial problems, particularly with the IRS, which was going after back taxes.

"I don't know what to do," she told me with a hint of desperation in her voice. "Is there any way you can help me, Grazia?"

Verita had once loaned Harold money before he became a writer, but she was hesitant to go to him, although I was certain he had enough money in reserve to meet her requirements. "I just can't ask him to help me," she lamented. "He has so many medical bills."

"Please, Grace," begged Verita, "please help me if you can."

I should have known better, but I volunteered to pawn one of my rings. Verita jumped at the offer. "I promise I'll pay you back," she told me. There was no question of her sincerity, but I should have realized from Harold's own losses through the years that a business in need of cash is a business in real trouble.

The money from the ring did not stave off Verita's creditors. She begged me again; I pawned another ring. It became a bottomless pit. I ended up hocking all of my jewelry, including a huge diamond that was worth more than $100,000.

Then one day when I arrived at her penthouse, I found her packing her bags.

"What are you doing?" I asked.

"The IRS boarded up the restaurant," she said despondently. "I'm out of business. They've sealed it closed."

I was dumbfounded.

"I'm so sorry," said Verita. "I'm still drowning in bills and I can't pay any of them."

Of course, my own bill was implicit in her words. My jewelry was in hock and the proceeds I had received and given to Verita were only a farthing compared to their real worth. I was in a fix, but there was nothing I could do or say. She went on to explain that she had also defaulted on her mortgage and the penthouse was reverting to the bank. She was heading to New Orleans.

"I'm so sorry," she repeated, and there was nothing more to say.

I left her place knowing I was in big trouble. I needed $50,000 to redeem my jewelry. It would be difficult to go to Harold. I had tried to tell him what I had done on several occasions, but each time he had called Jann into the room and I was not about to discuss Verita's misfortunes and my efforts to solve them in front of her.

Before she left town, Verita gave me as a partial payment a painting by Aldo Luongo, an up and coming artist. It was called *The Kiss*; although it had some value, Luongo's work at that time wasn't worthy of an auction by Christie's or Sotheby's.

I thought over my options. I had befriended a man who managed a restaurant in Palm Springs. Pierre thought he might be able to place the painting with one of his wealthy clients. Pierre was one of the few people who took an interest in my problems. We became confidantes at first, and later lovers.

No matter how confidential Pierre and I tried to be regarding the disposal of the painting, Harold found out about it. In all likelihood one of the gallery dealers in Palm Springs had told him.

"Has your boyfriend sold the painting yet?" he asked me bluntly one day.

"No," I said.

"Why are you selling it?" he pursued.

I confessed, explaining that I had pawned my jewelry to help Verita. To my surprise he sat very calmly in his wheelchair and listened, without once calling for Jann.

"How much will it cost to retrieve the jewels?" he asked quietly.

"Fifty-thousand dollars," I said.

He nodded, obviously letting it sink in.

"I'll get them back," he finally said.

I felt a great sense of relief.

True to his word, Harold redeemed the jewelry. For a man drowning in medical bills, he had no trouble coming up with the money. He simply wrote a check for $50,000. Once he had the jewels in hand, he called me back into his office.

"Here," he said. "This is for you."

He handed me an aquamarine.

"The rest," he continued, "is no longer yours."

What was no longer mine included a sixteen-karat marquise ring; a twenty-two-karat yellow canary diamond with settings and baguettes by Fred Joaillier; the small yellow diamond with emerald baguettes he had given me when we went to Colombia years before; and a dome-shaped sapphire with pave diamonds. Furthermore, earlier in the day and without my knowledge, Jann had wheeled him into the bank where we had a joint safety deposit box and he had removed what jewelry I had not pawned. It was all there, on display in his office.

I did not know what to say, but Harold did. He had mulled his words over so many times that it was now as though he were reciting from one of his books.

"If I could walk out on you, I would," he said, "but as you can see, I can't. So, you have to walk out on me, which I expect you to do. You can take what you want in the way of furniture and clothes, but do it now, not tomorrow, not next week." With that, after almost thirty years of marriage, it was over.

I did not argue with Harold, although I thought it was absurd for him to bring up Pierre. Harold had been philandering for years, and now he was with

Jann right under my nose. I didn't say a word, but only because Harold was too ill to withstand any kind of stress. He often said, "Stress will kill me." Our relationship had been finished for a long time, but I had been unwilling to face up to the facts. In a sense I was relieved. I gathered up my furs and some clothes and returned to his office.

"I want the piano," I told him, "but it will take a few days for me to find a place."

He stared at me a moment, and then nodded his approval.

Then I was gone, although I had no earthly idea as to where. I called a friend who was now living with her new husband in a condo in Los Angeles. Fortunately, her lease had not expired on her small studio apartment on King's Road in West Hollywood. I agreed to take over the lease.

What a change! The tiny pied-á-terre was a steep descent, almost a vertical fall, from our huge compound in Palm Springs, but I was glad to have it. For the very first time in my life I was living alone, with absolutely no one to turn to, yet I was consumed by a feeling of relief. I felt I had been treated shabbily, but living with Harold, with Jann always looking over my shoulder, had become unbearable. I was suddenly at peace with myself.

In May 1991, Harold and Jann gave an interview to the *Los Angeles Times*. I was flabbergasted. We weren't even divorced yet, and Jann was being quoted about "how romantic Harold is." She said, "he knows how to make a woman feel like a woman." I put down the paper. *If she had only known him when I knew him*, I thought. She was now talking about a seventy-five-year-old man who was confined to a wheelchair, a man who sucked on an oxygen mask every few seconds and jolted his body with electric shocks every five minutes to temporarily obliterate his pain.

Yes, I thought, *that's what Harold had really wanted—a nurse for life*.

In the final analysis, however, I knew that somehow Harold had come to replace my father, and that I, just as I had wanted to do when I was a little girl, had sought to placate him for his shortcomings, to love him regardless, and to do my best to make him happy. For the most part I had succeeded, until at last I had grown up and saw the relationship for what it was.

Not knowing what to do next, I thought I should at least try to protect myself. There comes a time when one must step back and ask, *what's best for me*. I decided to hire a lawyer and file for divorce. A few days later, after the papers had been served, Harold granted another interview. Army Archerd, the noted columnist for *Daily Variety*, asked him if it was true we were divorcing. "Yes," answered Harold, "but it will be very agreeable—with guns and knives!"

Meanwhile, in the midst of a great deal of anguish, serendipity lifted my spirits again. George Chakiris was the member of a troupe of artists who had been asked to perform for the queen at the Cole Porter Centennial Gala in England; it was a fundraiser for the Cancer Research Campaign in London, something, as Harold would say, was right up my alley.

"You love Cole Porter," said George. "Why don't you join us?"

It didn't take much persuasion. Other performers were Chita Rivera, Celeste Holm, Alice Faye, Rita Moreno, and Van Johnson. I signed up and flew to Britain. It was a wonderful trip, from beginning to end. Of all the countries Harold and I had been to, we had spent little time in England; our trips were almost exclusively related to book publicity stints. I took to the English people as I had the French, like a fish to water. I stayed with my good friends, Minda and Norman Lonsdale.

We rehearsed one week, and then went on stage. It was a spectacular gala evening, what with so many talented people. Each of us did a Cole Porter classic. When I went on stage and the orchestra struck up the music to my number, I thought briefly of Harold, and then I began singing. The words from my Cole Porter song were ironic. I kept my voice low and sultry, and if some extra and indefinable emotion came out, I couldn't help it. "My heart belongs to Daddy," was the song I sang.

After four grueling years I received my divorce from Harold. I got little monetarily, by no means enough to maintain the lifestyle I was accustomed to. Harold claimed he was totally broke due to his illness. I did not know that my lawyer, Marvin Mitchelson, was accommodating Harold to speed up the divorce so Harold could marry Jann. (Mitchelson later went to jail for tax evasion and was consequently disbarred.) After Mitchelson coerced me, the papers were signed and Harold married Jann.

He was never the same again. He wrote a couple of books, but they were obviously not from his own pen. Some of the more analytical critics alleged that a ghostwriter had written them. I knew Harold's imagination, the way he worked and wrote, and the energy he put into his books better than anyone else in the world. What was published under his name was no longer the work of the writer I loved.

EPILOGUE

Never Done . . .

"I'm never done; I just don't look back. I finish one project and start on the next. I'll do that until I die, and when I die, then I'll be done."

—Harold Robbins

On October 14, 1997, five years after our divorce became final, Harold died of pulmonary heart failure at Palm Springs Desert Hospital. He was eight-one years old. The most important man in my life was now gone and I can truly say I loved the man.

If Harold did not reach the stature of Hemingway or Fitzgerald or Faulkner, he was nevertheless an American storyteller of the first order. He did not think of himself as a literary figure, but he certainly thought of himself as a writer, a true storyteller. His imagination was enormous and often profound, and his fiction went far beyond his novels. He created much of the myth that surrounded his life, particularly incidents that he so glibly cast as absolute truths. In a way I think Harold came to believe them, as I truly did.

In a TV interview shortly after his death, his sister, Ruth, told the world that Harold fabricated his adventurous life. All of it was untrue, in fact, he was born and raised in a middle-class Jewish family. Blanche, his real mother and Ruth, his real sister. What? He was not the lonely, unwanted orphan who, as a newborn was left at the doorsteps of the Jesuit priests in Hell's Kitchen?

In the end I knew I was cast into a role with a man I did not fully know, but fully loved. Still, as I look back on my life, I can honestly say that I loved the Cinderella story that he created for me. It's not every woman who gets to live a life penned by Harold Robbins.

I am especially grateful for our beautiful and talented daughter, Adréana Robbins. (She too, like her father is a published author. Her book *Paris Never Leaves You* is incredible, and so is her wonderful husband, Jeffrey Greenberg.)

As with my life then, I love my life now, too. I am especially grateful for my most wonderful friends in Los Angeles, Palm Springs, New York, Las Vegas, and for the many other close relationships formed throughout my lifetime of travels and living. And, I am grateful for those who enrich and nourish my daily life, such as Gilbert Holmes—who I credit with encouraging me to get my book published. His talent, kindness and flair add flavor, fun and purpose to my life. How can I be more lucky?

And, of course, I have my adorable dog, "Luke Robbins"—who is the only "man" in my bed these days!

About the Author

For many years Grace Robbins made her home in various parts of the world before moving back to Beverly Hills, California in 2010. "I have wonderful friendships here and many lasting memories," says Grace, "and I enjoy being in the town where I spent the better part of my marriage to Harold and raised our daughter, Adréana."

A long time philanthropist, Ms. Robbins is credited for her work with charities such as the Thalians, the Princess Grace Foundation (where she was known for allowing her yacht to be action off as high-end vacation destination item). While in France, Grace founded the first charity for the children's orphanage in Cannes, aptly named A Tout Coeur ("With All My Heart").

Today, Grace enjoys spending time with her many friends, and attending chartable luncheons and black tie events, both in the US and abroad. She is also involved with the Motion Picture Home, a retirement home for actors.

To contact: www.cinderellaandthecarpetbagger.com

Other Books by
Bettie Youngs Book Publishers

The Maybelline Story—And the
Spirited Family Dynasty Behind It

Sharrie Williams

In 1915, when a kitchen stove fire singed his sister Mabel's lashes and brows, Tom Lyle Williams watched in fascination as she performed a "secret of the harem"—mixing petroleum jelly with coal dust and ash from a burnt cork and apply it to her lashes and brows. Mabel's simple beauty trick ignited Tom Lyle's imagination and he started what would become a billion-dollar business, one that remains a viable American icon after nearly a century. He named it Maybelline in her honor.

Throughout the 20th century, the Maybelline Company inflated, collapsed, endured, and thrived in tandem with the nation's upheavals—as did the family that nurtured it. Setting up shop first in Chicago, Williams later, to avoid unwanted scrutiny of his private life, cloistered himself behind the gates of his Rudolph Valentino Villa and ran his empire from a distance. Now after nearly a century of silence, this true story celebrates the life of a man whose vision rocketed him to success along with the woman held in his orbit, his brother's wife, Evelyn Boecher—who became his lifelong fascination and muse.

Captivated by her "roaring charisma," he affectionately called her the "real Miss Maybelline." Evelyn masterminded a life of vanity, but would fall prey to fortune hunters and a mysterious arson murder—that even today remains unsolved.

A fascinating and inspiring story of secrecy, ambition, and luck; a tale both epic and intimate, alive with the clash, the hustle, the music, and dance of American enterprise.

"A richly told story of a forty-year, white-hot love triangle that fans the flames of a major worldwide conglomerate." —**Neil Shulman, Associate Producer,** *Doc Hollywood*

"Salacious! Engrossing! Destined for film!" —*New York Post*

ISBN: 978-0-9843081-1-8 • $18.95
ePub ISBN: 978-1-936332-17-5

Diary of a Beverly Hills Matchmaker

Marla Martenson

Marla takes her readers for a hilarious romp through her days in an exclusive matchmaking agency. From juggling the demands of out-of-touch clients and trying to meet the capricious demands of an insensitive boss to the ups and downs of her own marriage with a husband who doesn't think that she is "domestic" enough, Marla writes with charm and self-effacement about the universal struggles of finding the love of our lives—and knowing it.

ISBN: 978-0-9843081-0-1 • $14.95
ePub ISBN: 978-1-936332-03-8

Amazing Adventures of a Nobody

Leon Logothetis

From the Hit Television Series
Aired in 100 Countries!

Tired of his disconnected life and uninspiring job, Leon leaves it all behind—job, money, home even his cell phone—and hits the road with nothing but the clothes on his back. His journey from Times Square to the Hollywood sign relying on the kindness of strangers and the serendipity of the open road, inspires a dramatic and life changing transformation.

"A gem of a book; endearing, engaging and inspiring." —**Catharine Hamm,** *Los Angeles Times* **Travel Editor**

"If you're looking to find meaning in this disconnected world of ours, this book contains many clues." —*Psychology Today*

ISBN: 978-0-9843081-3-2 • $14.95
ePub ISBN: 978-1-936332-51-9

Truth Never Dies

William C. Chasey

A Pulitzer-Prize entry!

A lobbyist for 40 years, William C. Chasey represented some of the world's most prestigious business clients and 23 foreign governments before the US Congress. Hired by a US company to forge communications between Libya and the US Congress, he takes a trip with a US Congressman for discussions with then Libyan leader Muammar Qadhafi. Upon his return, his bank accounts were frozen, and clients and personal friends had been advised not to take his calls.

Things got worse: the CIA, FBI, IRS, and the Federal Judiciary tried to coerce him into using his unique Libyan access to participate in a CIA-sponsored assassination plot of the two Libyans indicted for the bombing of Pan Am flight 103. Chasey's refusal to cooperate resulted in a six-year FBI investigation and sting operation, financial ruin, criminal charges, and incarceration in federal prison.

"A captivating story of international intrigue...and the abuses of state power."
—**Al Stoffel, producer**

"You'll never forget this book—nor the up-and-coming film." —**Donal Bailey, President, Forrest Motion Pictures**

ISBN: 978-1-936332-46-5 • $24.95
ePub ISBN: 978-1-936332-47-2

Out of the Transylvania Night

Aura Imbarus

A Pulitzer-Prize entry

"I'd grown up in the land of Transylvania, homeland to Dracula, Vlad the Impaler, and worse, dictator Nicolae Ceausescu," writes the author. "Under his rule, like vampires, we came to life after sundown, hiding our heirloom jewels and documents deep in the earth." Fleeing to the US to rebuild her life, she discovers a startling truth about straddling two cultures and striking a balance between one's dreams and the sacrifices that allow a sense of "home."

"Aura's courage shows the degree to which we are all willing to live lives centered on freedom, hope, and an authentic sense of self. Truly a love story!" —**Nadia Comaneci, Olympic Champion**

"A stunning account of erasing a past, but not an identity." —**Todd Greenfield, 20th Century Fox**

ISBN: 978-0-9843081-2-5 • $14.95
ePub ISBN: 978-1-936332-20-5

On Toby's Terms

Charmaine Hammond

On Toby's Terms is an endearing story of a beguiling creature who teaches his owners that, despite their trying to teach him how to be the dog they want, he is the one to lay out the terms of being the dog he needs to be. This insight would change their lives forever.

"Simply a beautiful book about life, love, and purpose."
—**Jack Canfield, compiler,** *Chicken Soup for the Soul* **series**

"In a perfect world, every dog would have a home and every home would have a dog like Toby!" —**Nina Siemaszko, actress,** *The West Wing*

"This is a captivating, heartwarming story and we are very excited about bringing it to film." —**Steve Hudis, Producer**

Soon to be a major motion picture!

ISBN: 978-0-9843081-4-9 • $15.95
ePub ISBN: 978-1-936332-15-1

The Morphine Dream

Don Brown with Boston Globe Pulitzer nominated Gary S. Chafetz

At 36, high-school dropout and a failed semi-professional ballplayer Donald Brown hit bottom when an industrial accident left him immobilized. But Brown had a dream while on a morphine drip after surgery: he imagined himself graduating from Harvard Law School (he was a classmate of Barack Omaba) and walking across America. Brown realizes both seemingly unreachable goals, and achieves national recognition as a legal crusader for minority homeowners. This intriguing tale of his long walk—both physical and metaphorical—is an amazing story of loss, gain and the power of perseverance and encouragement—a balm for those wanting to reboot their lives.

"An incredibly inspirational memoir." —**Alan M. Dershowitz, professor, Harvard Law School**

ISBN: 978-1-936332-25-0 • $21.95
ePub ISBN: 978-1-936332-26-7

Hostage of Paradox: A Memoir

John Rixey Moore

Few people then or now know about the clandestine war that the CIA ran in Vietnam, using the Green Berets for secret operations throughout Southeast Asia. This was not the Vietnam War of the newsreels, the body counts, rice paddy footage, and men smoking cigarettes on the sandbag bunkers. This was a shadow directive of deep-penetration interdiction, reconnaissance, and assassination missions conducted by a selected few Special Forces teams, usually consisting of only two Americans and a handful of Chinese mercenaries, called Nungs. These specialized units deployed quietly from forward operations bases to prowl through agendas that, for security reasons, were seldom completely understood by the men themselves.

Hostage of Paradox is the first-hand account by one of these elite team leaders.

"A compelling story told with extraordinary insight, disconcerting reality, and engaging humor." —**David Hadley, actor, *China Beach***

"Deserving of a place in the upper ranks of Vietnam War memoirs." —***Kirkus Review***

"Read this book, you'll be, as John Moore puts it, 'transfixed, like kittens in a box.'" —**David Willson, Book Review, *The VVA Veteran***

ISBN: 978-1-936332-37-3 • $29.95
ePub ISBN: 978-1-936332-33-5

Voodoo in My Blood
A Healer's Journey from Surgeon to Shaman

Carolle Jean-Murat, M.D.

Born and raised in Haiti to a family of healers, US trained physician Carolle Jean-Murat came to be regarded as a world-class surgeon. But her success harbored a secret: in the operating room, she could quickly intuit the root cause of her patient's illness, often times knowing she could help the patient without having to put her under the knife. Carolle knew that to fellow surgeons, her intuition was best left unmentioned. But when the devastating earthquake hit Haiti and Carolle returned to help—she had to acknowledge the shaman she had become.

This mesmerizing story takes us inside the secret world of voodoo as a healing practice, and sheds light on why it remains a mystery to most and shunned by many.

"This fascinating memoir sheds light on the importance of asking yourself, 'Have I created for myself the life I've meant to live?'" **—Christiane Northrup, M.D.**

"A fascinating read and personal insight into the world of shamans and spiritual healers." **—Dr. Marcia Hootman, the Chopra Center**

ISBN: 978-1-936332-05-2 • $24.95
ePub ISBN: 978-1-936332-04-5

The Girl Who Gave Her Wish Away
Sharon Babineau

The Children's Wish Foundation approached lovely thirteen-year-old Maddison Babineau just after she received her cancer diagnosis. "You can have anything," they told her, "a Disney cruise? The chance to meet your favorite movie star? A five thousand dollar shopping spree?"

Maddie knew exactly what she wanted. She had recently been moved to tears after watching a television program about the plight of orphaned children in an African village. Maddie's wish? To ease the suffering of these children half-way across the world. Despite the ravishing cancer, she became an indefatigable fundraiser for "her children."

In *The Girl Who Gave Wish Away,* her mother reveals Maddie's remarkable journey of providing hope and future to the village children who had filled her heart.

A special story, heartwarming and reassuring.

ISBN: 978-1-936332-96-0 • $18.95
ePub: 978-1-936332-97-7

The Tortoise Shell Code

V Frank Asaro

Off the coast of Southern California, the Sea Diva, a tuna boat, sinks. Members of the crew are missing and what happened remains a mystery. Anthony Darren, a renowned and wealthy lawyer at the top of his game, knows the boat's owner and soon becomes involved in the case. As the case goes to trial, a missing crew member is believed to be at fault, but new evidence comes to light and the finger of guilt points in a completely unanticipated direction.

Now Anthony must pull together all his resources to find the truth in what has happened and free a wrongly accused man—as well as untangle himself. Fighting despair, he finds that the recent events have called much larger issues into question. As he struggles to right this terrible wrong, Anthony makes new and enlightening discoveries in his own life-long battle for personal and global justice.

ISBN: 978-1-936332-60-1 • $24.95
ePub: 978-1-936332-61-8

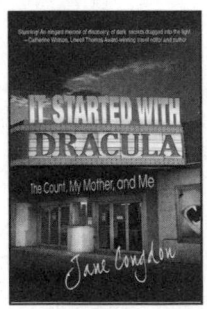

It Started with Dracula

The Count, My Mother, and Me

Jane Congdon

The terrifying legend of Count Dracula silently skulking through the Transylvania night may have terrified generations of filmgoers, but the tall, elegant vampire captivated and electrified a young Jane Congdon, igniting a dream to one day see his mysterious land of ancient castles and misty hollows. Four decades later she finally takes her long-awaited trip—never dreaming that it would unearth decades-buried memories, and trigger a life-changing inner journey. A memoir full of surprises, Jane's story is one of hope, love—and second chances.

"Unfinished business can surface when we least expect it. *It Started with Dracula* is the inspiring story of two parallel journeys: one a carefully planned vacation and the other an astonishing and unexpected detour in healing a wounded heart."
—**Charles Whitfield, MD, bestselling author of *Healing the Child Within***

"An elegantly written and cleverly told story. An electrifying read." —**Diane Bruno, CISION Media**

ISBN: 978-1-936332-10-6 • $15.95
ePub ISBN: 978-1-936332-11-3

MR. JOE
Tales from a Haunted Life

Joseph Barnett and Jane Congdon

Do you believe in ghosts? Joseph Barnett didn't, until the winter he was fired from his career job and became a school custodian. Walking the dim halls alone at night, listening to the wind howl outside, Joe was confronted with a series of bizarre and terrifying occurrences that puts his beliefs about self—*and ghosts*—to the test.

"Thrilling, thoughtful, elegantly told. So much more than a ghost story." —**Cyrus Webb, CEO, Conversation Book Club**

"This is truly inspirational work, a very special book—a gift to any reader." —**Diane Bruno, CISION Media**

ISBN: 978-1-936332-78-6 • $18.95
ePub ISBN: 978-1-936332-79-3

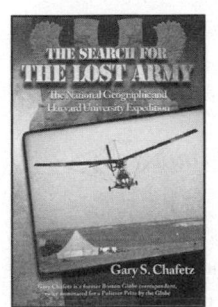

The Search for the Lost Army
The National Geographic and Harvard Expedition

Gary S. Chafetz

In one of history's greatest ancient disasters, a Persian army of 50,000 soldiers was suffocated by a hurricane-force sandstorm in 525 BC in Egypt's Western Desert. No trace of this conquering army, hauling huge quantities of looted gold and silver, has ever surfaced.

Nearly 25 centuries later on October 6, 1981, Egyptian Military Intelligence, the CIA, and Israel's Mossad secretly orchestrated the assassination of President Anwar Sadat, hoping to prevent Egypt's descent—as had befallen Iran two years before—into the hands of Islamic zealots. Because he had made peace with Israel and therefore had become a marked man in Egypt and the Middle East, Sadat had to be sacrificed to preserve the status quo.

These two distant events become intimately interwoven in the story of Alex Goodman, who defeats impossible obstacles as he leads a Harvard University/National Geographic Society archaeological expedition into Egypt's Great Sand Sea in search of the Lost Army of Cambyses.

ISBN: 978-1-936332-98-4 • $19.95
ePub ISBN: 978-1-936332-99-1

A World Torn Asunder
The Life and Triumph
of Constantin C. Giurescu

Marina Giurescu, M.D.

Constantin C. Giurescu was Romania's leading historian and author of the seminal *The History of the Romanian People*. His granddaughter's fascinating story of this remarkable man and his family follows their struggles in war-torn Romania from 1900 to the fall of the Soviet Union. An "enlightened" society is dismantled with the 1946 Communist takeover of Romania, and Constantin is confined to the notorious Sighet penitentiary.

Drawing on her grandfather's prison diary (which was put in a glass jar, buried in a yard, then smuggled out of the country by Dr. Paul E. Michelson—who does the FOREWORD for this book), private letters and her own research, Dr. Giurescu writes of the legacy from the turn of the century to the fall of Communism. We see the rise of modern Romania, the misery of World War I, the blossoming of its culture between the wars, and then the sellout of Eastern Europe to Russia after World War II. In this sweeping account, we see not only its effects socially and culturally, but the triumph in its wake: a man and his people who reclaim better lives for themselves, and in the process, teach us a lesson in endurance, patience, and will—not only to survive, but to thrive.

"The inspirational story of a quiet man and his silent defiance in the face of tyranny —**Dr. Connie Mariano, author of** *The White House Doctor*

ISBN: 978-1-936332-76-2 • $21.95
ePub ISBN: 978-1-936332-77-9

Crashers
A Tale of "Cappers" and "Hammers"

Lindy S. Hudis

The illegal business of fraudulent car accidents is a multi-million dollar racket, involving unscrupulous medical providers, personal injury attorneys, and the cooperating passengers involved in the accidents. Innocent people are often swept into it.

Newly engaged Nathan and Shari, who are swimming in mounting debt, were easy prey: seduced by an offer from a stranger to move from hard times to good times in no time, Shari finds herself the "victim" in a staged auto accident. Shari gets her payday, but breaking free of this dark underworld will take nothing short of a miracle.

"A riveting story of love, life—and limits. A non-stop thrill ride."
—**Dennis "Danger" Madalone, stunt coordinator for the television series,** *Castle*

ISBN: 978-1-936332-27-4 • $16.95
ePub ISBN: 978-1-936332-28-1

Fastest Man in the World

Tony Volpentest
Foreword by Ross Perot

Tony Volpentest is a four-time Gold Medalist and five-time World Champion sprinter. He carried the Olympic flame at the 1996 Atlanta Olympics. But it is not so much the medals he sports that make him admirable; it is the grit and determination that got him there. Though born without hands or feet, he is the fastest runner in the world. Tony shares his incredible journey, from the feet that Ross Perot built for him, to his 2012 nomination into the Olympic Hall of Fame.

"This inspiring story is about the thrill of victory to be sure—winning Olympic Gold—but it is also a reminder about human potential: the ability to push ourselves beyond the ledge of imagination, and to develop grit that fuels indefatigable determination. Simply a powerful story." **—Charlie Huebner, United States Olympic Committee**

ISBN 978-1-936332-00-7 • $16.95
ePub ISBN: 978-1-936332-01-4

Trafficking the Good Life

Jennifer Myers

An all-American, midwestern farm girl, Jennifer Myers had worked hard toward a successful career as a dancer in Chicago. But just as her star was rising, she fell for the kingpin of a drug trafficking operation. Drawn to his life of excitement, she soon acquiesced to driving marijuana across the country, making easy money she stacked in shoeboxes and spent like an heiress.

Steeped inside moral ambiguity, she sought to cleanse her soul with the guidance of spiritual gurus and New Age prophets—to no avail. Only time in a federal prison made her face up to and understand her choices. It was there, at rock bottom, that she discovered that her real prison was the one she had unwittingly made inside herself and where she could start rebuilding a life of purpose and ethical pursuit.

"Enthralling…and dramatic." **—Dennis Sobin, Director, Safe Streets Arts Foundation**

ISBN: 978-1-936332-67-0 • $18.95
ePub ISBN: 978-1-936332-68-7

The Rebirth of Suzzan Blac

Suzzan Blac

A horrific upbringing and then abduction into the sex slave industry would all but kill Suzzan's spirit to live. But a happy marriage and two children brought love—and forty-two stunning paintings, art so raw that it initially frightened even the artist. "I hid the pieces for 15 years," says Suzzan, "but just as with the secrets in this book, I am slowing sneaking them out, one by one by one." Now a renowned artist, her work is exhibited world-wide.

A story of inspiration, truth and victory.

"A solid memoir about a life reconstructed. Chilling, thrilling, and thought provoking." —**Pearry Teo, Producer,** *The Gene Generation*

ISBN: 978-1-936332-22-9 • $16.95
ePub ISBN: 978-1-936332-23-6

———

Blackbird Singing in the Dead of Night
What to Do When God Won't Answer
Gregory L. Hunt

Pastor Greg Hunt had devoted nearly thirty years to congregational ministry, helping people experience God and find their way in life. Then came his own crisis of faith and calling. While turning to God for guidance, he finds nothing. Neither his education nor his religious involvements could prepare him for the disorienting impact of the experience.

Alarmed, he tries an experiment. The result is startling—and changes his life entirely.

"In this most beautiful memoir, Greg Hunt invites us into an unsettling time in his life, exposes the fault lines of his faith, and describes the path he walked into and out of the dark. Thanks to the trail markers he leaves along the way, he makes it easier for us to find our way, too." —**Susan M. Heim, co-author,** *Chicken Soup for the Soul, Devotional Stories for Women*

"Compelling. If you have ever longed to hear God whispering a love song into your life, read this book." —**Gary Chapman,** *NY Times* **bestselling author,** *The Love Languages of God*

ISBN: 978-1-936332-07-6 • $15.95
ePub ISBN: 978-1-936332-18-2

DON CARINA

Ron Russell

A father's death in Southern Italy in the 1930s—a place where women who can read are considered unfit for marriage—thrusts seventeen-year-old Carina into servitude as a "black widow," a legal head of the household who cares for her twelve siblings. A scandal forces her into a marriage to Russo, the "Prince of Naples."

By cunning force, Carina seizes control of Russo's organization and disguising herself as a man, controls the most powerful of Mafia groups for nearly a decade. Discovery is inevitable: Interpol has been watching. Nevertheless, Carina survives to tell her children her stunning story of strength and survival.

"A woman as the head of the Mafia, who shows her family her resourcefulness, strength and survival techniques. Unique, creative and powerful! This exciting book blends history, intrigue and power into one delicious epic adventure that you will not want to put down!" —**Linda Gray, Actress,** *Dallas*

ISBN: 978-0-9843081-9-4 • $15.95
ePub ISBN: 978-1-936332-49-6

Living with Multiple Personalities
The Christine Ducommun Story

Christine Ducommun

Christine Ducommun was a happily married wife and mother of two, when—after moving back into her childhood home—she began to experience panic attacks and a series of bizarre flashbacks. Eventually diagnosed with Dissociative Identity Disorder (DID), Christine's story details an extraordinary twelve-year ordeal unraveling the buried trauma of her past and the daunting path she must take to heal from it. Therapy helps to identify Christine's personalities and understand how each helped her cope with her childhood, but she'll need to understand their influence on her adult life.

Fully reawakened and present, the personalities compete for control of Christine's mind as she bravely struggles to maintain a stable home for her growing children. In the shadows, her life tailspins into unimaginable chaos—bouts of drinking and drug abuse, sexual escapades, theft and fraud—leaving her to believe she may very well be losing the battle for her sanity. Nearing the point of surrender, a breakthrough brings integration.

A brave story of identity, hope, healing and love.

"Reminiscent of the Academy Award-winning *A Beautiful Mind,* this true story will have you on the edge of your seat. Spellbinding!" —**Josh Miller, Producer**

ISBN: 978-0-9843081-5-6 • $16.95
ePub ISBN: 978-1-936332-11-3

Bettie Youngs Books

We specialize in MEMOIRS

. . . books that celebrate

fascinating people and

remarkable journeys

In bookstores everywhere, online, Espresso, or from the publisher, Bettie Youngs Books.

VISIT OUR WEBSITE AT
www.BettieYoungsBooks.com

To contact:
info@BettieYoungsBooks.com